APOSTASY

in America

Solange Strong Hertz

Also by Solange Strong Hertz

The Star-Spangled Heresy: Americanism
Veritas Press, 1992

Utopia: Nowhere - Now Here
Veritas Press, 1993

The Thought of Their Heart
Veritas Press, 1994

Beyond Politics
Veritas Press, 1995

Sin Revisited
Veritas Press, 1996

On The Contrary
Veritas Press, 1997

ISBN : 1-883511-11-9

Published by:
Veritas Press
Post Office Box 1704
Santa Monica, California 90406
December 10, 1998

Printed and bound in the United States of America
By Little Jon Publications, Los Angeles, California

TABLE OF CONTENTS

ABOUT THE AUTHOR

An established writer before the Second Vatican Council, Solange Strong Hertz wrote for most major Catholic periodicals and had five books to her credit, one a selection of the Catholic Literary Foundation. When she refused to adjust her theology to the new "Spirit of Vatican II," her manuscripts almost overnight became unacceptable to her former editors. After a series on feminine spirituality for the old *Triumph* magazine, she continued speaking for tradition by successfully producing on her own *The Thought of His Heart* (1974) and *Sin Revisited* (1975). The former was republished in 1994 by Veritas Press under the title *The Thought of Their Heart* and the latter appeared once again in 1996.

In 1973 Mrs. Hertz began writing the Big Rock Papers, published privately throughout the next decade and the source of the highly acclaimed *Star Spangled Heresy*: Americanism (Veritas Press, 1992). In 1993 Veritas was privileged to publish her monumental collection on the confrontation between the universal republic and the reign of Christ the King, *Utopia*: Nowhere - Now Here, in 1995 *Beyond Politics* - A Layman's Guide to What Keeps on Happening, and in 1997 *On The Contrary*: What every revolutionary-in-reverse should know by now.

Mrs. Hertz is a regular contributor to *The Remnant* and her articles can be found abroad in *Apropos, Christian Order* and *Action Familiale et Scholaire*. She is universally regarded as one of traditional Catholicism's foremost contemporary writers.

As the title says,

this book is about apostasy, that gradual but radical dissociation of man from God whose history is as old as creation, having begun among the angels in heaven even before it began on earth in Eden. It would be impossible to tell it all, but what follows is an attempt to show some aspects of it from the perspective of America, where apostasy became as it were politicized by historical circumstance and burst out formally with a Declaration of Independence.

Readers of *The Remnant* will recognize in some of the chapters that follow the substance of articles which have appeared in the pages of that stalwart little Catholic periodical, which for the last thirty years has defended the cause of Christ the King in the land which gave Democracy to the world and Americanism to the Church. The second chapter, which deals with the origins of the Maryland Colony, is heavily indebted to research done by Lydia Logan Hertz, some of which was published under her name in 1975 as the Big Rock Paper "Lord Baltimore's Bungle."

The author is sometimes chided for the scarcity of her footnotes, but they will continue minimal – not for lack of proper source material, but because footnotes are unbecoming to children's books, especially books like this one, which was written for children after they are grown up!

Solange Strong Hertz
Big Rock,
Leesburg, Virginia
Feast of Our Lady of Victory, 1998

In Nomine Patris

et

Filii

et

Spiritui Sancti

YANKEE, COME HOME !

Although the soil beneath their feet was discovered and colonized by Catholics, some of it watered by Catholic blood, where the Faith is concerned Catholics in the United States tend unaccountably to behave as expatriates in their own country. Despite the fact that the Mother of God herself arrived literally on the heels of the first conquistadors to remind the inhabitants of America, "Am I not here, who am your mother?", they normally head for a shrine across the Atlantic when it is a question of making a pilgrimage to her of any consequence. To hear them tell it, anything directly pertaining to the universal Church always occurs, if not actually in Rome, at least somewhere outside America.

In diocesan school texts the only revolution which seriously affected the Faith was the French Revolution, and the last armed revolt against the enemies of the Church is now safely over and done with, having taken place more than two hundred years ago in the French Vendée. The import of the French Revolution must not be minimized, for it brought down the French king, Christ's constituted vicar in the temporal order. Had his throne endured, the collapse of Christian law and order which eventually left the Church everywhere at the mercy of the state would not have been possible. Nor must the martyrs of the Vendée be robbed of their glorious intercession on behalf of any stalwarts following in their footsteps, but it may be time to pay closer attention to what happened long before and after that in America.

Yankee, come home and listen to your Mother!

How is it that three hundred twenty-seven years before our Lady identified herself as the Immaculate Conception to St. Bernadette Soubirous at Lourdes, speaking a French *patois*, she had already proclaimed the mystery in America to a widowed Aztec convert in his native Nahuatl? There were four apparitions to him at the time, all of which took place in December, 1531 within the week the Church would one day consecrate as the Octave of the Feast of the Immaculate Conception. This cannot have been accidental, inasmuch as the first appearance virtually anticipated the formal definition of the dogma, made by Pius IX on December 8, 1854 to the effect that "the doctrine which holds that the most blessed Virgin Mary, at the first instant of her conception, by a singular grace and privilege granted by almighty God in view of the merits of Jesus Christ, the Savior of the human race, was preserved free from all stain of original sin is a doctrine revealed by God and therefore to be believed firmly and constantly by all the faithful."

When our Lady told St. Bernadette, "I am the Immaculate Conception," she was only putting into prescribed theological terms what she had already told the American Indian when she said, "I am the All-Perfect and Perpetual Virgin Mary, Mother of the true God." In France she drew a curative spring from the earth of Massabielle to testify to the truth of her words. In America she left imprinted on the cloth of the Indian's rough *tilma* a miraculous portrait of herself which like the Holy Shroud of Turin would provide its own authentication, not only by miracles, but by progressively revealing corroborative data mysteriously concealed in its folds.

In 1752, solemnly declaring Patroness of Mexico the beautiful Lady thus depicted, Pope Benedict XIV could find no words more appropriate to the occasion than those of the Psalmist, "He hath not done in like manner to every nation: and his judgments he hath not made manifest to them. Alleluia!" (Ps. 147:20). Indeed no other country was ever so favored, but inasmuch as the divine intervention happened at a spot situated at the exact geographical center of the American continents, we may suspect that it was intended for more than the immediate vicinity. Pius XII would formally recognize this fact by declaring her Empress of the Americas. In the light of subsequent developments throughout the world, however, it becomes increasingly difficult to view the Mexican phenomenon as an isolated event peculiar to America which bore no relation to the rest of Christendom.

Don Juan of Austria had borne her image on his banner at Lepanto against the Turks, for when Our Lady told the Indian that she was his mother, she made it clear at the same time that she had not come for his sake alone, but for "all the inhabitants of this land" and whoever invoked her with confidence. That her sole purpose was to introduce to the Faith large numbers of heathen "ethnics" who would not have ac-

2 APOSTASY

cepted it otherwise is not supported by the facts. Although it is true that the apparition sparked millions of conversions almost overnight, the Faith had already been firmly planted by zealous Spanish missionaries, and in the normal course of catechizing it would have made its way with relative ease into a society which had proved to be exceptionally open to God's grace.

The visionary himself was already a seasoned Catholic of outstanding virtue at the time of the apparition, having lived with his wife in perfect chastity from the time of his conversion. He had been baptized Juan Diego, and the story is that the "Juan" was conferred on him in deference to his former Aztec name "Singing Eagle" (or as some would have it, "He-who-speaks-as-an-eagle"), in which the missionaries perceived a cognomen for St. John the Evangelist, whose symbol is the eagle. No more suitable patron could have been found, for Juan Diego was destined to see vested in the apocalyptic signs the very same Woman pregnant with child whom the writer of the *Apocalypse* had beheld in his great vision of the latter days.

The late Don José de Jesús Manríquez y Zárate, first Bishop of Huejutla and ardent promoter of Juan Diego's cause, believed that this holy man had in fact been appointed by heaven as a permanent "mediator between herself and us." Writing from exile in San Antonio, Texas during the Calles persecution in October 1939, Bishop Zárate called him "the instrument of her mercies and the executor of her sovereign commands," cooperating in all her work "just as the Apostles of Jesus Christ cooperated in the Master's work." [1] In the second apparition the Mother of God had in fact told Juan Diego that although many others were capable of doing her bidding, she chose "you and no other." He was not to worry about anything: "Am I not here, who am your mother? Aren't you in my shadow? Am I not your salvation? Aren't you as it were on my lap? What more do you need?"

The time for massive recourse to Juan Diego's intercession may be at hand, for his beatification, which suffered a delay almost as long as St. Joan of Arc's, finally took place before the close of the twentieth century, and like hers would seem to augur a mysterious mediation reserved for the end times. This assumption is strongly supported by the fact that our Lady gave explicit instructions to Juan's uncle Bernardino that the icon left on the *tilma* be called "She who Crushes the Serpent." This was a full three hundred years before the Blessed Virgin instructed

St. Catherine Labouré in Paris to have the Miraculous Medal medal struck, depicting the Immaculate Conception crushing the Serpent under her foot. In Spanish the closest approximation of the Nahuatl words to Bernardino turned out to be "Guadalupe," but their import was clear enough at the time, promising deliverance from the Serpent deity who had exacted ritual human sacrifices in the thousands as the price of his rule.

The message should be even clearer today, when the phenomenon of Guadalupe can be seen in broader context as a pivotal point in world history, and not merely as an outstanding example of Our Lady's motherly compassion for the most abandoned of her children. Occurring so far in advance of the great apparitions in Europe at the rue du Bac, la Salette, Lourdes and Fatima, those in America marked nothing less than the inauguration of the Marian Age, which would see the final battle between our Lady and Satan foretold by God in Eden when He warned the Serpent, "I will put enmities between thee and the woman, and thy seed and her seed: she shall crush thy head, and thou shalt lie in wait for her heel" (Gen. 3:15).

The staggering truth is that our Lady chose to open hostilities, not in Rome, the Holy Land or elsewhere, but on American soil, attacking the primordial Adversary in territory which till then had been his last undisputed preserve. The first skirmish ended in a crushing defeat for him. Not only did the human sacrifices he doted on come to an end, but the way was cleared for the incorporation of millions of his former subjects into the Kingdom of the Incarnate God whom he had refused to serve in heaven. It would be a long time, however, before the end was in sight. As our Lord told His Apostles, "When you shall hear of wars and rumors of wars, fear ye not, for such things must needs be: but the end is not yet.... These are the beginnings of sorrows" (Mark 13:7-8). By the time our Lady appeared at Lourdes as the Immaculate Conception, urging the recitation of her Rosary, battle had been joined for three and a quarter centuries. Hell had re-grouped its forces and seemed to be winning.

St. John the Evangelist, who was privileged to foresee the future combat in vision, clothes his account in metaphor, relating how "the serpent cast out of his mouth after the woman, water, as it were a river: that he might cause her to be carried away by the river. And the earth helped the woman, and the earth opened her mouth and swallowed up

4 APOSTASY

the river, which the dragon cast out of his mouth," whereupon "the dragon was angry against the woman and went to make war with the rest of her seed" (Apo. 12:15-17). Without presuming to attempt the exegesis of so obscure a passage, we may hope that "her seed" refers to Catholics everywhere, and those of America in particular, for although the Great Apostasy had not been conceived in America, having been brought here from Europe by the same evil forces which brought it to earth from heaven, it is in America that apostasy was forged into a political weapon and institutionalized.

+

This was not the first time the devil had put together a common-wealth under his headship apart from God. His first attempt had succeeded so well that God "repented... that he had made man on the earth" (Gen. 6:6) and obliterated all memory of it by the Flood. Returning to the task at Babel, Lucifer was prevented from going further until the Incarnation was accomplished. A Christian empire was established on earth which endured for over a thousand years, but now the time of his revenge has arrived, during which he will labor to destroy Christ's kingdom as God had destroyed his. America, which may have been predisposed to such a destiny, would figure as a major base of operations.

Evidence mounts that the fabled island empire known to Plato, Pliny and ancient scholars as Atlantis had once actually existed, filling nearly the whole of what is now the Atlantic Ocean. If the conclusions of the French hieroglyphist Fernand Crombette prove correct, this huge land mass became an important outpost of the ancient world empire founded in Egypt after the Flood by Noah's reprobate son Cham and grandson Misraim. Masters of the black arts inherited from Cain and Lamech through Noah's wife (who was later repudiated by her husband for idolatry and licentiousness), they established a dynasty which would rule the world unchallenged for centuries in the devil's name. (Significant remnants of this demonic culture are still extant, among them the gigantic statues on Easter Island whose origin was finally determined by Crombette.)

Atlantis' very name betrays its demonic affiliation, for it is derived from that of the Titan Atlas who, like his brother Prometheus, was one of classical mythology's outstanding rebels against the established order. Doomed to bearing the weight of the heavens on his shoulders for having disobeyed the father-god Zeus, Atlas was an unmistakable impersonation of Lucifer, who in the beginning had been cast to earth for refusing to submit to his Creator. Wherever the sounds "atl" are found in language or nomenclature, the influence of Atlantis may be suspected, and Nahu*atl,* the language of the Aztecs, whose serpent god was known as Quetzalcó*atl,* is no exception.

According to Crombette, mighty Atlantis vanished into the ocean depths to be seen no more on April 2, 1226 B.C., submerged by the same divine miracle which simultaneously parted the waters of the Red Sea for Moses and the Israelites and by reflux drowned the army sent by Pharaoh to pursue them.[2] After the Sargasso Sea, an impenetrable mass of seaweed generated from the silt of the sunken continent, gradually formed over the empty expanse left in the wake of the catastrophe, the flow of communication which till then had existed between the lands on either side came to an abrupt end. All knowledge of the great colony's location was lost to western cartographers. Only in the east was it remembered, whence it seeped providentially into the maps of the second century geographer Ptolemy and others whose works became known to Columbus.

To believe, however, that every last vestige of Atlantis' sophisticated culture plunged with it into the sea is to fly in the face of the evidence. Filling a large part of the ocean space now left between Europe, Africa and North America, the island had not only linked these continents and their respective hemispheres in close communication, but constituted the nucleus of a vast empire which spawned satellites in its own image and left telltale artifacts throughout the contiguous territories. Its shores, however, lay closest to those of Europe and America, at some points only a short distance away. After the cataclysm it is not unreasonable to suppose that survivors on the coasts opposite, especially in what is now England and the eastern seaboard of the U.S., would have continued living there, and that their descendants are probably there today.

Their lifeline to civilization cut off, the highly cultured Atlanteans on America's east coast would have gradually degenerated into "primitive" Indian tribes which modern sociologists could pass off as less evolved specimens of the human chain. In England they would simply have merged with other elements of the population and eventually been Christianized by European missionaries. Both contingents, however,

6 APOSTASY

must have retained the old luciferian dream of world empire as part of their genetic heritage, for to deny that evil tendencies are normally transmitted from generation to generation would mean denying the doctrine of original sin. Constituting a hidden but real bond between Mother England and her future colonies to which the devil was privy, their common affinity may well have been cunningly exploited by him for the accomplishment of his own ends. At any rate it might serve to explain the strange propensity of the English monarchy to regard itself as a component of "the Atlantic community" rather than a part of Europe.

Looming up literally from the sea like the first beast of the Apocalypse, England was the vanguard of the Great Apostasy. Although the Reformation is usually blamed on Germany, the record points inexorably to England, the land of Wycliffe and William of Ockham. Nor was France the first Christian nation to put its anointed Catholic monarch to death. Here again, Christendom's first regicide occurred in England, with the execution of Charles I. And so with modern Freemasonry, concocted by no Adam Weishaupt in the eighteenth century, but by a bevy of Englishmen in the previous century — those "able pens" and adepts who wrote Shakespeare's plays and sonnets, the King James Bible and for all we know, *Don Quixote* and Montaigne's essays, not to mention hatching the prestigious Royal Society of London for Improving Natural Knowledge which to this day propagates the old scientific spirit of Atlantis.

It is these latter day sons of Cham who forged revolution into a political instrument. When it failed of its full purpose in England under Oliver Cromwell, what better expedient than to transfer it to the colonies across the Atlantic? There, with the help of the "Indians," it could be brought to full flower in far less restricted circumstances than at home. The Iroquois in particular possessed a particularly well developed form of democratic government whose taproots may easily have lain in old Chamite Atlantis. Of all the major American tribes they proved the most resistant to Christianity and the cruelest persecutors of Catholic missionaries and Indian converts. The particularly barbarous martyrdoms suffered by the French Jesuits St. Jean de Brébeuf, St. Isaac Jogues and their companions in what is now New York state and Canada, not to mention several Spanish Jesuits to the south in Virginia, offer ample testimony of their ferocity.

By a kind of preternatural attraction these primordial heathens, whose numbers always exceeded the Catholic Indians of the east coast, would almost invariably side with the English, Dutch and Swedish heretics to the detriment of the Faith in the New World. The Iroquois confederations throughout the east, which included groups as diverse as the warlike Mohawks in the north and the agricultural Cherokees in the south, all spoke versions of a common language and maintained a loose organic unity inherited from former times. There were basic racial differences, however, which may account for their divided allegiance to the newcomers. This meant that the balance of power in the east between heretics and Catholics in those crucial early days lay for all practical purposes in the hands of the natives, with enormous consequences both political and religious.

This facet of American history deserves better study, for the outcome of the struggle proved decisive for the French and Spanish Catholic spheres of influence throughout North America, and indeed for the whole world. By 1763 Spain had lost the Floridas to the British, and all of New France in what is now Canada, and parts of the U.S. followed suit. Cut off from her mother country and the rest of Christendom, bereft of leadership after her aristocracy was supplanted by foreigners, French Catholic Canada did well to salvage her faith. To make matters worse, by 1776 when the English colonists formally disassociated themselves from both Mother England and her Church, a New Atlantis was born in the New World.

+

That the old Atlantis would rise from the deep before the end of time had been predicted for centuries, but even those few who were aware that it had once existed gave such prophecies little credence. Even after the algae subsided sufficiently to allow passage to Columbus (who was well aware of its former location), no signs of resurgence were noted, but to say that Atlantis is still underwater is to dodge overwhelming evidence to the contrary. Although its material residue may not have surfaced, its spirit is visibly active, reasserting ever more forcefully the ancient hegemony it once enjoyed.

The first clear indication of its resurrection was the publication of the original Latin version of Francis Bacon's *New Atlantis* in 1627.

8 APOSTASY

When it appeared in English two years later, there was no mistaking its implications. A remarkable treatise on utopian world government, it projected a future ideal commonwealth called Bensalem which was based purely on scientific knowledge and presumably patterned after the fabled Atlantis once renowned the world over for beauty and prosperity. The luciferian inspiration is easily detected in the work's recurring emphasis on "light." When Bacon, a master of the conceits and ciphers which so fascinated the Elizabethans, exalts light as "God's first creature," he is obviously identifying it with the great fallen angel himself, created before man and supreme grand master of the *illuminati* of every age.

Because for the enlightened, perfection is looked for in knowledge and not in love, "merchants of light" are dispatched at regular intervals from Bensalem to glean scientific information from every corner of the globe. These occult missionaries "maintain a trade, not for gold, silver or jewels, nor for silks, nor for spices, nor any other commodity of matter, but only for ... light: to have light, I say, of the growth of all parts of the world." Refusing to accept matter as the instrument of the Incarnation of the Son of God when the mystery was first made known in heaven, the devil remains forever unreconciled to it. As incapable as anyone else of either creating or destroying matter, Lucifer therefore seeks to "spiritualize" it out of existence by force of intellect.

On the pretext of eliminating the heavy burdens and limitations imposed by matter, he has pretended to show earth-bound men, sentenced to eat bread "by the sweat of thy face... till thou return to the earth out of which thou wast taken" (Gen. 3:19), how to escape their punishment by constructing a worldwide push-button society more and more subject to the mind alone. In a previous work, the *Novum Organum*, Bacon envisaged what he called a great "Instauration," proposing nothing less than the complete reconstruction of human learning by a new scientific method of interpreting nature which would displace divine revelation as ultimate source of truth. All things would be instaured in Satan. When St. Pius X opened his pontificate in the twentieth century by announcing his intention to "*Instaurare omnia in Christo*," was it a reversal of Bacon's "Instauration" that he actually had in mind? Very likely, for the *Novum Organum* was nothing other than the fetal form of Modernism, which the holy Pope targeted so accurately in the counter-revolutionary encyclical *Pascendi*.

Anti-Aristotelians who considered syllogistic reasoning from the general to the particular fundamentally unsound, and who despised any knowledge based on authority to begin with, Bacon and his adepts would aim at truth by reasoning inductively from observation rather than deductively from accepted premises. In other words, learning would be democratized in tandem with the social base, ascending henceforth from the bottom up instead of descending from the top down. No longer would truth be bestowed on men"from above, coming down from the Father of lights, with whom there is no change nor shadow of vicissitude," as St. James said, for it would be plentifully gleaned by unaided human effort. Not without reason did the Apostle preface his words with the warning, "Do not err, therefore, my dearest brethren. Every best gift and every perfect gift is from above!" (Jas. 1:16-17).

The *New Atlantis* had been left purposely unfinished, for it was only a beginning. A second part, which was never published, is said to have been secretly buried in the earliest foundations of Williamsburg, Virginia, English America's first colonial capital, now restored by the Rockefellers and a major national shrine. The manuscript has yet to appear in public, but its geographical location is singularly apt, for Bacon situated his ideal island republic to the west of sunken Atlantis, precisely in the area where in due time a secular republic conceived in the spirit of Atlantis would materialize under the aspect of that most desired of nations, the U.S.A.

+

Yankee, come home! In 1634, a century after the first annunciation of the Immaculate Conception and a mere five years after the publication of the English version of Bacon's *New Atlantis*, our Lady appeared once more with an apocalyptic message for the world. Here again, it was delivered not in Europe, but in America, this time on the South American continent in Quito, Ecuador. On the feast of her Purification she divulged to Mother Mariana of Jesus in her convent chapel the main substance of the famous message known as the Secret of la Salette, which would be confided only two hundred years later to little Mélanie Calvat in the Alps above Grenoble.

Warning of a future crisis in the Church due to a hiatus of some kind in the Papacy, our Lady spoke at the same time of a Great Pope to come.

A likely reason for making predictions of this kind in America so long before making them known in Europe may be guessed from the message's explicit reference to democracy: "At the end of the 19th century and for a large part of the 20th," Mother Mariana was told, "various heresies will flourish on earth *which will have become a free republic.*" It is well known that democracy's cradle was no European nation, but one concocted in America for that very purpose, and as we have seen, it was already being manufactured even as these words fell from our Lady's lips.

In a passage clearly foreshadowing la Salette, she goes on to say, "The precious light of faith will go out in souls because of the almost total moral corruption.... The licentiousness will be such that there will be no more virgin souls in the world.... By having gained control of all the social classes, the sects will tend to penetrate with great skill into the heart of families and destroy even the children.... Priests will abandon their sacred duties and will depart from the path marked out for them by God. Then the Church will go through a dark night for lack of a Prelate and Father to watch over it with love, gentleness, strength and prudence."

Worth noting is the Mother of God's mention of "various heresies" in the same breath with the forthcoming free world republic, as if the two were organically related. There is a school of thought which holds that any form of government is unobjectionable provided it recognizes the rights of God above those of the nation and its rulers. By this token, to become pleasing to Him, elected constitutional government need only be "baptized" as it were by acknowledging the Faith. It so happens that such a government was actually set up in Ecuador in the nineteenth century, and our Lady must have been referring to it when she predicted to Mother Mariana, "Satan will gain control of this earth through the fault of faithless men, who, like a black cloud, will darken the clear sky of the republic consecrated to the Most Sacred Heart of my divine Son."

For fifteen years, under the Presidency of the virtuous Catholic reformer Gabriel Garcia Moreno, the Church operated freely in this unusual republic without governmental constraint or interference, but the benevolent regime came to an abrupt end on the Feast of the Transfiguration, August 6, 1875 when he was assassinated by Masonic terrorists. Hamish Fraser, editor of *Approaches*, called Moreno "the most outstanding statesman the post Reformation world has known," who "governed Ecuador as no South American country has ever been governed before and as no South American country has ever been governed since," when it enjoyed "a quite unprecedented period of peace and prosperity ... derived from his seeking first the kingdom of God, from his uncompromising respect for the social rights of Christ the King."[3]

It would appear, however, that even when well intentioned, democracy as a political system does not command the same blessings accorded by God to monarchies. That democracy is structured less closely to natural law than monarchy is not the only reason, for there is another far more serious. When Garcia Moreno summed up his political philosophy as "freedom for everything and for all except for evil and evil-doers," he promised more than any free democracy, by its very nature, can deliver, for our Lady had prophesied what would inevitably come to pass in Catholic Ecuador: "This republic, having allowed entry to all the vices, will have to undergo all sorts of chastisements; plague, famine, war, apostasy and the loss of souls without number."

She does not blame these ills on Ecuador's form of government directly, but by saying it "allowed entry to all the vices," she put her finger on democracy's fatal flaw, one for which there is no remedy, for it is congenital. Built squarely on equality and religious liberty as governing principles, democratic government in due course of time proves utterly incapable of protecting its citizens from harm within or without, for a system which grants equal rights to individuals and freedom to all beliefs has no legitimate means of *excluding* either error or its consequences from the body politic. In other words, democracy promotes and encourages evil by the very way it works, without necessarily intending it. Sooner or later republics auto-destruct for want of an auto-immune system. To dissolve them, nothing beyond the original sin at the heart of each of its citizens is required. Democracy is to politics what usury is to economics.

Against this backdrop it is easy to see why the first successful political onslaught against Christ the King took place in the New World rather than in the Old, and specifically in the New Atlantis. It was, after all, the American Revolution and not the French Revolution which set off all the others. The *encyclopédistes* who manufactured the French revolt and put together the French Constitution of 1791 freely acknowledged the English as originators of the revolution then in progress. In

1788 one of their number, the Marquis de Condorcet, actually authored a work entitled *The Influence of the American Revolution on Europe*, which has incurred no refutation.

That Thomas Jefferson and James Madison launched a newspaper from the United States called the National Gazette for the express purpose of whipping up enthusiasm for the French Revolution even as its atrocities were being perpetrated, is well known to historians of the period. On his deathbed Jefferson wrote commemorating the 50th anniversary of the American Declaration of Independence, "May it be to the world what I think it will be ... the arousing of men to burst the chains under which monkish ignorance and superstition had persuaded them to bind themselves, and to assume the blessings of security of self government.... All eyes are opened, or opening, to the rights of man."

Crucial as was the fall of the French monarchy, it therefore did not initiate the domino effect which within the space of a hundred years literally leveled Christendom's every fortification. This is a fact of history which Catholics of the U.S. find difficult to grasp, living as they do in a land blessed with "religious freedom" of a kind to be found nowhere else on earth, where the Faith is practiced without hindrance on an equal footing as one of any number of other religions. Surely the enemy must be looked for somewhere else and not in the United States!

The *Declaration of Independence*, whose ideology lay at the bottom of Bacon's Bensalem and the ideal free republic which our Lady prophesied at Quito would take over the world, was mostly an emotional outburst against the reigning English sovereign George III. Penned by a disloyal subject and unanimously approved by a covey of like-minded others, it is seldom read in its entirety by those it aimed to benefit, but it served its purpose by formulating into quasi-juridical eighteenth century jargon the new democratic principles which would be used to circumvent the rights of Christ's kingship. If they played well in America, they could be applied with all the more telling effect back home in Europe. The document's treasonable intent was evident to all, for even as it was being signed, the group's ringleader Benjamin Franklin had quipped, "Gentlemen, let's hang together, or we'll all hang separately."

According to this unprecedented Declaration, "governments are instituted among men" not to facilitate their way to heaven, but "to secure [their] rights ... deriving their just powers" not from God, but "from the consent of the governed; that whenever any form of government becomes destructive of these ends, it is the right of the people to alter or abolish it, and to institute a new government, laying its foundations on such principles, and organizing its powers in such form, as to them shall seem most likely to effect their safety and happiness." In other words, the document would claim that men possess an inborn right to revolution because authority originates from themselves. It is Lucifer's *non serviam* in political dress.

With some humor Christopher Hollis notes in The *American Heresy* how its author Jefferson, "at his wits' end to give a reason for doing what he wanted to do, solved the difficulty by writing, 'We hold these truths to be self-evident.' " Needless to say the name of Jesus Christ, who assured us that all authority comes from God, is nowhere to be found in the *Declaration*, nor is it found in the utopian Constitution of the United States of America, which the revolutionaries worked out on paper and imposed on themselves thirteen years later as the law of the land. Hollis points out that with such a political philosophy, "America is an example of how the principles of liberty and equality, unregulated by religious authority which can adjust their competing claims, may destroy a state. For it was inevitable that, since he had not reason to compel assent, each man would restate these principles as it suited his convenience."

Omitting by design the name of God and the Son to whom "all power is given ... in heaven and in earth" (Matt. 28:18), the Constitution formally denies the rights bestowed on Christ the King from all eternity by almighty God. Is it any wonder that within less than a hundred years of its inception the new nation founded on revolution as principle began falling apart? That it still endures at all can only be attributed to the residual Christianity of its citizens and the preservation of unity at gunpoint after four years of bloody, fratricidal civil warfare. It stands today as a model of the free society where divorce, contraception, abortion, sodomy and other crimes crying to heaven for vengeance enjoy the protection of the law in the name of liberty. The truth is, the United States is dying young of its own genetic disease after infecting the whole world.

Democracy has metastasized, just as our Lady of Quito came to tell America it would. Cardinal Pie once said, "When a country's Christianity is reduced to the proportion of domestic life, when Christianity is no longer the soul of public life, of the power of the state and of public institutions, then Jesus Christ will treat such a country as He himself is treated. He will continue to bestow His Grace and His blessings on those who serve Him, but He will abandon the institutions and authorities that do not serve Him. And such institutions, authorities, kings and races become like sands in the desert or like the dead leaves of autumn which can be blown away by a gust of wind."

+

So far the United States has produced only one canonized saint. She is Elizabeth Ann Seton, a convert from Episcopalianism née Bayley of a Tory family in New York in 1774. Now acclaimed as the foundress of the American parochial school system, she had hoped to affiliate her community with St. Vincent de Paul's Sisters of Charity in France, but on solicitations emanating from the See of Baltimore had been persuaded to abandon the project. What was wanted in the new free republic was indigenous, all-American orders without foreign ties which would conform more closely to the democratic ideals of the nation. It was not unusual to encourage foreign priests not wholly persuaded of the blessings of democracy to undertake parish work in the more westerly territories of Kentucky and beyond, or to evangelize the Indians.

Mother Seton obediently complied with what was expected of her, and today she is the sole American saint in the calendar born in the territorial U.S. With the friendly cooperation of the Vatican, her canonization was scheduled to coincide with the U. S. Bicentennial celebration in 1976, hallowed anniversary of the aforesaid *Declaration of Independence*. On November 11, 1997 the process for a second politically correct canonization was opened for another U.S. born candidate, Mother Marie Henriette Delille, a "free person of color" who founded the Sisters of the Holy Family for black women in New Orleans in the 1800's. The Church in the United States has yet to produce a martyr.

Or dare we say, none officially recognized. For a significant period between 1820 and 1860, however, the prospects looked only too good, for the more irascible elements of the eastern Wasp establishment seemed bent on reviving in America the bitter religious wars which had taken place in Europe in the wake of the Reformation – especially the Battle of the Boyne between the Orange and the Green. Their motivation may not have been entirely religious, originating to some degree in resentment over the loss of jobs to large numbers of invasive Irish immigrants who happened to be Catholic rather than in outright hostilty to the Faith, but the net result was the same.

Open, violent persecution broke out on August 11, 1831 when a convent school run by four Ursuline nuns outside Boston in Georgetown, Massachusetts was sacked and burned to the ground, despite the fact that four-fifths of the student body were upper class Protestants. According to the authors of *Progress of the Catholic Church in America* published on the occasion of the Columbian Exposition, "It was well known that the nuns had been most scrupulously careful not to meddle with the religious opinions of their scholars, and that not one conversion to the Church could be ascribed to their influence," yet when "a Miss Harrison had, from excessive application to music, become partially demented," the time was deemed right for active retaliation.

Miss Harrison soon recovered from her indisposition, but the incident was followed by desecrations of Catholic graveyards, riots, assaults and burnings of private residences in adjacent areas. Spreading into New York, the disaffection gradually took over the whole country, moving westward to Kentucky and Catholic St. Louis in Missouri, where a local paper reported, "For forty-eight hours the city has been the scene of one of the most appalling riots that has ever taken place in the country. Men have been butchered like cattle, property destroyed and anarchy reigns supreme.... The military and police have thus far been unable to check the onward march of lawlessness and crime."

In Philadelphia in 1843, a nativist group offended by Bishop Kenrick's request that Catholic public school children be allowed to use the Douai Bible instead of the Protestant version, engaged some tough Irish street fighters in a three day brawl which ended in a fatality and scores of wounded. Whole blocks of Catholic homes and two churches fell prey to arson. Another altercation in Southwark required the intervention of the state militia. There was less trouble in the agricultural south which, prior to the massive "steamboat" immigrations to the industrial north, was inhabited by the largest percentage of Catholics, yet outbreaks occurred even as far as Louisiana.

By 1850 militant political enclaves had begun forming to save America the Beautiful from the Pope. When the Holy Father sent Archbishop Cajetan Bedini, Papal Nuncio to Brazil, on an ill-timed visit to the U.S. in 1853 to report on internal conditions in the Church, certain factions pronounced the danger imminent and called for action. The following year the "Know-Nothings," a secret society operating under cover of the newly formed American Party, perpetrated a major outrage on the Convent of Mercy in Providence, Rhode Island, succeeded by yet another on a German church in Newark, New Jersey, where a Catholic was killed. In Maine a Jesuit who had entered into a controversy over public schools was stripped naked, ridden on a rail, tarred and feathered and left for dead.

Shortly after midnight on March 6, 1854 nine members of the Know-Nothings stole onto the grounds of the Washington Monument then under construction in Washington. D.C. Having poisoned the watch dog and tied up the watchman at gunpoint, they took sledge hammers to a marble slab from the ancient temple of Concord which happened to be Pius IX's contribution to some 195 other memorials donated worldwide to face the inside walls of the Monument. According to an interview with one of the surviving conspirators which was published in the Washington Post in 1883, the Pope's stone was carried to the river, which in those days was less than 100 yards away, and taken by boat to the vicinity of what is now the 14th Street Bridge, where it was dumped overboard. No one was ever prosecuted, and no trace of the stone was ever found, although parts were allegedly confided to the Smithsonian and perpetrators are said to have kept pieces of it.

According to the *New York Times* the Know-Nothing party, "Without presses, without electioneering, with no prestige or power ... has completely overthrown and swamped the two old historic parties of the country." In *History of Bigotry in the United States*, Gustavus Meyers writes, "The strength of the Know-Nothings was shown in the elections of 1854.... They elected Governors in nine states and filled legislatures and Congress with Know-Nothing adherents. A clear majority of 33,000 was reaped in Massachusetts. In Congress eight of the sixty-two members of the Senate were avowed members of this party, and 104 of the 234 members of the House of Representatives. Many other Congressmen were too timid to oppose Know-Nothingism." [4]

The political zealots were ably supported by voluminous rhetoric from Protestant pulpits and publishers. Besides established newspapers like the *New York Herald*, periodicals like "The American Crusader" and the Reverend Sperry's "American Anti-Papist" were launched specifically to further the cause, not to mention inflammatory "exposés" allegedly revealing the scandalous carrying on of priests and nuns inside religious houses. The defamatory *Six Months in a Convent* by the apostate "Sister Mary Agnes" was surpassed only by Maria Monk's notorious fabrication *Awful Disclosures*, which not only turned out to be the *Uncle Tom's Cabin* of the nativist movement but was put back into circulation a century later when the Catholic President John Kennedy was running for election.

Although many hot-headed Irishmen injudiciously confronted their persecutors with their fists or better during this hectic time, theirs was never a course of action recommended by their prelates, whose defense strategy seems to have consisted mainly in loudly protesting the high quality of their Americanism rather than any truths of the Faith. The unfortunate Archbishop Bedini was openly insulted in the press and in the streets throughout his visit, not to mention being burned in effigy in Cincinnati and threatened with assassination in New York; yet, as John Cogley relates in *Catholic America*, "Not one American bishop ... came to his defense publicly during his turbulent stay." [5] The Archbishop's subsequent report must have provided Pius IX much food for thought, some of which may have found its way into the *Syllabus of Errors*, published eight years later. The American Catholic ecclesiastical establishment has never deviated from its support of the Masonic government, even at the height of the anti-Masonic sentiment which swept the country after the Morgan affair in the 1830's. Under the leadership of Protestant journalists like Thurlow Weed and Henry Dana Ward, a former Mason, not only was the number of lodges in New York state reduced almost overnight from 600 to 50, but an anti-Masonic political party was formed which merged with the Whigs in 1834. Commenting on a preliminary meeting in Baltimore, the *Anti-Masonic Review* had sounded the clarion note by openly declaring in October 1830, "The ministry is corrupted, the church is defiled, Christianity is supplanted in the affections and confidence of this generation, by the arts of Free Masonry," but these words found no echo in the Catholic hierarchy, which maintained a neutral stance throughout the entire period. In fact, anti-Masonic Catholic literature of any kind was virtually non-existent throughout the 1800's.

18 APOSTASY

Among the first ecclesiastical spokesmen for the Catholic cause was the Irish-born John England, Bishop of Charleston, South Carolina, who in 1826 founded our first Catholic periodical, "The United States Catholic Miscellany" for the express purpose of refuting what Protestants saw only too clearly, namely that, "Republicanism and Catholicism have no affinity or relationship whatsoever, nor can they ever be cordially united because of their basic differences." In 1843 Fr. Charles Pise published a series of eighteen letters under the title *Aletheya* which attempted to demonstrate how Catholics can sincerely support democratic institutions without prejudice to their Faith. As persecution mounted, countless other clerics preached in the same vein, presuming to hold the enemy at bay by confirming their flocks in the heresy which in due time would be identified as Americanism.

All stood squarely on the precedent set by the nation's first Bishop, the liberal John Carroll, whose appointment had been maneuvered by the Founding Fathers in a shrewd bid for Catholic cooperation. Not that the Fathers ran any risk of compromising their convictions, for under a Constitution specifying that "Congress shall make no law respecting an establishment of religion, or prohibiting the free exercise thereof," how could there ever be any recognition, let alone enforcement, of the exclusive rights of Christ the King over society and every individual in it? Under the partisan leadership of the Americanist establishment operating from the See of Baltimore, the Catholics of the New Atlantis were gradually brought to accept as their very own the political agenda of the Masonic *Novus Ordo Seclorum*.

Even as the persecutions were gathering momentum in the 1830's, Alexis de Tocqueville would report that Catholics "constitute the most republican and democratic class in America." This is still true today, when the Catholics who arrived on the last boats prove more likely to defend the now near-defunct Constitution than descendants of the earliest settlers. An Americanist parochial school text used prior to the Second Vatican Council gloried that, "The very existence of a hierarchy distinctive for its particular American national character, independent of the Apostolic Bishopric in London, of the ecclesiastical jurisdiction of the neighboring French Bishopric in Quebec and of the trusteeship of the French Episcopacy, has eloquently proved the patriotic loyalty of the Catholic clergy in the new, expanding Republic." [6]

Had the Civil War not broken out when it did, it is impossible to say what would have been the immediate outcome of a situation in some respects similar to the one raging in Northern Ireland today. After Ft. Sumter, however, when both North and South found themselves in sudden desperate need of conscripts, religious differences tended to dissolve into the national emergency. In the evangelical North, where the war was extremely unpopular, the persecution of Catholics was quickly diverted into forcing them into the ranks of the military. With, we might add, the able aid of their religious mentors. Archbishop Hughes of New York, a personal friend of the, possibly, apostate Catholic Abraham Lincoln, declared unequivocally, "The Union must and will be preserved!" He enthusiastically supported the draft, assuring the faithful, "This is not cruelty but mercy. This is humanity.... You must be loyal and patriotic and do for your country what the country asks. Divine benedictions will reward those who fulfill their duties without hesitation and without violating any of the divine, human laws."

+

After the Union victory the Catholic establishment did not rest on its laurels, but redoubled its efforts to prove its wholehearted dedication to the democratic ideology and America's "manifest destiny." A climax of sorts was reached in 1884, when the Fathers of the Third Plenary Council in Baltimore addressed an official letter to the Catholics of North America, urging parents to educate their children "in the history of our country. We regard the crowning independence of our country, the winning of liberty and the adopting of its laws as the masterpiece of a special Providence because its architects, building even more wisely than they themselves realized, *had the hand of God to guide them*." Thus it would seem that the Constitution of the United States, which rigorously excludes religion from government and never mentions the name of God, was nonetheless divinely inspired. This being the case, the Council Fathers averred, "If the heritage of freedom which they left us should ever be in danger, heaven forbid! Our Catholic citizens will find themselves on their feet, out in front as one person, ready once more to give their lives, their fortunes and their sacred honor, etc., etc."

Needless to say, the politically correct apostasy known as Americanism had acquired enormous impetus during the troubled pre-Civil War period and was a preponderant factor in forming this mentality among Catholics. In no wise hatched in the United States, it was a heresy which, like the American Revolution itself, had been brought over from England. Lydia Logan has shown in "Lord Baltimore's Bungle" how it arrived here in the Ark and the Dove as the constituent principle of the "ecumenical" Catholic colony established in Maryland by Lord Calvert, long before the sovereign States entered into union. [7] As we shall see in the next chapter, it was this Maryland colony which provided the working model for the religious freedom clause which was incorporated into the Bill of Rights at Bishop Carroll's suggestion and which figures as the original Constitution's first amendment.

In great part through the efforts of Fr. Isaac Hecker and the Order of Paulists which he and other converts from Protestantism founded in 1858, Americanism claimed many liberal areas of the Church, not only in the U.S. but in Europe as well, not excepting Rome itself. Even after the heresy was formally condemned by Leo XIII, its principles continued to be disseminated by means of the Americanist media founded by Bishop England and a parochial school system second to none in the world. In due time articulate prelates like Archbishop John Ireland of St. Paul, wielding "the Bible in one hand and the Constitution in the other" under the benign gaze of Cardinal Gibbons, led the generality in the pews to believe that the interests of Christ the King and those of Atlantis had always been more or less the same.

Thus far the disedifying tale of the Faith as practiced in the United States of America, which need not be pursued further here, beyond noting that Catholic persecution did not cease with the Civil War. In 1889 the well known American Protective Association was put together on a platform postulating that "the support of any ecclesiastical power of non-American character with equal or greater sovereignty than the government of the United States is irreconcilable with American citizenship," and that political office should therefore be denied to anyone "subject to or in support of said ecclesiastical power." Whoever believes this spirit of intolerance has finally subsided, need only dip into *An Ugly Little Secret* by Fr. Andrew Greeley, who without descent into subterfuge calls anti-Catholicism "as American as blueberry pie." It is part and parcel of the American heritage and here to stay, yet "most Catholics are not concerned about anti-Catholicism," says he, because "they are not hurting." [8]

They are not hurting because when they were under heavy persecution they learned, or were taught, not how to embrace martyrdom, but how best to accommodate their Faith to the demands of those they were supposed to convert. Catholics today who with clear consciences vote pro-abortion candidates into public office are direct lineal descendants of those who were taught in parochial schools to accept revolutionary principles as part of their religion. Where Church and state operate independently, why not morality and law? Under such a system, they will argue, why does legal have to be right?

By the time the Second Vatican Council convened, the Catholics of the United States had learned so well how to live peacefully as one religious denomination among others in a pluralistic society that they felt honor bound to teach the rest of the Church how to share religious liberty with their fellows rather than impose their convictions on them. With the able help of the American Jesuit Fr. John Courtney Murray and a few others, the old spirit of Atlantis found its way into the pronouncements of the Council, emerging therefrom newly–fledged as "the spirit of Vatican II." There is only slight exaggeration in saying that the practical details of the accommodations to the world which are preached in the Pastoral Constitution on "The Church and the Modern World" had been worked out long ago in the U.S. in the days of the "Know-Nothings."

Never have American Catholics got on so well with everybody. Rather than calling them "expatriates," perhaps a better word would be "ex-patriots," for it is difficult to see how true love of country can coexist with indifference to the eternal salvation of com-patriots, let alone the fate of the nation as a whole. Do they reflect that the soil they tread was consecrated to the Most Blessed Trinity and claimed for Christ the King nearly three hundred years before the Constitution was ratified? Do they reflect that this Consecration has never been revoked and must still be honored? And for future reference, let them not rely too heavily on the Constitution's guarantee of freedom of religion, for it applies only to laws made by Congress, specifying nothing in regard to executive orders of the President or judgments handed down by the Supreme Court.

If persecution does not show its face openly as it once did, that is because so few Catholics are any longer so, but "Protestants who go to Mass," as Hamish Fraser put it. Triumphant they may be, but hardly

Suffering and certainly not Militant. Yet we know that true Catholics will always draw persecution, for as St. Paul said, "All who will live piously in Christ Jesus shall suffer persecution" (2 Tim. 3:12). These are drawing it today, at every level of society, especially in families, but it is camouflaged and comes from a new breed of heretics, the "reformed" Catholics of the *Novus Ordo Seclorum*, their faith recast in the spirit of the Council and the conciliarist Popes.

A holy angel is said to have told Maria Valtorta in 1947, "Consider that the apathy, continual bad habits or open hypocrisy of false or weak Christians are more injurious to religion than the violent stabs of the enemies of God. Religion and the church are injured by the lukewarmness of the faithful more than by the aggression of enemies. Do not turn confession [of the Faith] into a party weapon. See what happened when Israel made the Hebrew confession a political instrument. Never give holy things for profane uses. But be holy, though, in public life as well, so that the dark forces will not prevail and morality and the Faith will be defended." [9]

In the fall of 1979 the Pope of Rome in the person of John Paul II met with the President of the United States in that nation's capital city, where His Holiness celebrated Christ's redeeming Sacrifice on the great mall midway between the Capitol and the phallic obelisk known as the Washington Monument, on a Sunday which happened to be the Feast of the Most Holy Rosary. The previous Wednesday had found Christ's Vicar in Battery Park, New York, addressing a large outdoor audience in words he thought proper to conclude with a heartfelt "*Shalom!*" He spoke in full view of the Statue of Liberty Enlightening the World, the great Anti-Mary of the Americas who keeps fearful watch over sunken Atlantis with her back turned to the Lady of Guadalupe who bides her time on the opposite side of the continent. A proper luciferian idol whose halo is an illuminated spiked crown, she brandishes in her right hand a giant electric torch and in her left hand a book inscribed with the date July 4, 1776, birthday of the *Declaration of Independence* and the New Atlantis.

In the presence of this hallowed false goddess, at the dedication of whose effigy the U.S. President had promised, "We will not forget that Liberty has here made her home; nor shall her chosen altar be neglected," the Catholic Pope delivered his own *akathistos* of praise, saying, "My visit to your city would not be complete without coming to Battery Park, without seeing Ellis Island and the Statue of Liberty in the distance. "Every nation has its historical symbols. They may be shrines, or statues or documents; but their significance lies in the truths they represent to the citizens of a nation and in the image they convey to other nations. This is an impressive symbol of what the United States has stood for from the very beginning of its history; this is a symbol of freedom.... On this spot I wish to pay homage to this noble trait of America and its people: its desire to be free, its determination to preserve freedom, and its willingness to share this freedom with others. May the ideal of liberty, of freedom remain a moving force for your nation and for all the nations in the world today!"

And His Holiness noted particularly that "the right to religious liberty is deeply rooted in your country." Indeed it is. As we have seen, Catholics led the way in accommodating the Faith to the principles of democracy, first at home, and then throughout the Church. Had the crowd wished to burst out at the close of the Pope's talk with a hearty, "LONG LIVE CHRIST THE KING, SON OF THE LIVING GOD AND OUR IMMACULATE EMPRESS OF THE AMERICAS! there was no law on the books anywhere in the United States to restrain them. But no one did. In the New Atlantis, who is Christ the King?

LORD BALTIMORE'S UTOPIA

When John Paul II told the crowds assembled in Battery Park that "the right to religious liberty is deeply rooted in your country," he was telling only part of the story, for that liberty was never planted on these shores by Protestants, who with few exceptions in colonial times had been noted for rigorous intolerance. Much less the fruit of the Constitution eventually adopted in 1789, religious freedom was introduced into that very Constitution by way of an amendment embodying a principle laid down a hundred and fifty years before by the founders of Maryland, the Union's only Catholic colony. In other words, the seeds of ecumenism, religious pluralism and heretical Americanism were not brought to these shores by the Mayflower, but by the Ark and the Dove, not by fanatical Puritans, but by tolerant Catholics.

By the time the Constitution was ratified, the results in Maryland had already proved what could be expected from such an experiment. Skeptics need only visit St. Mary's City today, tucked within a beautiful inlet on St. Mary's River in southern Maryland. Once the scene of violent confrontations, here in 1634 the prosperous Lord Baltimore had invited English Catholic and Protestant settlers alike to establish the first non-sectarian community in the New World. Envisioned as what might be described as a little Catholic utopia existing within the greater Atlantean one, it occupied the site of what was originally an Indian village, renamed in honor of our Lady by Jesuit missionaries.

Now that the little town has become one of the nation's shrines to democracy, the visitor is greeted by an oversized statue of a young nude Apollo emerging triumphantly from a roughly quarried stone with his eyes uplifted to the heavens. Erected by the Maryland counties for their Tricentennial celebration in 1934, the monument proclaims a formidable message, spelled out on its base in the words, FREEDOM OF CONSCIENCE. The Catholic faith has somehow survived throughout the Maryland population, in which are numbered countless descendants of early Indian converts, but buildings dating from St. Mary's inception which are still Catholic are nowhere to be found. The charming chapel called Trinity near the river is Protestant Episcopalian, as is famous St. Mary's College to the right. Resting on its laurels and tidy lawns, St. Mary's now presents the appearance of a snug, well-endowed Anglican enclave.

Except for those Catholics dead to this world whose remains lie beneath the chapel or here and there under headstones in the old cemetery, Christ's faithful have obviously gone elsewhere. As for Lord Baltimore's vision of peaceful co-existence, where does it lie? Rather than search through the grounds of St. Mary's for telltale artifacts, more conclusive results can be obtained by examining the deeds and misdeeds of milord and his fellow dreamers as they emerge from the archives of the period. Who will not learn from history, as they say, is doomed to repeat it, and this particular little segment of history is being repeated by Catholics on an unprecedented scale pretty much everywhere today.

+

Lord Baltimore's story yields a mass of contradictions which historians have been powerless, or perhaps unwilling to resolve, and needless to say they do not coincide in many respects with the popular version agreed upon for dissemination throughout the parochial and public school systems. The zealous, enlightened and fearless Catholic convert who in his new-found fervor wrested permission from James I, a Protestant monarch noted for his religious intolerance, to found a sanctuary where persecuted papists could flourish in peace, simply refuses to stand out clearly from the existing documents. What does arise is the suspicion that this idealized Calvert may be an Americanist creation, calculated to adjust Catholic thinking to the prevailing Masonic naturalism in which the United States of America was conceived.

Like other political figures who seemed to spring full blown out of nowhere to wield sudden power in an England summarily cut off from its spiritual head in Rome, George Calvert has exceedingly obscure origins. He is known to have been the son of a Leonard Calvert, or Calvaert, of Flemish origin, as the name would imply, who resided in Yorkshire in the days of Elizabeth and married an English Protestant by the name of Alicia

Crossland. Nothing is known for certain of his prior antecedents beyond the fact that Leonard's father was called John. Leonard's son George, however, married one Alice Mynne (or Mayne) who happened to be the granddaughter of Sir Thomas Wroth, the English commissioner to Ireland under Elizabeth, and apparently on the strength of his connections with the new "abbey-burning" aristocracy rising to prominence in England at the time, he entered public service.

While studying on the Continent he had formed a long-standing friendship with Robert Cecil, son and successor of Elizabeth's infamous Secretary of State Sir William Cecil, after whom he named his first son Cecilius. His fortunes rose rapidly thereafter. The Maryland historian William Hand Browne says in *George Calvert and Cecilius Calvert*, that he "became Cecil's private secretary and was appointed by the king clerk of the Crown and of assize in County Clare, Ireland, an office of importance resembling that of an attorney-general. This was the first link connecting Calvert with Ireland, in which kingdom he was afterwards to hold considerable estates and a place on the role of nobility." After Cecil's death "he was appointed clerk to the Privy Council and was sent on a mission to Ireland to report on the success of James' new policy of bringing the Irish to conformity with the religion and obedience to the law of England."

His reports "dwell especially on the harmful influence of the Jesuits; a point worth noting, as we shall see later that his son and successor entertained a strong suspicion and dislike of that order."[10] Becoming a favorite of the anti-Catholic King James, George Calvert found himself employed in important diplomatic missions. In 1617 he was knighted and succeeded the powerful Cecils as principal Secretary of State. According to the French ambassador Tillières, the control of all public affairs passed into his hands and those of Lord Buckingham. In addition to an important treasury post, he occupied seats in Parliament, for Yorkshire in 1621 and Oxford in 1624, having by that time been rewarded for his services with a 2,300-acre estate in Ireland in County Longford, on condition that all settlers "should be conformable in point of religion."

Given the political turbulence of the times, meteoric rises to power from obscure backgrounds were not unusual. William Cecil's own career had been similar to Calvert's. As William Thomas Walsh notes in his biography of Philip II, the name Cecil had undergone many spellings, ranging from Sissill to Cecill to Sissille and others, and his coat of arms bore a remarkable resemblance to that of the prominent Israeli family of Toledo whose most famous son would turn out to be the Benjamin Disraeli who gained an ascendancy over the widowed Queen Victoria similar to the one Cecil had exercised over Elizabeth. The Marrano historian Cabrera states as common knowledge that most of the heresiarchs and heretics of the day were in fact Jews; and Abrahams in *Jewish Life in the Middle Ages* says the first leaders of the Protestant sects were everywhere known as *semi-Judaei*, men of Jewish descent being as prevalent among them as they had been among the Gnostics of earlier times – and later among the Communists.

Be that as it may, it was the policy of Cecil and his friends, with the able help of a growing body of international usurers like Sir Thomas Gresham, to underwrite subversive movements within Catholic countries. Cecil's agents were everywhere. One named Borghese was secretary to the Spanish ambassador. Sir Thomas Sackville served in Rome, and others moved among the seminarians and students of the expatriate Catholic colleges in Douai and Rheims or at Louvain. Others, presenting themselves for ordination with that very end in view, succeeded in infiltrating the Jesuits. A priest named John Cecil, a graduate of the English Catholic college at Valladolid, even gained the confidence of the shrewd Fr. Robert Persons, Superior of the underground Catholic missions in England. Others worked among the Spanish friars.

These being the forces propelling George Calvert's career from the start, his success should occasion no surprise. At its height, however, the incredible is supposed to have happened. Proclaiming himself a convert to the Church of Rome, he apparently asked to be relieved of his office. He surrendered his Irish manor, but only to receive it again with the religious clause omitted. The exact date of his conversion has, however, never been fixed with any certainty. According to the Aspinwall Papers he was received into the Church secretly in the North of England in February of 1625, having been converted some time before by Sir Francis Bacon's lifelong intimate Sir Tobie Matthews. Son of the Anglican Archbishop of York and furthermore well known to Robert Cecil, Sir Tobie was himself a sudden convert who had been ordained to the priesthood in 1614 by no less a personage than Cardinal St. Robert Bellarmine. Strange to say, this radical turnabout did not prevent his being knighted nine years later in a land where it was against the law even to worship as a Catholic!

George Calvert's story presents like anomalies. English Catholics finding themselves hopelessly torn between loyalty to their Faith and their natural patriotism, were often catapulted against their wills into dangerous compromises with the enemies of their souls, but this seems not to have been the case with Calvert. His Anglican sovereign not only retained him in the Privy Council, but elevated him to the Peerage as Baron Baltimore of County Longford, "nearly considering in person of our well-beloved and entirely faithful councillor George Calvert, knight, gravity of manners, singular gifts of mind, candor, integrity and prudence, as well as benignity and urbanity towards all men, and also reflecting in our mind with how great fidelity, diligence and alacrity he has served us...."

King James died not long after, having urged Calvert to retire in comfort to the pleasures of the country under the royal protection, but his protégé was not to be lulled by encomiums. Although he had resigned the Secretaryship, it was not for the religious reasons generally presumed, but in order to devote himself to Avalon, an ecumenical colony he had established on a plantation purchased in Newfoundland in 1620. Designed for commercial profit, the enterprise was in many ways similar to a failed settlement which Sir Humphrey Gilbert had planted there in 1583 in conjunction with two Catholic entrepreneurs, Sir George Peckham and Sir Thomas Gerard, on land originally allocated by Elizabeth to Sir Francis Bacon. Although Baltimore provided both Catholic and Protestant pastors for his settlers, unlike the community started at Plymouth by the Pilgrims at about the same time, Avalon made no pretense of harboring the religiously persecuted.

The Hon. John P. Kennedy, a severe critic of Baltimore, noted in a discourse delivered to the Maryland Historical Society on December 9, 1845 that Baltimore was for a long time "a member of a company concerned with the colonization of Virginia.... One of the Committee of Council for the plantations, he had ample opportunities to become acquainted with the character of these enterprises which very few possessed. There is indeed abundant evidence that these schemes of colonization were a favorite speculation of his. He was engaged in them from the date of his early manhood until the close of his life." Furthermore, as Proprietary and absolute Lord of Avalon, "He possessed the patronage and avowedsons of all churches and chapels, and to cause them to be consecrated according to the ecclesiastical laws of England."

Kennedy, a Scotch Presbyterian who was once the Historical Society's Vice-President, had the misfortune to publish his research at the height of the nativist uproar, drawing a barrage of fulminations from the Irish Americanist contingent not unlike those in circulation today. One indignant reviewer called his biography of Baltimore "the dullest of his works of fiction, full of grave invention, without wit or humor to enliven it," but, alas, he musters no arguments against Kennedy's contentions. Descending instead to the customary *ad hominem* bombast, he impugned the historian's patriotism by declaring, "And far more honorable to his love for his native state, had he withheld the unfilial, though impotent hand which has been extended to deprive the founders of our commonwealth of their glory and fame, as examples to the world in the establishment of a state upon principles alike sacred to liberty and sanctified by the charities of religion, etc., etc." [11]

Meanwhile, the questions raised in regard to George Calvert remain unanswered. If he was a Protestant at the time he was climbing the ladder of success, his preferment is not to be wondered at, but was he? Kennedy believes "there is proof extant to show that he had always been attached to the Church of Rome, or at least from an early period of his life." If so, then Baltimore would have merely headed the long list of indifferent American Catholics who throughout the history of the nation would not allow their religious convictions to color their political life. Among other discrepancies, Kennedy points out that he could never have retained King James' favor as he did, had he really left the Church of England for Rome.

"There were several Catholic noblemen who enjoyed the confidence and friendship of James," who felt no animosity "against such Catholics as had been bred and nurtured in that Faith ... but he was noted for avowal of particular hostility against such as had been converts from the Protestant Church." In a speech at Whitehall James excoriated the latter as "apostates," vowing, "I can never show any favorable countenance to them!" In his speech to the Star Chamber in 1616 he said, "I can love the person of a papist, being otherwise a good man and honestly bred, never having known any other religion, but the person of an apostate papist I hate!"

Unable to unearth any proof that Baltimore was ever a Protestant, Kennedy asks whether he was not rather "one of those who did not choose to make any very public exhibition of his faith." As it is, the sole authority for Calvert's alleged conversion is Fuller's *Worthies of England*, on which the entire assumption hangs. All Baltimore's children passed for Catholic, most of them already grown at the time of their father's supposed changeover. Is it likely that they too were converted at the same time? These inconsistencies have been dismissed without refutation or explanation by Americanist historians, yet they refuse to go away. Why was it expedient for George Calvert to proclaim himself a Catholic at the risk of his career if he had always been one? And if his conversion did indeed take place, why did it prove to be no obstacle to his advancement?

A third possibility exists in the light of what history reveals of secret Jews and others who found it advantageous to pose as Catholics, but it is highly speculative, and so far there is no evidence whatever of Jewish ancestry in the Calverts' lineage. We might note, however, that the only known portrait of the first Lord Baltimore is one by King James' court painter Mytens, which found its way into the possession of, here again, Francis Bacon's heirs the Earls of Verulam. Is it possible that the early Calverts had occult affiliations which their descendants would openly acknowledge only a century later? The annals of Masonry list a Calvert among the seven adepts who founded the Grand Lodge of London in 1717, and on April 11, 1730 *The Weekly Journal* or *British Gazeteer* carried the following item:

"A few days since, their Graces the Dukes of Richmond and Montagu, accompanied by several gentlemen, who were all Free and Accepted Masons according to ancient custom, formed a lodge upon the top of the hill near the Duke of Richmond's seat at Goodwood in Sussex, and made the Right Hon. the Lord Baltimore a Free and Accepted Mason." This would have been Charles, fifth Lord Baltimore, Protestant son of the apostate fourth Lord, Benedict Leonard. The first papal Bull forbidding the faithful to become Masons was promulgated only in 1738, so it is not impossible that before that date Catholic Calverts had been affiliated with the Craft without prejudice to their conscience.

+

In the face of the severe winters and the unfriendly French, who rightly resented the illegal English presence, the colony at Avalon failed as miserably as had Gilbert's, but Baltimore was not to be deflected from the ideal to which he was dedicated. He obtained from King James another grant of land in a better climate farther south, in what now comprises parts of Maryland and Virginia around Chesapeake Bay. In fact before undertaking the settlement in Maryland, Calvert would sponsor a second failure in Virginia in 1629, losing his wife and part of his family at sea on the return to England. The final Maryland charter was actually granted to his son Cecil and confirmed by King James' son Charles I, for both George Calvert and his royal benefactor had died before the transaction could be officially approved. By its terms the second Lord Baltimore was made absolute ruler of the new grant as he had been at Avalon, receiving extraordinary powers from a ruler who was accustomed to deal very cautiously with declared Catholics.

According to the historian William T. Russell, Baltimore and his heirs were given what amounted to the rights of a king in the new domain, "confirmed in the proprietorship of the land, islands and islets, the lakes, rivers and bays; they were given ecclesiastical jurisdiction over the Palatinate and power to ordain, make and enact laws with the advice and assent of the freemen of the province, while in certain cases it lay within their right to legislate independently of the freemen assembled; with them rested the power to appoint judges, justices, magistrates and officers, to pardon and release either before or after judgment had been passed ... to hold pleas in the execution of the laws if it be necessary to deprive of member or life...." [12]

The seventeenth century community planner had indeed been declared "absolute Lord of Maryland," yet how explain that King Charles dared favor a papist so openly? What was the real relationship between the Calverts and the royal family, where the queen was a French Catholic and the king himself was suspected of Catholic leanings? Were the two families in fact bound by secret Catholic sympathies? Or were there occult forces at play behind the scenes, intent on promoting their own agenda by encouraging religious equality in the colonies? In *History of a Palatinate*, William Hand Browne says that shortly before Charles I's execution, "the Close Committee of Parliament held a secret meeting at which Baltimore and two or three other Catholics were present," as a result of which they "sent a message to Charles in prison that if he would recede from his firm stand and own himself to have been in some measure in the wrong, they would save his life and if possible his crown."

Charles I's downfall is generally attributed to his uncompromising treatment of forces hostile to him in Parliament, but the English historian Macauley suggests that his death was not without religious overtones. What sort of stand, exactly, did Calvert wish his royal friend to recede from? Charles refused, carrying the nature of the request to the grave, as well as the true state of affairs between the two families, but after his execution his son Charles II, who died a Catholic, considered Calvert a rebel. According to Browne, the new King proceeded to confer "lands given by his father to Calvert to Sir William Davenant the English poet. Davenant actually set sail for the province, but was seized in the British channel by a Parliament cruiser and his plans brought to an untimely end."

Did the second Charles suspect Calvert of playing a double game? His father Charles I had wanted the new colony to be called *Marianna*, but George Calvert had opted strangely enough for *Crescentia*. Eventually they compromised by naming it Maryland in honor of the Queen, Henriette Marie, daughter of Henri IV and sister of Louis XIII of France. Some like to think that the name was tacitly understood to refer to our Lady, but if so, history is silent on the matter. Choosing to direct affairs from England so as to keep an eye on the vagaries of Parliament, George Calvert's son Cecil appointed his young 26-year-old brother Leonard as Governor of Maryland, on whose soil freedom of conscience would supposedly first see the light of day, brought forth to the modern world under Catholic auspices.

In "Maryland Two Hundred Years Ago," another discourse to the Maryland Historical Society delivered in Baltimore on May 20, 1852, seven years after Kennedy's, Sebastian F. Streeter categorically denied that this was the case. He says, "The assertion has long passed uncontradicted that toleration was promised to the colonists in the first conditions of plantation; that the rights of conscience were recognized in a law passed by the first Assembly held in the colony; and that the principal officers from the year 1636 or 7 bound themselves not to molest, on account of his religion, anyone professing to believe in Jesus Christ. I can find no authority for any of these statements." He maintains that no such act was passed "until fifteen years after the first settlement, at which time a Protestant had been appointed Governor and a majority of the Burgesses were of the same faith; and when for the first time a clause involving a promise not to molest any person professing to believe in Jesus Christ and 'particularly a Roman Catholic' was inserted by the direction of Lord Baltimore in the official oath."

Before that time, avers he, only *practical* toleration could have existed. He would accord the honor of toleration to neither Catholic nor Protestant, but only to outright necessity and the force of circumstances beyond anyone's control. Lord Baltimore simply had no choice, and the laws "were drawn up in deference to the progressive doctrines and increasing political strength of the Independents in England, as well as to meet the wants of the mixed population." It was plain civil necessity without religious character and "an unavoidable consequence of the provisions of the charter, the peculiar position of the Proprietary and the mixed religious opinions of the people."

Whatever the truth of the matter, the Baltimores accorded Catholics no special privileges in their so-called "Catholic" colony, where religious discussions were strictly prohibited to all. The second Lord's well known dislike of the Jesuits furthermore added materially to that Order's difficulties in the conversion of souls. In defiance of the Bull *In caena Domini*, in which the Pope asserts the Church's full jurisdiction over ecclesiastics, Baltimore insisted that the Fathers be subject to the common law like everyone else. He refused them the right to own property, nor would he contribute to their support, even petitioning Rome for their removal in favor of a secular clergy. Today Maryland is still the only state where no land may be owned by a religious body without the consent of the legislature.

Like Streeter, John Kennedy persisted in denying that "in the planting of either Avalon or Maryland Lord Baltimore was moved by a special desire to provide asylum for persecuted Catholics, as many have alleged," and finds, "no reason to believe that he was a very ardent or zealous follower of his faith." Be that as it may, many English Catholics, by that time worn out from nearly a century of specious compromises which always ended by worsening their position, were drawn to compromise once more and take refuge in the ecumenical exile offered to them in the New Atlantis by their persecutors. No doubt most of them viewed their decision as a simple matter of facing facts in treacherous political terrain still remaining to be charted.

The Catholic Church will on no account place error on the same level as truth and accord it equal rights, but never has she been against toleration on principle in the civil domain. On June 20, 1888 Leo XIII would teach clearly in the encyclical *Libertas* that "right is a moral power which ... it is absurd to suppose nature has accorded indifferently to truth and falsehood, to justice and injustice," yet he would also say, "In view of the common good and for that reason alone, the laws of men may, and even should tolerate evil." When it is impossible to eliminate an evil entirely, the age-old principle of the lesser evil comes into play, allowing a minor ill to subsist rather than cause society a greater one directly contrary to the common good. This is why King St. Louis IX of France permitted bawdy-houses within his realm, and why Protestant churches were eventually countenanced in Catholic countries.

The directive in such cases was laid down by Our Lord himself in the parable of the cockle and the wheat, where the master forbids his servants to pull up the weeds, "lest perhaps while ye gather up the cockle, you root up the wheat also together with it. Let both grow until the harvest" (Matt. 13:29-30). As in Solomon's judgment between the two harlots, each laying claim to the same infant as her own, the Church always acts like the rightful mother, who is willing to relinquish the child to the false mother rather than see him perish by being cut in two to satisfy them both. (3 Kgs. 3:16 ff.) As Admiral Berger recently pointed out, "Civil tolerance is a rule and practice of political prudence in the service of orthodoxy," [13] and for that very reason, as Pope Leo said, it must be "rigorously circumscribed within the limits of ... the public good."

This is the problem which a handful of Catholics hoped to resolve by running away from it at home, jumping, as it turned out, from the frying pan into the fire. The interfaith colony designed to rid England of unemployment and Catholic recusants, which had been contemplated first by Sir Humphrey Gilbert and then by George Calvert, finally materialized, not in Newfoundland in defiance of the French Catholics as originally planned, but at the very heart of the new Masonic utopia already beginning to taking shape on America's southeastern flank. Among those arriving aboard the Ark and the Dove to lay the foundations of Maryland would be Richard Gerard, son of the Sir Thomas Gerard who had collaborated so actively in Sir Humphrey Gilbert's ill-fated venture.

The two ships had not always served purposes as peaceful as their names would suggest, for they had seen heavy duty at Avalon some years before under the first Lord Baltimore, when the French Admiral de la Rade[14] and "the flower of Normandy's youth" attacked the illegal English fisheries and outlaying stations in Newfoundland. As the Proprietor later wrote Lord Buckingham, the French raid would have been successful, "had I not sent ... assistance with two ships of mine, one of three hundred and sixty tons and twenty-four pieces of ordnance, and another a bark of sixty tons with three or four small guns in her, and about a hundred men aboard us in all." Although not referring to the ships by name, they were, of course, the Ark and the Dove, the latter pressed into service as supply ship to the other.

Advised that de la Rade was "committing more spoil" in Conception Bay, "I sent forth the great ship again, with all the seamen I had here, and one of my sons with some gentlemen and others that attend me in this plantation." Joining forces with "Captain Fearnes, a man of war," the Ark succeeded in capturing six French ships "in a harbor called Trépassée ... near ready to return homewards. These we took for the hurt they have done us, and have sent them now to England, where they shall arrive safely, I hope, within your Grace's admiral jurisdiction." From this incident may be judged the reality of the warfare between Catholics of differing nationalities which by now had spread from the Old World to the New.

Before Leonard Calvert and his band of pioneers were allowed to leave the port of Gravesend and sail for Maryland in November of 1633, an oath was administered to all one hundred twenty-eight persons on board by a Mr. Watkins, a conscientious London "searcher" whose duty it was to see that no one left England without duly swearing. According to Russell, a writer with Americanist bias, this oath was one of simple allegiance to the king. He assumes that the Calverts took it routinely, all the while avoiding the Oath of Supremacy which acknowledged the king as head of the Church in England. It is interesting, however, that Fr. Henry More, a member of the expedition said to be descended from St. Thomas More, stated that by far the greater number of passengers aboard the ships were heretics. By "heretics" was he referring only to the many Protestants aboard, or did he include in their number Catholics who took Mr. Watkins' oath without demur?

We may wonder whether this oath was the innocuous one Russell assumes it was, or whether it was in fact the Oath of Supremacy, which no faithful Catholic could take without risk of apostasy and which had been the occasion of so many English martyrdoms. "This supremacy," according to Macauley, "was nothing less than the whole power of the keys. The king was to be the pope of his kingdom, vicar of God, the expositor of Catholic verity, the channel of sacramental graces. He arrogated to himself the right of deciding dogmatically what was orthodox doctrine and what was heresy, of drawing up and imposing confessions of faith, and of giving religious instruction to the people. The king was the way, the overseer, the very shepherd whom the Holy Ghost had appointed and to whom the expressions of St. Paul applied."

If such was indeed the substance of Mr. Watkins' oath, what could Catholics with proper scruples have done to avoid it? As a matter of record some of the passengers, both Jesuits and laymen, did not board at Gravesend at all, but at the Cowes on the Isle of Wight off the coast, where the ships later stopped to take on extra provisions. By so doing they would have been able to by-pass Mr. Watkins' ministrations entirely, and it is possible that those who availed themselves of this stratagem were the more conscientious Catholics of the new colony.

Once past the Isle the two ships were separated during a severe storm, but they were eventually re-united, and in March 1634 on the feast of the Annunciation, the colonists reached St. Clement's Island off the Maryland coast, where a Mass was offered in thanksgiving for a safe journey. An eye witness left a detailed account of the event, which took place with every evidence of heartfelt devotion: "After we had completed the Sacrifice, we took on our shoulders a great cross which we had hewn out of a tree, and advancing in order to the appointed place with the assistance of the Governor and his associates and the other Catholics, we erected a trophy to Christ the Savior, humbly reciting on our bended knees the litanies of the Holy Savior with great emotion."

After a brief stay on St. Clement's the colonists proceeded to the territory of the Yacomicos, with whom they bartered for choice green areas. Oddly enough the Indians were only too happy to surrender these, trading half their town immediately and offering the other half after the harvest. "The settlers and the savages," cites Russell, "then promised each other to live in peace and concord, and thus, with a solemn covenant of faith to be kept and mutual assistance rendered, was founded upon justice, peace and charity the little town of St. Maries." A secure charter, grateful passengers, an abundance of fertile land and Indians bent upon pleasing the white man made for a situation entirely out of the ordinary.

Fr. Andrew White, a Jesuit member of the expedition, deemed it miraculous "that barbarous men a few days before arrayed in arms against us should so willingly surrender themselves to us like lambs and deliver up to us themselves and their property. The finger of God is in this, and He purposes some great benefit to this Nation." As a Jesuit he could hardly have been unaware that a century before, on the Feast of the Purification in 1571, the Spanish Jesuit Vice-Provincial of Florida, Fr. Juan Bautista Segura, together with a Fr. de Quiros and six religious Brothers had been martyred not far from there in the Tidewater area of "Ajacan" by an apostate Indian chief whom they had befriended and educated.

The destruction and abandonment of the Spanish mission unfortunately removed the last obstacle to English encroachment in what had been till then, at least juridically, exclusively Catholic territory; but the blood of these martyrs, whose sole objective had been the conversion of the natives, may well have been the price paid for the unexpected docility of those encountered later by Lord Baltimore's colonizers. Whatever the reason, the relationship between the colonists and the Indians around St. Mary's City continued on the whole to be peaceful and joyous, in marked contrast to that found in other English settlements, where far more effort seemed to be expended on expelling or exterminating the red man than on converting him to Christianity. To this day many families descended from Indian converts can be found throughout that region of Maryland.

+

Because a governing body of some kind was of the utmost priority in order to fulfill the terms of the charter and regulate practical day to day living, one of Leonard Calvert's first official acts in 1635 was to put together a representative assembly which would at the same time carry out the intentions of his father and his older brother Cecil. Inasmuch as their declared policy was that officials impart justice without regard to the religious persuasions of any parties involved, Leonard insisted that the colony's office holders take oaths binding themselves to execute their duties in the tolerant spirit of the Calverts. A sample oath relayed by Russell reads, "I will not by myself or any other person directly or indirectly trouble or molest or discountenance any person believing in Jesus Christ for or in respect to religion." Although such a pledge would have excluded Jews, their numbers would in any case have been negligible, and no discrimination against them was ever recorded. As a matter of fact in 1663 a Jew named Jacob Lumbroso would be granted full citizenship by Cecil's son Charles, third Lord Baltimore.

The spirit behind the pledge is reflected in many of the court decisions handed down at that time, the "Lewis Case" being often cited as an example. William Lewis, a Catholic, had a serious dispute with his Protestant servants regarding the character of the Sunday services they were holding among themselves. As they had no minister, it was their custom to read aloud from a book of Protestant sermons which was vehemently anti-Catholic in tone and abusive of the Pope and the Jesuits, whom it designated as antichrists. This quite understandably angered Lewis, and although he never resorted to physical violence, he was nonetheless brought before the court for calling Protestant ministers "ministers of the devil," and for arguing openly about religious matters. He was fined 300 pounds of tobacco and placed under bond for an additional 3,000 pounds to keep him quiet, but neither chastisement nor reprimand were visited on the Protestants.

In fact a certain Fr. Copley, alias Philip Fisher, a Jesuit present at the proceedings, publicly chided Lewis for his intransigence. Perhaps the priest felt it his duty to help keep the peace at all costs in the budding colony, but at this distance from the event, a Catholic may wonder whether it was not also his duty to defend the Faith when it was under open attack, especially in what was supposed to be a "Catholic" community headed by professed

Catholics. The incident, however, is strangely prophetic of the policy which would be adopted generally by the Catholic hierarchy when persecution raised its ugly head in the future United States. It is not in Puritan New England, but in Catholic Maryland that the first stirrings of heretical Americanism became evident.

Fr. Copley himself is a mysterious figure, apparently leading a life curiously free of the many hardships and entanglements which were the daily lot of his fellow Jesuits in their dealings with the settlement. He would have had powerful friends at court, for it is a matter of record that he was related to no less a person than Queen Elizabeth, one of his older cousins being moreover her godchild. Nevils states in *Miniatures of Georgetown* that on Fr. Copley's arrival in Maryland two years after that of the Ark and the Dove, he was able to lay claim to forty-eight men as his portion in the construction of the colony, entitling him to 10,000 acres of land. Nevils admits that his position was highly unusual, for although he was a professed member of the Society of Jesus under vows, he retained his worldly rank, by which he was recognized both in England and Maryland.

It would be gratifying to ascertain whether George and Cecil Calvert's animosity towards the Society should not be laid at the door of exceptional Jesuits like Frs. Copley, Cecil and Matthews rather than blamed on the Order itself, within whose ranks a strange favoritism also seems to have been prevalent. Whereas Fr. Andrew White and his Jesuit companions were among those boarding ship from the Isle of Wight, presumably in order to avoid the Oath of Supremacy, Fr. Copley apparently left from an English port two years later without encountering any difficulties whatever. When organized persecution eventually broke out in the colony against its Catholics, Fr. White and Fr. Copley were both clapped in irons and deported to England, but whereas the former Jesuit languished in prison to die later a physically broken old man in Belgium, the latter returned to active life in the colonies. What sort of Jesuit could have commanded such privileges from the hands of the anti-Catholic authorities who governed the England of his day? What were his objectives?

It remains that Copley Hall on the campus of Georgetown University in the capital of the United States is named after him. He died long before this first seat of Catholic learning was founded in the American utopia, but he had worked hard for its establishment, having in fact chosen the site on which it stands. (His first choice had been preempted by the Founding Fathers for the U.S. Capitol.) Founded in 1789 at the close of the American

Revolution by Jesuits under Fr. John Carroll acting as "the Incorporated Clergy of Maryland," during the time when the Society was suppressed by papal edict, the University has consistently propagated the ecumenical spirit first launched in America by the Maryland colony. The University's official seal, an eagle encircled by thirteen stars with a cross clutched in its left talon and a globe overlaid by a compass in its right, may provide sufficient indication of the institution's inspiration.

+

With true Americanist fervor William Russell writes, "Religious liberty was the statute paramount" in Maryland, "guarded by the Catholic authorities with the most absolute fidelity and with the most jealous care. They seem to have had an extreme sensitiveness concerning any, even the least, infringement of its provisions, and justice moved swiftly to punish the offender who rashly dared to assail the cardinal principle of the colony's foundation. Thus was the sacred fire of religious freedom guarded by the Catholics, who had first kindled the spark upon the shores of the New World."

In 1642, when the prominent Catholic landowner Thomas Gerard was accused of taking the key to the ecumenical chapel in which Protestants were allowed to hold services, together with their books, he was found guilty of a misdemeanor. Not only was he forced to return both key and books, but he was required to "relinquish all title to them or the house, and ... pay for a fine 500 lbs. of tobacco *towards the maintenance of the first minister as should arrive.*" In the same spirit Governor Calvert denied the Jesuits ownership of the lands given to them by the Indians, a decision in which he was warmly backed by Rome. This precedent eventually resulted in a Maryland law to the effect that, "No ecclesiastic may sit in the General Assembly, no gift, sale or devise of land nor gift nor sale of goods or chattels to take effect after the death of the donor or seller can be effective without ratification by the Assembly."

In Maryland it would seem that Catholics were the first to discriminate against Catholics, so true is it that the worst enemies turn out to be those of the household. Were the Calverts fearful of arousing the leaders of the Reformation in England by overt favoritism to members of their own faith? Were they caught in a desperate situation, perhaps pressured by hidden spiritual forces stronger than they knew? Being of a noble, rather sentimental nature, did the young Governor Leonard sincerely believe that insistence on strict separation of Church and state as practiced during his administration, would eventually dissolve all prejudices and win over the opposition? What is the real explanation of his endorsement of St. Mary's church as a shared place of worship where all faiths might meet? Why his obsessively tolerant, not to say pro-Protestant courts? His dread of church-owned property?

Whatever the answers to these questions, it should be clear to any unbiased student of the period that all the seeds of the Americanist heresy which would eventually draw Leo XIII's formal condemnation were not only planted, but carefully nurtured and disseminated from the Union's sole Catholic state. After Leonard's death, when active persecution began within the colony itself on the part of the elected Protestant officialdom, his kinswoman and executrix Margaret Brent, a lady now unfortunately claimed as one of the nation's first champions of women's rights, was emboldened to petition for a vote. A staunch, high-spirited Catholic who foresaw the grave problems lying in store for her co-religionists, who now found themselves at the mercy of a Protestant majority in the Assembly, could she have turned the tide? Probably not, but we shall never know, for she was firmly denied suffrage, and years later she left in disgust for Virginia.

Matters had already gone from bad to critical in 1645, when the pirate Richard Ingle suddenly appeared in the harbor in an armed ship called the Reformation, laden with goods entrusted to him by a leading Maryland colonist named Cornwaleys and a commission from Parliament for carrying food to the colonists in sympathy with the Parliamentary party. Taking the town by force of arms and imprisoning a number of its inhabitants, he despoiled the Baltimore supporters of their estates and banished many of them. The following year, in what must have been an embarrassing reversal of his peaceful policy, Leonard Calvert was forced to lead a small force of armed men in an attack against St. Mary's to regain his rights. Firmly committed to re-establishing lawful authority, he cleared the area of undesirables, but rather than fortify the city against future molestations, he sought to strengthen its position by inviting the rebellious Puritans from Virginia to settle within its Catholic confines!

The Puritans were only too happy to avail themselves of so providential an opportunity, for their fanaticism had become a problem in Virginia, where the Anglicans, not laboring under the ecumenical delusions of their Catholic neighbors, had no scruples about forcibly expelling them. Hear the Virginia legislation: "For the preservation of the purity of doctrine and unity of the Church, it is enacted that all ministers whatsoever, which shall reside in the colony are to be conformed to the orders and constitution of the Church of England and not otherwise to be permitted to preach or teach publicly or privately and that the Governor and Council do take care that all non-conformists upon notice of them shall be compelled to depart the colony with all convenience."

Thus always "the children of this world are wiser in their generation than the children of light" (Luke 16:8). Focussing not only on political control, the Anglicans had a care for "the preservation of the purity and doctrine and unity" of their heretical church, whereas in regard to their Holy Catholic Church, the Calverts evidently held these concerns secondary to the all-important – and equally heretical – principle of religious liberty condemned till then by every Pope and Council. Until the adoption of the U.S. Constitution imposed freedom of conscience indiscriminately on all consciences, Virginia stuck to her guns, as did most of the other thirteen colonies.

Either unable to learn from bitter experience or too deeply infected by the pluralism to which he was dedicated, the Governor of Maryland persisted in turning the Assembly over to all – Catholics, Episcopalians, Presbyterians, Quakers, and now Puritans, a full century before the egalitarian takeover in 1776. His next move was a new act drafted by the colony's ethical authority Fr. Copley, which postulated once more, "No persons professing belief in Jesus Christ shall be in any way troubled, molested or discountenanced for or in respect of his religion, nor the free exercise thereof." Although the document mentions our Lady and disapproves of blasphemers, it exudes far more religious indifferentism than commitment to the defense of the Faith.

Needless to say, the Puritans in their turn soon gained control of the Maryland Assembly, repaying their benefactors by passing their own religious edict in 1654, which read that "none who professed and exercised the Popish (commonly called Roman Catholic) religion could be protected in the province by the laws of England ... but were to be restrained from the exercise thereof." Only Catholics were singled out for discrimination, for the act further stated, "Such as profess faith in God by Jesus Christ, though differing in judgment from the doctrine, worship or discipline publicly held forth, should not be restrained from, but protected in the profession of faith and the exercise of their religion." Any brand of Christian heresy, yes; the true Faith, no.

From that time forth the faith in which the colony had been conceived was officially proscribed. Of the persecutions unleashed by the Puritans and later by the Church of England the less said the better. As Bishop John Carroll's relative Charles Carroll, a Maryland Catholic who was one of the Masonic signers of the Declaration of Independence, remarked regarding the harsh treatment meted out between 1654 and 1776, "We remember and we forgive." This was not entirely dictated by political expediency, for during this harrowing period Catholics had displayed truly outstanding charity and goodness towards their Protestant neighbors, despite loss of homes, goods and Holy Mass. As a result Jesuits in secular garb were in fact able to convert many Protestants avid for truth and good example, who turned in disgust from the kind of ministers being sent to them from England.

So closes a most unflattering chapter in our nation's history for the Reformers, but a heroic one in many ways for those Catholics who despite all remained in the Faith, and whose descendants enjoy the fruits of their fidelity today. Some, like Margaret Brent, left for less hostile surroundings among Anglicans. Others settled to the west in the Emmittsburg area, where their posterity was privileged to be educated by St. Elizabeth Seton and her nuns. Whatever their options, the future was not hard to predict. The Crown suspended the charter as unsafe in Catholic hands, restoring it eventually to the aforesaid Charles, fifth Lord Baltimore, who was not only an Anglican like his father, but also a Mason. Anglicanism became Maryland's state religion in 1692, and by the time the sixth and last of the Lords Baltimore, the dissolute Frederick Calvert, died without legitimate issue in 1771, popery was judged a serious slander against the Proprietorship.

Degenerating both physically and spiritually, the Calvert family therefore did not survive to see their dream become the law of the land under the U.S. Constitution. Sad to say, large numbers of the Catholic citizenry followed them into apostasy, and such is the force of example, probably for pretty much the same reasons. So much for Lord Baltimore's little Catholic utopia on St. Mary's River, which contributed so substantially to the greater one on the banks of the Potomac. "The church of St. Dunstan, Fleet Street, London, where Baltimore was buried," wrote Browne in 1890, "has since been destroyed by fire, and no statue, bust or monument on either side of the Atlantic perpetuates the memory of George Calvert." An obelisk honoring his Catholic son Leonard, however, Maryland's first Governor, stands fittingly in the churchyard of Trinity Episcopal Church on the spot where the first colonists, Protestant and Catholic, assembled in common brotherhood to build a new order of the ages.

Like the Civil War a century later, the Revolutionary War never enjoyed popular support, but was engineered by the proverbial active, well organized minority intent on its peculiar agenda, who "while men were asleep" or otherwise occupied in earning a living, "oversowed cockle among the wheat" (Matt. 13:25). On January 30, 1648, when Charles I of England was "put to death by the severing of his head from his body" as ordained by the Death Warrant issued by Oliver Cromwell and his Republicans, the assembled multitude, "far from accepting the executioner's invitation to 'rejoice at the death of a traitor,' uttered a dismal universal groan such as one hearer had never heard before nor desired to hear again. She was only twenty when she heard it, and she never forgot the sound." [15] A similar reaction on the part of the people would occur at the execution of Louis XVI of France in 1789, so firmly is monarchy rooted in natural law and so ingrained in Catholic hearts is love for their anointed kings.

Had Maryland's political elite kept the Faith in its integrity, one cannot help wondering whether they might not have been able to check, or even withstand the onslaught of the Revolution as did the French Catholics of Canada, who so indignantly refused the seditious overtures of Benjamin Franklin and the future Bishop John Carroll. Had Maryland followed their example, an effective counter-revolutionary base for royalist sentiment – which actually predominated throughout the Colonies before large numbers of loyalists took flight for Canadian Ontario – might have taken shape in what became the United States. By then, of course, it was too late. The Revolution promised the Maryland Catholics the same freedom they had held out to others, and they not only welcomed it with open arms, but succeeded in winning to its cause every Irish immigrant who hated England more fervently than he loved his Catholic faith.

The Catholic founders of St. Mary's City are now revolutionary heroes in American history books, whereas they might have been martyrs and saints. The Maryland experiment is living proof of our Lord's words that "Every kingdom divided against itself shall be made desolate: and every city or house divided against itself shall not stand." And almost in the same divine breath He said, "He that is not with me is against me, and he that gathereth not with me scattereth" (Matt. 12:25,30). As Maryland went, so goes the nation, for under the principle of religious freedom, God and Satan are accorded equal rights before the law.

44 APOSTASY

INCULTURATION USA

Two centuries later the unprecedented congress of world prayer hosted by the Catholic Church at Assisi in 1986 would send tremors through the ranks of the faithful everywhere. When a Buddha was placed over the tabernacle at one of the local churches to facilitate the worship of some participating bonzes, the tremors turned to shudders. But of course, Holy Mother Church had been in the throes of "inculturation" for some time. Ardently welcomed by Modernists as a healthy manifestation, the malady is hardly new. Something of a chronic fever first brought on in Apostolic times by the Ebionites, it flares up periodically in different times and climes and has never been thrown off for good. One of its most celebrated attacks was in China under the Jesuit missionaries Ricci and de Nobili, who sought to incorporate Mandarin elements into Catholic worship, but like all the others it was quickly brought under control.

Only the delirious "spirit of Vatican II" has ever permitted it to rage unchecked. The Declaration *Nostra Aetate* begins, "In our times, when every day men are being drawn closer together and the ties between various peoples are being multiplied, the Church is giving deeper study to her relationship with non-Christian religions," and in Article 2 asserts, "The Catholic Church rejects nothing which is true and holy in these religions." She therefore "has this exhortation for her sons: prudently and lovingly, through dialogue and collaboration with the followers of other religions, and in witness of Christian faith and life, acknowledge, preserve and promote the spiritual and moral goods found among these men, as well as the values in their society and culture."

Notably in Zaire, the former Belgian Congo, the progress made in "acknowledging, preserving and promoting" elements of native spirituality soon allowed native substances to be substituted for the Eucharistic species of wheat bread and grape wine. In India the priest was permitted to sit in the lotus position of the Yoga adept throughout the Mass, even for the Consecration, and if he so chooses, to wear orange or brown, as do Buddhist monks. Some Masses began to open with the sacred word *om*, traditional invocation of the god Krishna, and with the recitation of appropriate *mantras*. There may be dancing, and chants in Sanskrit before images of the Indian Trinity – surely not the Father, the Son and the Holy Ghost, but Brahma, Vishnu and Siva.

An Indian Jesuit, one Fr. Hirudayam, was quoted in the March 1988 issue of *La Croix* as saying, "There will be no true liberation without genuine inculturation. One religion should not dominate another. On the contrary, all are made to complement one another." Traditional American Catholics may find this disturbing, but take comfort in applying it only to the welter of souls on the other side of the globe who are still waiting to be Christianized. Here at home, where society is considered basically Christian to begin with, inculturation is not required. This may be true, for in the United States the Church was long ago inculturated, not by the Spirit of Vatican II, but by its forerunner the Spirit of '76.

It took a Pope to point it out to us after the revolutionary leaven had already been at work for over a century: Leo XIII, in the condemnation of Americanism which he addressed to Cardinal Gibbons in 1899, voiced the suspicion "that there are some among you who conceive of and desire a church in America different from that which is in the rest of the world." He warned us against the insidious notion that, "in order the more easily to bring over to Catholic doctrine those who dissent from it, the Church ought to adapt herself somewhat to our advanced civilization, and, relaxing her ancient rigor, show some indulgence to modern popular theories and methods."

This is the essence of inculturation, of which Americanism is a form so pernicious that in due time it infected the whole Church. Like AIDS, the democratic virus seems not to attack the Mystical Body in any one organ, but rather to attack them all by weakening its immune system. Heresies which were once violently resisted on contact are simply absorbed and taught as developments of Catholic doctrine. Every aberration of pluralism, collegiality, vernacularization, situational ethics, morality by majority rule can be traced to the revolutionary mystique which for two centuries has quietly and invisibly permeated the Church by way of the American environment and American influence in the world.

In the U.S. before the Council there was no question of incorporating extraneous elements into the liturgy to make worshippers feel at home in the wasp atmosphere around them. As far as eye could see and ear could hear, the sanctuary remained intact – except for the presence of the Stars and Stripes at the Altar, never officially permitted by Rome, but allowed by the American hierarchy regardless. As far as can be ascertained, for many generations it was the only instance where the national emblem of a temporal government – and a revolutionary one at that – was accorded ecclesiastical standing. Before long it was gracefully balanced at the other side of the Altar by another temporal banner : that of the Papal State. Despite the psychological effect Old Glory must have exerted on congregations, it can hardly be credited with the virulent spread of Americanism, even allowing the weakness for the vernacular and for preaching in Protestant pulpits exhibited by prelates like Cardinal Gibbons and Archbishop Ireland, not to mention Bishops Carroll and England before them.

Amid these incidental aberrations, never did the clerical leadership propose tampering with rites. They went deeper. In the final analysis, inculturation for them meant accommodating the supernatural, God-given Faith of the Apostles to the purely natural, man-made principles of nativist America's Spirit of '76. No one purposely sets out to be a heretic, so we may assume they sincerely believed, as did Orestes Brownson and Fr. Isaac Hecker, that the Spirit of '76 was of God. Once purified by the Faith, democratic America was destined, they felt sure, to transfuse her incomparable new vitality into the Church and the whole world. Under God, this for them was the national vocation of the United States, its "manifest destiny."

Leo XIII was well aware of these misguided aspirations when he wrote Cardinal Gibbons, "Beloved Son, the project involves a greater danger and is more hostile to Catholic doctrine and discipline, inasmuch as the followers of these novelties judge that a certain liberty ought to be introduced into the Church, so that, limiting the exercise and vigilance of its powers, each one of the faithful may act more freely in pursuance of his own natural bent and capacity. They affirm, namely, that this is called for in order *to imitate that liberty which, though quite recently introduced, is now the law and the foundation of almost every civil community.*" The Pope is referring here, of course, to revolutionary democracy, which, following its first success in North America, raged through Europe and South America and was establishing itself throughout Christendom. "On that point we have spoken very much at length in the Letter[16] written to all the Bishops about the constitution of States; where We have also shown the difference between the Church, which is of divine right, and all other associations which subsist by the free will of men."

In desperate need of the generous Peter's Pence by then forthcoming from America, Leo XIII deemed it prudent to mention no heresiarchs by name. Cardinal Gibbons kept the document to himself as long as possible, apparently with no intention of making it public. Only after a copy had been leaked to the secular press did he speak of it, dutifully voicing agreement with the Pope but maintaining that its contents did not apply to the American clergy. Nonetheless, staunch defenders of the Faith, led mostly by the Germans of the Midwest and Archbishop Corrigan of New York and his Suffragan Bishop McQuaid of Rochester, pressed their advantage. A reaction set in. The Americanist contingent were forced to retire from their more outspoken positions on their side of the Atlantic, and in Rome Archbishop Ireland was denied the Cardinal's hat he had so long coveted.

Democratic inculturation was arrested for a time, remaining dormant as it were, until the close of the Second Vatican Council. Then the Spirit of '76 – ably assisted by the spirit of Fr. John Courtney Murray – wafted where it would. Today the American Church has at its disposal the brand new, do-it-yourself democratic Mass of Paul VI, celebrated in part by the people themselves in the vernacular, with a consecrating Presider. Several secular holidays have been canonized and bid fair in many parishes to become holydays alongside Christmas and Easter. For the divine Sacrifice the American Sacramentary now provides a special "Preface for Independence Day and Other Civic Observances" which is a masterpiece of inculturation, reading,

> *Father,*
> *all-powerful and ever-living God,*
> *we do well to sing your praise for ever,*
> *and to give thanks in all we do*
> *through Jesus Christ our Lord.*
>
> *He spoke to men a message of peace*
> *and taught us to live as brothers.*
> *His message took form in the vision of our fathers*
> *as they fashioned a nation*
> *where men might live as one.*

This message lives on in our midst
as a task for men today
and a promise for tomorrow.

We thank you, Father, for your blessings in the past
and for all that, with your help, we must yet achieve, etc.

Thus far the liturgical expression, *in sacris*, of the Americanist belief in the divine inspiration of the Constitution of the United States of America.

+

Admirable as the Constitution may be in many respects, and under God as binding upon its citizens as was Caesar's authority in all things save sin, no one acquainted with the primary sources of American history could rightly contend that it is a document of Christian – let alone Catholic – inspiration. Only Americanists and some Protestant fundamentalists seriously hold such a view. The Church has never held the Faith to any particular form of government, wisely leaving the choice to the temporal authorities; yet today, after two centuries of inculturation, there are Catholics in America who cling to their Constitution as if it were an article of faith, apparently holding the Founding Fathers in no lesser regard than the Fathers of the Church. For such an attitude credit is due to the American parochial school system, whose history texts were not only patterned on those of the secular schools, but were at pains to teach that there were no inherent contradictions between the faith and modern liberal democracy.

A correspondent to *The Remnant* once wrote in all sincerity, "The enemies of God's Church are one and the same enemies of the system of government handed down from our Founding Fathers." The corruption of the American political system, now too obvious to be denied, is viewed by such patriots as a lapse from the principles of '76, caused by Communists, Jews, the Federal Reserve System, special interests, infiltrators or other invasive factors. They will admit no congenital defect in the great American experiment itself. Nonetheless, the fact remains that historically it was a choice blossom of eighteenth century Masonic Enlightenment. Rooted in the organized naturalism which dates back to the days of St. Joan of Arc and before, it began as a movement directed specifically against the Kingship of Christ. The principle of death was in it from the beginning, as in all merely natural things, and the decline we witness today is that of unsupported nature taking its course.

We have the word of the Founders in our first treaty with Tripoli to the effect that, "the Government of the United States of America is not in any sense founded on the Christian religion." [17]   Certainly in its ingenious structure of checks and balances between the executive, legislative and judiciary branches of government, the U.S. Constitution bears more than a passing resemblance to the Utopia delineated by the English Rosicrucian John Harrington, a copy of which can be found in the Folger Shakespearean Library in Washington, D.C. The ideas he propounded were quite simply those of Sir Francis Bacon's seminal "college of the six days," the secret society of adepts spoken of in the first chapter, who dreamed of a universal, self-governing republic based on brotherhood like that of ancient Babel and Atlantis.

The occultist Manly Palmer Hall (pseudonym of Paul Connolly, a.k.a. Tom Wicker) says of Bacon in *The Secret Destiny of America*: "He made sure that the American colonists were thoroughly indoctrinated with the principles of religious tolerance, political democracy and social equality. Through carefully appointed representatives, the machinery of democracy was set up at least a hundred years before the period of the Revolutionary War." These representatives, who were drawn not only from England, but from Germany, France and Holland, numbered in their ranks alchemists, cabalists, Rosicrucians, Pietists and of course Freemasons. We might add that their ideas took root easily in the prevailing atmosphere of Calvinism, which was a revolutionary movement in itself, containing all the seeds of modern democracy.

"The brotherhoods met in their rooms over inns and similar public buildings... These American organizations were branches under European sovereignty, with the members in the two hemispheres bound together with the strongest bonds of sympathy and understanding... Quietly and industriously, America was being conditioned for its destiny - leadership in a free world. Any account of secret societies in America would have to include tribute to the man who has been called the 'First American Gentleman' – Benjamin Franklin.... Historians have never ceased to wonder at the enormous psychological influence which Franklin exercised in colonial politics.... Franklin was not a lawmaker, but his words became law.... The rise of American democracy was necessary to a world program. At the appointed hour, the freedom of man was publicly declared." [18]

It may be well to interpolate here that America's first Catholic bishop, John Carroll, an ardent partisan of ecumenism and the vernacular, had been thoroughly indoctrinated in democratic ideals in the English expatriate schools abroad, where Sir Francis Bacon's friend Fr. Tobie Matthews had long ago laid the groundwork. Fr. Carroll was a personal friend of Franklin, who made known to the Vatican that he was the sole episcopal candidate acceptable to the new government, a nomination which Rome reluctantly ratified after five years of diplomatic stalling. The date of his consecration might be taken as the formal inauguration of the American Church. Through the influence of Georgetown University, founded by him, the revolutionary mystique eventually impregnated the entire Catholic educational system in the U.S., especially the seminaries. Although Freemasonry had already suffered papal condemnation, Bishop Carroll's kinsmen Daniel and Charles Carroll were active members. Daniel signed both the Articles of Confederation and the Constitution.

Sovereign Grand Master Henry Clausen credits "enlightened Masons" with laying both "the intellectual and spiritual foundations of America. When Benjamin Franklin went abroad as an envoy to France and met there with his Brethren in Masonry, it was with the moral strength gathered in Masonic Lodges for individual action outside the Lodges. Similarly, George Washington and his most trusted generals and Alexander Hamilton, Robert Morris, Paul Revere, John Marshall, John Hancock and many of the co-signers of the *Declaration of Independence* were Masonically so inspired." [19] Of the fifty-five deputies working on the American Constitution in 1787, thirty-one are known to have been Masons, as were twenty of the thirty-nine signers.

According to Hall, that they "had the fundamental teaching of the Fraternity in mind when they labored to produce a fundamental law to act as a cement never to give way, between Peoples and States of greatly varying size, power, wealth, industry, climate, ideas and ideals, is not only understandable – it was inevitable." In other words, the United States of America was from its inception a mini-world republic, a blueprint for the self-governing one world of the future. A Masonic Service Association Bulletin reads, "By the facts of its history, no less than by the spirit of its laws, America must know nothing of the Saxon race, nothing of the Teutonic race, nothing of the Slavic race. It must know only the Human Race, of whose future and fulfillment it is the last great hope and promise... "

The Preamble to the *Declaration of Independence* imputes this political miracle not to rulers, or even to deputies, but to a new order of sages designated as "We the People" – future source of all political power and authority. "The note of democracy thus struck at the very outset is truly the Masonic teaching of 'meeting upon the level and parting upon the square' without reference to creed or place or power or position," runs the Bulletin. The Bill of Rights guaranteeing Americans their individual freedom was of the same revolutionary inspiration, its first, fourth and fifth amendments designed particularly to safeguard, not the Christian religion, but Masonry. "Without this guarantee Freemasonry could not live," reads another Masonic bulletin. Under its provision, "No civil authority may arrest a Freemason, throw him in jail, punish him in any manner, for being a Freemason," – as had happened many times in other countries in the Americas and abroad who were sufficiently alerted to the threat.

"Can you think of any country where Freemasonry has been able to flourish except in a democracy, whether it be a constitutional monarchy or a federal republic like ours?" asked Wallace Kent, Grand Master of Michigan Masons in 1960. "Our Fraternity has grown only where men are free.... We must maintain both our democratic form of society and our Fraternity, because they are the only two that can co-exist. If Freemasonry disappears, democracy as we know it in this country cannot possibly survive. And equally, if democracy in this country disappears, Freemasonry cannot survive. Freemasonry came into existence with democratic forms of government."

+

The American historian George Bancroft called the American Revolution an American "Revelation." In a Bicentennial lecture at Southern Connecticut State College, history professor Arthur Kelsey noted that the Revolution occurred in "a religious climate" and that it "was a religious thing.... Bancroft knew what he was talking about when he likened the coming of its ideals into the stream of history almost to the way the Christ event entered into history." A Catholic may well ask, how else would Antichrist, the displacer of Christ, enter?

Long ago Masonry's hallowed *Old Charges* declared that the only religion recognized in Freemasonry was "that natural religion in which all men agree." As a Masonic Bulletin explains, "He who worships the God of Abraham, he who kneels to Buddha, he to whom Allah is the One True God, and Mahomet his prophet, he who subscribes to Confucius, as well as that mighty host who bow the head and bend the knee before the gentle Man of Galilee, are alike welcomed before the Altar of Freemasonry." Of such stuff is the Spirit of Assisi. And again, "In nothing was the founding of our Republic more significant than in the new relation which it established between Church and State. Our fathers separated the two forever, but they gave equal liberty and honor to all elevating and benign religions." [20] Under the Constitution this is the only religious freedom accorded the one true Faith revealed by God, and the one which Catholic Americanists are pathetically pleased to accept on principle in a pluralistic society.

It will be objected that the Founding Fathers did believe in a God of some kind, but as we shall see in the next chapter, so do all pagans. The Deity is mentioned four times in the *Declaration of Independence* under the titles "Nature's God," "Creator," "Supreme Judge of the World," and "Divine Providence." He is hardly Christian, however, for "He is no sectarian God; He is the Father of all men; He is the energizing and controlling Force of all the universe. It was that concept of Deity which Masonry adopted as early as 1723 in Anderson's *Constitutions*," another Bulletin tells us. This was the God whom our Founding Fathers venerated publicly and whom Hollywood proposes for our veneration today in the Star Wars prayer, "May the Force be with you!" As for the Founders' alleged private practice of Christianity, the reader is referred to the chapter "The American Way?" in the author's book *Utopia*. Suffice it to say here that there is no documentary proof of such practice in the lives of the major protagonists, and in fact overwhelming evidence to the contrary.

George Washington wrote his Brothers of King David's Lodge in Newport, Rhode Island in 1790: "Being persuaded that a just application of the principles on which the Masonic Fraternity is founded, must be promotive of private virtue and public prosperity, I shall always be happy to advance the interests of the Society, and to be considered by them as a deserving Brother." So far among Washington's successors in the Presidency, at least sixteen have certainly been Masons and therefore subscribers to similar sentiments. Given this power base at the executive level, and spread throughout the legislative and judiciary, it is hardly surprising that American common life and iconography are redolent with the aroma of revolutionary democracy, inhaled by every newborn with his first breath.

The three public structures in the nation's capital which every American schoolchild associates most intimately with his country are certainly not cathedrals, but nonetheless houses of worship. They are the U.S. Capitol, the White House and the Washington Monument, to which must be added that incomparable American idol, the Masonic Madonna of the Americas known as the Statue of Liberty. All these were dedicated – the Capitol no less than three times – with Masonic ceremonies, and they supply the background to the elaborate democratic mythology expounded in every school text, both public and parochial. A guide book to the Lincoln Memorial put out in 1973 with the cooperation of the U.S. Parks Service is actually called *In This Temple*. As for the Great Seal of the United States, it is unique in the annals of heraldry in that it is two sided like a medal, both sides of which are of Masonic inspiration – the reverse in particular, whereon figure the truncated pyramid and the All-Seeing Eye.[21]

Next to the Fourth of July in dignity in the democratic liturgical cycle stands Thanksgiving Day, proof positive, Americanists will maintain, that the United States is a basically Christian nation, since once a year it thanks God officially for His blessings. Laudable as may be the intent, this God is unfortunately nowhere defined as the Father, the Son and the Holy Ghost of Christian revelation, whereas he bears a striking resemblance to the supreme deity once worshipped in pagan Greece and Rome. The religious origin of Thanksgiving Day is in any case highly dubious. No historical documentation exists beyond a mention of the Pilgrim settlers joining some Indians for a harvest feast of some kind, at which most of the next winter's supplies were consumed, and no thanks to God were recorded.

There is, however, a curious passage in the prophecies of Nostradamus designating America as "the Land Which Keeps the Thursday." Manly Hall believes this "refers to the unique American holiday, Thanksgiving, which always falls on a Thursday. And this is the only holiday which expresses thankfulness for freedom of religion, freedom of opportunity, and freedom of life." He says Nostradamus prophesied in the Platonic tradition that this nation "would free itself from the bonds to its mother country" and eventually "would become a great power in a pattern of world peace and would be looked up to by other nations for leadership against the common evils of the time." Be that as it may, Thanksgiving Day has become the national Holy Thursday, if not the *Habeas Corpus Christi* of its body politic. At one time in New England it displaced the feast of Christmas, whose celebration became punishable by fine or imprisonment. Today the American Catholic Church accords it liturgical status along with Independence Day, with a special Preface which runs,

> *Father,*
> *we do well to join all creation,*
> *in heaven and on earth, in praising you,*
> *our mighty God through Jesus Christ our Lord.*
>
> *You made man to your own image*
> *and set him over all creation.*
> *Once you chose a people and gave them a destiny*
> *and, when you brought them out of bondage to freedom they carried*
> *with them the promise*
> *that all men would be blessed*
> *and all men could be free.*
>
> *What the prophets pledged was fulfilled*
> *in Jesus Christ, your Son and our saving Lord.*
> *It has come to pass in every generation*
> *for all men who have believed that Jesus,*
> *by his death and resurrection*
> *gave them a new freedom in his Spirit.*
>
> *It happened to our fathers,*
> *who came to this land as if out of the desert*
> *into a place of promise and hope.*
> *It happens to us still, in our time, as you lead all men*
> *through your Church to the blessed vision of peace.*

+

The aforementioned correspondent to *The Remnant* also wrote, "I defy anyone to examine the Constitution in the light of the founders' premise and find enough Masonic or other non-Catholic principles to render the government of our heritage less in conformity with the 'laws of nature and of Nature's God' than any other secular government on the face of the earth." Granted, for that is precisely the point. To paraphrase the traditional liturgy for Pentecost, "The spirit of the Revolution has filled the whole earth!" and is substituting naturalism for the true religion. As our Lady predicted at Quito, virtually all governments today are contaminated with republicanism. If we can credit the prophecies of St. Louis de Montfort and similar saints, the latter days are upon us, and a battle to the death for the Social Kingship of Christ has indeed been engaged.

It is a battle against the pervasive, satanic naturalism which makes the state a law unto itself, without even minimal statutory recognition of that indirect power over government which the Church holds from God. Although many citizens would readily concede that all authority ultimately comes from God, in democratic government "it resides primarily in the people," says St. Pius X in *Our Apostolic Mandate*, "and expresses itself by means of elections or, better still, by selection. However, it still remains in the hands of the people. It does not escape their control. It will be an external authority, yet only in appearance. In fact it will be internal because it will be an authority assented to." Incontrovertible proof of his contention lies in the fact that under the U.S. Constitution the people always retain the power to impeach those they have elected to office.

St. Pius reminds that "Leo XIII absolutely condemned this doctrine in his Encyclical *Diuturnum illud*... in which he said, 'Modern writers in great numbers, following in the footsteps of those who called themselves philosophers in the last century, declare that all power comes from the people; consequently those who exercise power in society do not exercise it from their own authority, but from an authority delegated to them by the people from whom they hold it. Quite contrary is the sentiment of Catholics, who hold that the right of governing derives from God as its natural and necessary principle.'

56 APOSTASY

"But besides its being abnormal for the delegation of power to ascend, since it is in its nature to descend, Leo XIII refuted in advance this attempt to reconcile Catholic doctrine with the error of philosophism. For, he continues, 'It is necessary to remark here that those who preside over the government of public affairs may indeed, in certain cases, be chosen by the will and judgment of the multitude without repugnance or opposition to Catholic doctrine. But whilst this choice marks out the ruler, it does not confer upon him the authority to govern; it does not delegate the power, it designates the person who will be invested with it.' For the rest, if the people remain the holders of power, what becomes of authority? A shadow, a myth.... "

This political fantasy is compounded by the rigorous separation of Church and state which reduces all religions to private status and places them on the same footing before the law. No intrusion of religion in any institution enjoying public funding can be tolerated – especially not in the nation's classrooms, where the next generation is formed. In this kind of "government without benefit of clergy," where the people are the sole source of authority, national morality rises and falls with public opinion. Being independent of any objective standards, it must always sink to the lowest common denominator. Need we seek further for the headwaters of the moral chaos engulfing us both publicly and privately?

Such ideology categorically denies the Kingship of Christ. It is unprecedented in world history in that even among pagans, no Nebuchadnezzar, no Caesar, no tribal chief ever denied religion a place in government. Opposed in principle to the natural hierarchical order which reigns throughout Creation, revolutionary democracy would furthermore abolish all class distinctions based on anything but so-called individual merit. Legislating marriage as if it were a mere civil contract, it now dares to legislate the right to life itself by countenancing abortion, and already, euthanasia. Such are the end products of the movement loosed by the Spirit of '76, formally condemned by Popes from Pius VI on down.

+

The fatal cleavage was not discernible at first. For several generations, during which Christian morality was still the accepted public norm,

American politics was able, like the camel lost in the desert, to live off the hump of its Christian heritage. Certain truths were held, as in the *Declaration of Independence*, as "self-evident," and democracy, because of its leftover Christian components, "worked" for a while. It even prospered. With the constant application of the principle of separation of Church and state, however, which denied Christianity any possibility of correcting the aberrations of the state, fallen nature could only take its course. Public morality fell to the level we know, for private citizens soon began exhibiting the same schizoid condition which plagued their government. Today a fullblown moral schizophrenia allows Catholics in public office to declare themselves, for instance, "personally against abortion," but unwilling to oppose it for fear of trampling the constitutional rights of those who disagree with them.

Religion, however, is not a private matter, much less a private opinion. At the very moment of His Ascension, our Lord's parting command to the Church He left on earth was to "teach all *nations*" – not just individuals. In 1925, when the evil was already very far advanced, Pius XI established the feast of Christ the King by his encyclical *Quas primas*, in which he said, "Nations will be reminded by the annual celebration of this feast that *not only individuals, but also rulers and princes are bound to give public honor and obedience to Christ.* It will call to their minds the thought of the last judgment, wherein Christ, who has been cast out of public life, despised, neglected and ignored, will most severely avenge these insults; for His kingly dignity demands that the State should take account of the commandments of God and of Christian principles, both in making laws and in administering justice, and also in providing for the young a sound moral education."

The converted Communist Hamish Fraser, in an editorial in *Approaches* for February 1976, bicentennial year for the United States, deplored that, "*Quas primas* was all but completely ignored, especially by the so-called Catholic nations and by the Catholic clergy. In fact, *Quas primas* proved to be the greatest non-event in the entire history of the Church." The episcopate, "instead of resolutely seeking to make the State conform to 'the commandments of God and Christian principles'... preferred rather to play down the more unacceptable implications of the Church's teaching and at all costs to avoid a confrontation with Caesar, particularly in the decisive and sensitive sphere of Church-State relations. And being as circumspect as they were, bishops chose to act by omission: by *not* intervening to ensure that the doctrine of Christ's social kingship be given the emphasis it deserved in the seminaries and other institutions of higher learning under ecclesiastical control."

As late as 1958, Pius XII was warning against the pitfalls of denying God and rejecting religious principles under an appearance of patriotism. In *Ad Apostolorum Principis*, his Encyclical to the Chinese living under the Communist yoke, he reminds, "The power of the Church is in no sense limited to so-called strictly religious matters; but the whole matter of the natural law, its institution, interpretation and application, in so far as the moral aspect is concerned, are within its power. By God's appointment the observance of the natural law concerns the way by which man must strive toward his supernatural end. The Church shows the way and is the guide and guardian of men with respect to their supernatural end."

The end of government cannot therefore be merely the "life, liberty and pursuit of happiness" envisaged by the *Declaration of Independence*, whose original draft, incidentally, read "pursuit of property!" These are legitimate ends, but quite secondary to the main purpose of government, which, as St. Thomas lays down, is to order temporal society so as best to prepare its members for their eternal destiny with God. A government functioning independently of any supernatural authority, as if the supernatural did not exist, floats in a utopian dream from which the ultimate, transcendent reality is excluded on principle. It is not a political state at all, but a deranged state of mind.

+

The Fr. Hirudayam previously quoted maintains that there can be no liberation without inculturation, but the exact opposite is true. Inculturation traps souls in the miasma of their own immediate temporal surroundings, propelling them inward into themselves instead of outward to freedom. Intellectually, spiritually, nay, even physically, it confines them to their own meager resources and ends by suffocating them. The Church, on the other hand, all the while carefully preserving authentic cultures, promotes what might be called exculturation in the sense that she is universal, eternal in scope, not tied to any provincial ethnicity, ideology, time frame or vernacular. The rites which express her faith are not from the here and now, but from the beginning. Prefigured and prescribed in detail under the Adamic natural dispensation and again under the Mosaic Old Covenant, they permit man to worship God as He wishes to be worshipped, and not merely as man wishes to worship Him. Her universal culture offers a worldwide reprieve from the fragmentation, multiplicity and narrowness which are the sad legacy of Babel. Drawing us out of ourselves towards our eternal destiny, even here on earth the Church invites us to a larger life.

Witness the inculturated American Catholic: the Spirit of '76, which promised freedom to the common man, long ago cut him off from the full dimension of political life. He knows little or nothing of the city of God on earth as a St. Joan of Arc delineated it. For him American history begins with English colonialism. He is not even adequately acquainted with the Catholic past of his own continent, not only discovered and colonized by Catholics, but accorded the special heavenly protection of the Immaculate Lady of Guadalupe, Patroness of the Americas. Nor has he ever heard the whole of the political message given by the Sacred Heart to St. Margaret Mary, Claire Ferchaud and so many others. Authentic papal teachings on democracy, like St. Pius X's Letter *Our Apostolic Mandate*, receive no mention even in the Catholic schools of the nation. Whatever forthrightly condemns revolutionary democracy in unequivocal terms is deemed "counter-productive" and "divisive," *i.e.*, un-American, as if being a good American meant living in lifelong error.

The American, or shall we say, the *Usan* – United Statesian – Catholic has been taught to revere, along with the saints, a bevy of anti-heroes acting in concert to remove Christ the King from politics. As a child an Orwellian litany was indelibly fixed in his mind which runs, "King - bad, president - good; upper class - bad, common man - good; monarchy - bad, democracy - good; submission - bad, revolution - good; social classes - bad, equality - good; minority - bad, majority - good," and so on. Under pressure of early cultural conditioning he can view with equanimity political iconography which would otherwise outrage his Catholic sensibilities. To take but one example, Brumidi's blasphemous apotheosis of George Washington, depicted on the interior of the dome of the Capitol in the guise of God the Father reigning in the clouds of heaven amid the revolutionary blessed. He is unaware of any conflict with his Catholic principles, because inculturation, like all psychological conditioning, by-passes the intellect. Led to identify the ideals of democracy affectively with those of the Faith, the neo-Americanist must be forgiven for mistaking the sudden clamor for democracy now resounding in Moscow for the long awaited conversion of Russia prophesied by our Lady at Fatima!

Inculturation is by nature non-violent, insidious and nothing new to the Church. Some sixteen centuries ago St. Hilary said in reference to Arianism, "The cross and the breaking of every bone of my body should not have made me a coward, for the good thief would have encouraged me," but "nowadays we have to do with a disguised persecutor, a smooth-tongued enemy who scourges us, not with lashes, but with caresses; who instead of robbing us, which would give us spiritual life, bribes us with riches... who thrusts us not into the liberty of a prison, but into the honors of his palace... who tears not our flesh, but our hearts.... He confesses Christ the better to deny him; he tries to procure a unity which shall destroy peace.... he honors bishops that they may cease to be bishops.... By a strange, ingenious plan, which no one had ever yet discovered, thou hast found a way to persecute without making martyrs."

No Catholics anywhere in the world are so prosperous, so socially accepted, indeed, so *inculturated* as those in the United States of America. This alone should lead them to wonder whether their faith is intact. The American Constitution notwithstanding, God has always shown a vital interest in politics here below. He dictated legal statutes and prescriptions to Moses, chose the Judges of Israel, and established the royal line of David. St. Joan of Arc was directed from on high to accomplish the coronation of the King of France at Rheims. At Paray-le-Monial at the end of the seventeenth century, when the democratic insanity was already seeping from England into France and the rest of Europe, our Lord demanded reparation to His Sacred Heart for the disregard shown Him, all the while promising, "I shall reign in spite of Satan and all opposition!"

Nearly three centuries later, in 1928, He ordered through His Vicar Pius XI a formal act of reparation to be recited annually throughout the world on the feast of His Sacred Heart. The faithful were enjoined "to make amends," not only for personal sins against their Savior, but "*for the public crimes of nations who resist the rights and the teaching authority of the Church.*" Outside this Church our Lord founded there can be no culture worthy of man, no universal brotherhood, no freedom and certainly no salvation. A political system which is nothing more than a "government of the people, by the people, for the people" must inevitably "perish from the earth," for the Truth who alone can make us free has told us plainly, "Without Me, you can do NOTHING!"

THE PERILS OF PAGAN PIETY

Why gnostics of every age have ascribed the creation of matter to an evil god is no harder to understand than why gnostics have always been with us. The truth is, matter has caused a lot of trouble from the beginning. Evil can be said to have come into existence with the mere thought of matter, for when God revealed to the angels that He would create it so that His Son might assume it and associate it with all His works, a rebellion broke out in their ranks whose effects were felt not only in heaven, but even more so on earth, where matter and spirit meet one on one.

Composed as they are of material bodies compacted to immaterial souls, even the best of earth's inhabitants must contend with congenital double vision in everything they do. Praising the God who "knoweth all knowledge" and hath "no need of any counselor," Jesus the son of Sirach had to admit that He who "hath made nothing defective," had nonetheless by His one almighty word "made all things double, one against the other" (Ecclus. 42:19, 25). Inasmuch as everything received is received according to the make up of the recipient, it certainly seemed that way to him, composite being that he was.

King David recognized the basic duality underlying his own human nature and everything accosting his senses when he sang in the Psalm, "God hath spoken once," yet, "two things have I heard." Even God, who is pure act, supremely one and simple, is apprehended by man under twin aspects, one of "power" and the other of "mercy," because He renders "to every man according to his works" (Ps. 61:12). Thus the Valiant Woman in Proverbs, figure of the Mother of God and divine wisdom, sees to it that "all her domestics are clothed with double garments" (Prov. 31:21), for in this world they require double protection from every threatening evil. Praying for deliverance from his persecutors, the prophet Jeremias by the same token begged God to "destroy them with a double destruction" (Jer.

17:18), because really to obliterate enemies, you have to kill them twice, not only physically but spiritually.

Under the circumstances it is therefore not surprising that St. John in his *Apocalypse* speaks of not one, but two deaths to which mankind is liable. The first is inevitable, but not irremediable. The death of the body is the common lot, the wages of original sin which sooner or later must be paid by all. Occurring when the body separates from the soul which is its life principle, it terminates sense life on earth, but does not necessarily entail separation from God. When body and soul are reunited at the Resurrection both may in fact find their union with Him prolonged into eternity. Final separation from God takes place definitively after the Last Judgment, when the "first earth was passed away" and a new heaven and earth established.

The Apostle was told, "This is the second death!" which was shown to him under the figure of a pool of fire into which "whosoever was not found written in the book of life was cast." Although sin is the common cause of both deaths, the second death is the reverse of the first in that it is irremediable, but not inevitable. Man is given a choice in the matter, for at the start of the revelation the Spirit had been heard saying to the seven churches, "He that shall overcome shall not be hurt by the second death... He that shall overcome... I will be his God, and he shall be my son" (Apo. 21:1; 20:14-15; 2:11; 21:7).

In the final analysis, to "overcome" is to accept with all its consequences the invitation to the cosmic wedding of matter and spirit prepared by God the Father for His Son, the very same invitation refused by the fallen angels. The whole of Creation may be viewed in terms of marriage with God, for the moment matter was joined to spirit by the divine omnipotence, heaven and earth were betrothed. They engaged themselves to enter into an indissoluble contract whereby body and soul, the seen and the unseen, the mortal and the immortal, the physical and the spiritual, the natural and the supernatural would one day merge at every level of being.

Our Lord laid this down as doctrine when He said, "The kingdom of heaven is like to a man being a king, who made a marriage for his son," who sent his servants to "tell them that were invited: Behold I have prepared my dinner; my beeves and fatlings are killed, and all things are ready: come ye to the wedding!" (Matt. 22:2-4). To St. John, taken "up in spirit to a great and high mountain" in the *Apocalypse*, the same wedding was revealed as the marriage "of the Lamb ... which was slain from the beginning of the world," for which "his wife hath prepared herself. And to her it is granted that she should clothe herself with fine linen, glittering and white. For the fine linen are the justifications of the saints" (Apo. 21:10;13:8;19:7-8).

St. Paul, who had been "caught up into the third heaven ... and heard words which it is not allowed man to utter" (2 Cor. 12:2,4), would not hesitate to call marriage itself "a Great Sacrament." He adds, however, "but I speak in Christ and in the church," as a theologian of the new law of grace, for human marriage consummated in the Sacred Humanity of God's Word made Flesh was designed by God to determine the configuration of all created reality (Eph. 5:32). By it rocks are put into relation with angels, and men with God in view of the final Transfiguration which terminates all Sacraments in an indissoluble union of matter with spirit. If sin brings death, it is because it puts asunder what God has been pleased to join. Whereas by definition physical death is the separation of the material body from its animating spirit, spiritual death is the separation of both these partners from God.

Not that elements He puts together can ever really be separated, for like any divorced couple, their relationship remains regardless of circumstances. If there were not always a basic connection between the body and the soul especially created for it, the Catholic Church's veneration of the relics of her saints would rest on dubious premises indeed, as would her indulgences granted for visiting grave sites. In her marriage laws the Church permits separations for just cause, but divorce she will not allow, because only God can part what He has joined. After the Resurrection body and soul enter heaven together, and together they are cast into hell, where their greatest suffering is the pain of separation from God. Even so, if they were ever entirely divorced from Him, they would not continue in existence. As the Psalmist said, "If I descend into hell, thou art present!" (Ps. 138:8).

Thus our Lord said, "Fear not them that kill the body and cannot kill the soul: but rather fear him that can destroy both soul and body in hell" (Matt. 10:28). Having introduced the "first death" into the world by persuading Eve to act independently of her husband, Satan now labors to prepare the "second death" which admits of no repentance. Using the same strategy which served him so well the first time, he would like to finalize the divorce from God by transforming the Great Sacrament into the Great Apostasy.

The laws governing society being no different from those governing individuals, St. John in his *Apocalypse* saw looming ahead for mankind not only two deaths, but two beasts who would be given power on earth to rule "over every tribe and people and tongue and nation." As might be expected in a society peopled by men with souls attached to bodies, these monsters represent a church and a state, the one wielding spiritual authority and the other political authority. The first one, "coming up out of the sea," which in Scripture usually represents the world, is described as having seven heads, being obviously a secular confederation of some kind. In the wake of this first beast arrived "another beast coming up out of the earth," who "had two horns like a lamb" but spoke "as a dragon," functioning in conjunction with the former as the devil's mouthpiece.

Of the state-beast the Apostle says, "And I saw one of his heads as it were wounded to death: and his deadly wound was healed." This gratuitous detail might pass unnoticed were it not that the Apostle returns to it twice in the text with some insistence. The action turns on it as on a pivot, for the church-beast "caused the earth and them that dwell therein to adore the first beast, whose deadly wound was healed," as if this healed wound were somehow a prerequisite for what follows. That the tableau represents an inverted working arrangement of church and state to be put in operation at some future time, soon becomes clear. Operating in collusion with the infernal dragon "which gave power to the [first] beast," the church-beast would effect the transfer of man's primary allegiance from the church back to the state, as had been the case in pagan times.

This is what the healing of the state-beast's strange wound makes possible. St. John was told the wound was "deadly" and caused by the sword, yet "the beast ... lived" (Apo. 13:1-14), for the wound signifies the death blow to paganism dealt by Christ, from whose "mouth came out a sharp two-edged sword," twice beheld by St. John in his vision (Apo. 1:16; 19:15). Although incapacitated in one of its heads, the beast nevertheless lived on in the Roman Empire, which was eventually replaced by Christendom, the first regenerated human society where Church and state worked side by side in proper order under God. The vision warned that the injury would eventually "heal," and the resurgence of paganism would make it possible for the state to reassert the supreme authority it once wielded over the souls of men.

+

A brief but significant preview of the ultimate pagan revival occurred in the fourth century when the Emperor Julian the Apostate, grandson of

Constantine the Great, rose to power at the height of the Arian heresy. Convinced that he was under the direct guidance of the gods to restore the Roman Empire to the religious traditions of its fathers, he claimed to have received a divine mandate to that effect from the sun-god Mithra, into whose gnostic mysteries he had been initiated while he was governor of Gaul, and to whom he had consecrated himself as a spiritual soldier. The surprising support he elicited from pagan quarters led many Catholics to believe that the end times were already upon them.

Although he grew up under his predecessor the Emperor Constantius who, like most of his teachers and probably his mother, was an Arian, he had been only too well educated in the faith, and his was no mean intellect. St. Cyril of Jerusalem considered Julian an especially formidable adversary, not so much because he was "naturally gifted in rhetoric," but because "before he became Emperor he was numbered among the believers. He was worthy of Holy Baptism and trained in the Scriptures.... Even those who are strong in faith are troubled because they thought he knew the Holy Scriptures. He heaped up many testimonies from them ... although he did not understand what they meant." [22] His *Contra Galileos*, in which he contemptuously portrayed Christians as a Galilean sect which had apostasized from Judaism, was penned in the tradition of the neoplatonic philosophers Celsus and Porphyry whose systematic argumentation against the Faith commanded so much attention on the part of Origen, St. Jerome, St. Augustine and other Fathers of the Church. Their works and Julian's proved so dangerous to men's minds that eventually the Emperor Theodosius ordered them burned wholesale, so that today they survive only as fragments quoted by Christian apologists.

After a brief but energetic reign of only one year and eight months Julian providentially met his death at the age of thirty-two in a campaign he was waging against the Persians, but just as providentially, he retained his place in history as a portent of things to come. He began restoring the cults of the ancient gods by undertaking a massive reform of the pagan priesthood and reviving the old liturgy in all its erstwhile splendor. Taking an active part in the public ceremonies, he was known to sacrifice a hundred bulls at a time, leaving people to wonder whether there would be enough animals in the whole empire to satisfy his zeal. He soon realized, however, that such measures would not suffice of themselves to uproot Christianity, which after nearly four hundred years had more than carved a place for itself in the general culture.

An astute politician, he guaranteed freedom of conscience for all, advising Christians and other factions to compose their differences and live peaceably together, although according to Ammianus Marcellinus, he did so only "in order that he might have no fear thereafter of a united populace, because such freedom increased their dissensions, and he knew from experience that no wild beasts are so hostile to mankind as are most Christians in their savage hatred for one another." [23] Determined to remove Christian influences from the education of the young, he issued a rescript decreeing that "whoever wishes to teach should ... be approved by the judgment of the council and obtain a decree of the curials, by common agreement and the consent of the best of men. For this decree will be referred to me to deal with, so that they may take up their posts in the city schools with my approval as a higher kind of commendation." [24] When protests were raised, Julian made it clear that "now that the gods have granted us freedom, it seems to me absurd for men to teach what they disapprove. If they are real interpreters of the ancient classics, let them first imitate the ancients' piety toward the gods. If they think the classics wrong in this respect, then let them go and teach Matthew and Luke in the church!"

Setting norms of competence for the teaching profession was nothing new in ancient Rome, but his was the first attempt to dictate to private consciences. By specifying that "schoolmasters and teachers should excel in morality in the first place," his fiat in fact dictated the imposition of pagan morality. By the same token, the appointment of Christians to public office was firmly, if unofficially discouraged. In a letter to a provincial governor Julian writes, "I declare by the gods that I do not want the Galileans put to death or unjustly beaten, or to suffer anything else, but still I emphatically maintain that those who reverence the gods must be preferred to them. For through the folly of the Galileans nearly everything has been upset, whereas through the good pleasure of the gods we are all preserved."

He also undertook the restoration of the Temple in Jerusalem, not because of any predilection for the Jews or their faith, but because he wished to discredit Christ's prophecy, "There shall not be left here a stone upon a stone that shall not be thrown down" (Matt. 24:2). The project had to be abandoned almost immediately, however, for as one witness reported, "Frightful balls of flame kept bursting forth near the foundations of the temple and made it impossible for the workmen to approach the place, and some were even burned to death. And since the elements persistently drove them back, Julian gave up the attempt."

According to some historians, as Julian lay dying of his battle wounds, he cried out, "Galilean, thou hast conquered!" According to others he reproached his "father Mithra" with, "Helios, thou has ruined me!" Both quotes are probably apocryphal, but as his biographer Dom Ricciotti says, "They poetically sum up in a telling manner Julian's endeavors." [25] We can hope they prefigure the end of paganism in our own time, destroyed once more by Christ with the unwitting aid of the devil. The measures Julian took to restore paganism, ably supported by its intelligentsia, are disturbingly similar to those used by secular forces today. Then as now, they by no means operate in a vacuum, for although Constantine had enfranchised the Catholic faith by the Edict of Milan, it was far from being universally practiced throughout the Empire, which continued to subsist politically on the old natural pagan principles and to observe the official festivals on which its culture had rested for so long. Living by two calendars, the one secular and the other ecclesiastical, as Christians do today, is nothing new.

Although visibly declining in Rome and the adjoining provinces, paganism flourished virtually unhindered in the west until the fifth century, when Clovis, King of the Franks, laid the first foundations of Christendom by declaring himself the imperial lieutenant of Christ the King in the temporal order. To him and not to Constantine is due the establishment of the new Holy Roman Empire on the law of the Gospel, for the first time in history tempering the rule of justice with that of love. It was by force of arms that he finally dispatched Arianism, which had been bleeding the Faith white in much the same way that Protestantism bleeds it today by proliferating varieties of "Christians."

The "sharp two-edged sword" issuing from the mouth of Christ was literally directed to its target by the hand of Clovis, who by both word and deed delivered the fatal wound to the head of the state-beast. By means of the Catholic monarchy begun in him and his queen St. Clothilde, God invested the body politic with a Christian soul as vivifying principle. Anchored like the rest of creation in the union of matter and spirit, society would henceforth rest secure not only in indissoluble fidelity between man and wife in the private sector but between clergy and laity in the public domain. For so long as this cooperation was maintained, Christian society perdured.

Not that there can ever be actual separation between religion and civil law, whatever legal distinctions may be made between Church and state, for they are like man and wife. The close rapport between the state-beast and the church-beast in the apocalyptic vision demonstrates how even the powers of evil cannot act otherwise, for a false state automatically calls forth a false church. History testifies that only in relatively recent times has an outright rupture between them been seriously contemplated. Even so, it subsists as little more than an acceptable fiction, for no government in history has ever maintained any degree of integrity without benefit of clergy of some kind. Man was created to worship, and if he is to be governed at all, he must be tethered to something beyond himself.

The root meaning of the word *religio* is to bind. Where the religion is not supernatural, the state may indeed live, but only temporarily, like an animal endowed with a natural soul. This was the general rule in all the great empires which rose and fell before the advent of Christianity, and it remains the rule in a few areas of the globe. To refer to the godless as pagans, or the pagans as godless, as if the words were interchangeable, betrays a myopic ignorance of what only the past can teach. The pagan was anything but godless. What he suffered from was in fact a super-abundance of gods. He worshiped almost anything. Deeply aware of his own dual material-spiritual nature and the intimate communication between these two elements in creation, he was religious in the real sense of the word. He peopled the heavens, the world and the underworld with crowded hierarchies of beings ranging all the way from a Supreme Being through lesser Olympian gods and goddesses, *daemones*, stars and deified heroes on down to woodland deities and the lowly *lares* and *penates* residing in every household, each exercising his specialty like the patron saints of the Catholic Communion.

In the Roman Empire the tribal gods of conquered nations were more than welcome to assume a position in the official pantheon, for the government literally ran on civic piety. As a matter of fact, any nation prepared to jettison its old gods on accepting Roman rule was by that very fact regarded as untrustworthy. Porphyry and Julian distrusted the early Christian for this very reason, branding him with impiety and atheism for allegedly apostasizing from the judaic traditions of his fathers to coin a religion without links to any particular nation or people. Today we forget, if we ever knew, that prominent Romans like Cicero and Pliny, along with Greeks like Plutarch, who was a priest of Delphi, were members of a state priesthood whose duty it was to offer communal sacrifices. The functions of the Augurs in defining public policy is well known. Diviners were called in to lay out the reconstruction of the Capitol, which was begun in the presence of the Vestal Virgins.

What's more, pagans were not only sensible of the citizen's moral obligations to the state, but the state's reciprocal obligation to promote the moral life of the citizen. In a society where philosophers were not mere academicians, but practicing spiritual directors, Socrates was sentenced to death for impiety, on the grounds that he was subverting the youth of Athens. All schools of thought, whether Stoic, Platonist or Epicurean, peddled a specific way of life founded on the natural virtues as they saw them. As St. Paul noted, "the Jews require signs, and the Greeks seek after wisdom" (1Cor. 1:22), determined like the gnostics to attain salvation through knowledge. Godless, however, they were not. Taking religion out of politics was unthinkable, for as Cicero said, "In all probability disappearance of piety towards the gods will entail disappearance of loyalty and social union among men as well, and of justice itself," (Nat. D. 1,4).

So insecure is government without religion that when the old paganism recovered from its wound and resurrected as the United States of America, it set about almost immediately to constructing a mythology for itself. In its capital city today already a number of deified men preside in temples dedicated to them under the names of Washington, Jefferson, Lincoln and others. Certain days having been allocated to their memory in the secular sanctoral cycle, they are in the process of becoming "gods" in the selfsame way that the men of Olympus, with all their deadly virtues and all too human vices, were gradually transformed into Zeus, Apollo and the whole panoply of the pagan heavens. There are official hymns and many emblems, and a great goddess known as the Statue of Liberty guards the major seaport against the great *Oriens ex alto*, "the Just One from the east" who "shall rule kings" (Is. 41:2).

+

So, if pagans are so religious, and their religion similar to Christianity in so many respects, why don't they become Christians the moment they hear the Gospel? The answer is that thousands do, but other thousands don't. Whatever the obstacles to their conversion, however, belief in one supreme Deity is not one of them. Not only was His existence universally recognized among pagans, but their concept of Him was not too far from that of St. Thomas. Porphyry called him "the first God," and described him as "incorporeal, immovable and invisible... in need of nothing external to himself," being "above all things." In fact he considered Him so spiritual that he believed sacrifices and external observances were to be offered only to lesser deities, in whose "divine qualities" some men "in the long reach of time, because of supreme excellence, after being purified," might eventually share to some degree.

He went so far as to say, "Neither is vocal language nor internal speech adapted to the highest god... but we should venerate him in profound silence with a pure soul and with pure conceptions about him" (Abst. 2:37-42). For the pagan, this constituted worship "in spirit and in truth." Nor was so exalted a conception of the Godhead a prerogative of Greek and Roman intellectuals. In his *Origin and Growth of Religions*, Dr. Schmidt found "a clear acknowledgement and worship of a supreme being" in most primitive cultures. "The supremacy of this being is so comprehensively and energetically expressed that all other supernormal beings are far inferior and invariably subject to him." [26] Far from having evolved from polytheism, belief in one god above others inheres in polytheism and is in fact a distinguishing mark of paganism.

Christians tend to think that someone who "believes in God" is showing at least a glimmer of supernatural life and is unconsciously headed for heaven, especially if he gives evidence of living a virtuous life, but there is nothing supernatural about the merely spiritual or the merely righteous. As Fr. Gabriel of St. Mary Magdalen points out in his *Divine Intimacy*, "The moral virtues can make a man honest and virtuous, and can regulate his actions according to reason, but they can in no way bring him into friendship with God or even give him the possibility of meriting eternal life." If the words pagan and godless are not interchangeable, the words pagan and immoral are even less so. Many pagan philosophers, like Socrates, were noted for irreproachable morals, but this did not make them Christians. They were only obeying the natural law in the light of natural reason, and it is natural for man to worship.

But how believe *in* God without believing God, which is faith by definition? Without accepting the conditions He has laid down for salvation? Sometimes the pagan demonstrates a real love of God, but why shouldn't he love the one who provides his very life and sustenance? Didn't our Lord say, "If you love them that love you and... do good to them that do good to you," don't "sinners also do this?" (Luke 6:32-33). It's only natural to take a benevolent attitude toward God for a sign of supernatural life, but precisely because it's only natural, it has turned out to be one of the worst follies of the current ecumania, spawning far more scandals and sacrilege than converts.

Commenting on the passage in St. Matthew's Gospel where our Lord says, "If therefore they shall say to you: Behold he is in the desert: go ye not out... believe it not" (Matt. 24:26), St. Jerome interpreted that to mean that if we are told Christ dwells in the desert, we are to lend no credence because the desert represented the pagan world and its teachings, in which *Christ is never to be found.*: "If they assure you that Christ resides in the desert of the gentiles and in the doctrines of philosophers... don't believe it!" [27] What this doughty Father of the Church would say of the Second Vatican Council's startling exhortation in *Gaudium et Spes* "to hear, distinguish and interpret the many voices of our age" can be imagined. Could he believe that, "Thanks to the experience of past ages, the progress of the sciences and the treasures hidden in the various forms of human culture... new roads to truth are opened?" To think that to preach the Gospel the Church "must rely on those who live in the world, are versed in different institutions and specialties, and grasp their innermost significance in the eyes of both believers and unbelievers," is quite simply to think like a pagan. [28]

Soon after he began preaching to the gentiles St. Paul learned the hard way that monotheism was a natural deduction of human reasoning and in itself no predisposition to the faith (*Acts* 17:18 ff.). Invited to the Areopagus by some Epicurean and Stoic philosophers to acquaint them with the new religion he had been preaching in the synagogues and market-places, he thought it expedient to open with a reference to their supreme god by saying, "Ye men of Athens, I perceive that ye are in all things over-religious, for passing by and seeing your idols, I found an altar also on which was written: TO THE UNKNOWN GOD." In his inexperience he tells them, "What, therefore you worship without knowing it, that I preach to you." Reinforcing their conviction that the God of all is pure spirit, he speaks of Him as one who "dwelleth not in temples made with hands, nor is he served by the hands of men as though he needed anything..." in whom "we live and move and have our being: as some also of your own poets said: For we are also his offspring."

Although he appeared "to be a preacher of new gods," and even went so far as to exhort his listeners to penance, St. Paul elicited no serious objection from them until "they had heard of the resurrection of the dead." Being met with outright mockery on that score, he stopped talking and "went out from among them." Only "certain men adhered to him and believed," for in his sermon three aspects of the Christian God had been introduced which rendered Him totally unacceptable to the pagan mentality: 1. He had created everything out of nothing solely by His will, 2. He is the only God there is, and 3. He has somehow entered into partnership with matter and would allow the world to be judged by a Man.

A *Creator ex nihilo*, who not only "made the world and all things therein" out of absolutely nothing, God therefore also has the power to resurrect what He has made. A century later the philosopher Celsus would ask, "What sort of body, after being corrupted, could return to its original nature and that same condition which it had before it was dissolved?" He accused the Christians of "escape to a most outrageous subterfuge by saying that 'anything is possible to God'," for like our modern pagan scientists today Celsus held that God is bound to the laws of nature like everything else that exists.

Galen regarded our Lord's affirmation that "God is able of these stones to raise up children to Abraham" (Matt. 3:9) as ridiculous superstition. Hoping to demonstrate in a book he wrote on anatomy that "nature does nothing without a reason," he argued, "For it is precisely this point in which our own opinion and that of Plato and of the other Greeks who follow the right method in natural science differ from the position taken by Moses, for the latter it seems enough to say that God simply willed the arrangement of matter and it was presently arranged in due order, for he believes everything to be possible with God, even should he wish to make a bull or a horse out of ashes. We, however, do not hold this. We say that certain things are impossible by nature and that God does not attempt such things at all but chooses the best out of the possibilities of becoming" [29]

Such was the declared position of the pagan, for whom God's relation to the universe was not that of a Creator, but rather that of the Masonic "Architect of the Universe" who simply assembled the cosmos out of pre-existing chaos and put it in proper order. In pre-Christian times the poet Lucretius had already laid down as principle in his *De Rerum Natura* that "Nothing can ever be created by divine power out of nothing." Sounding for all the world like a modern evolutionist, he says that once this is accepted as fact, "we shall have a clearer picture of the path ahead, the problem of how things are created and occasioned without the aid of the gods." In other words, we are at liberty to fathom for ourselves the process by which the world literally creates itself.

Using his Catholic background to fullest advantage, the apostate Julian hoped to induce Christians to rethink the sources of their faith by alleging that the Mosaic account of creation dealt only with the physical world. Departing from the exegesis of the Fathers by refusing to recognize the creation of spiritual beings in the opening words of the Bible, "In the beginning God created the heavens and the earth," he maintained that, "according to Moses, God is the creator of nothing that is incorporeal, but is only the disposer of matter that already existed." Denying God's power to create from nothing, he thus more or less identified Him with the evil god of the gnostics who was held responsible for introducing evil and inequality into the world by introducing matter.

Inasmuch as both Greeks and Romans tolerated a wide variety of philosophical opinions and gloried in spirited discussions on every conceivable subject, no Christian need have feared to voice his convictions regarding the genesis of the world, which to them remained a speculative question with little practical application. As Robert L. Wilken points out in *The Christians as the Romans Saw Them*, "Christians readily entered the public arena and adopted the accepted standards of truth as the basis for discussion.... That pagans continued to write books against the Christians for three hundred years is evidence that they took the ideas of Christian thinkers seriously. This made a genuine dialogue possible." [30]

To polemicists like Porphyry, such peculiarities as the dogma of the Incarnation or the abolition of animal sacrifice presented no serious obstacles to incorporating Jesus of Nazareth's new religion into the official system, nor to making room for Him in the imperial Pantheon as modern syncretists do. Anyone could become divine, and diversity of worship was taken for granted. Celsus had seen "nothing wrong if each people observes its own laws of worship." The more the merrier. Obviously, religious freedom was not made in the U.S.A., nor was it taught to the world by the U.S. Constitution. As we have seen, the Empire had no problem with tribal gods as such. The pagan state literally subsisted on what Eusebius called "political theology," taking for granted that religion was a patrimony linked to the traditions of every city and people. Citizens moving to a new locality were simply expected to add the regional gods to their own without making a fuss.

Although pagan nations were often at war, it was rarely if ever over religion. It was universally understood that a victor absorbed the gods of the vanquished into his own pantheon, in some cases even according them preference. As Jean-Jacques Rousseau pointed out, "This is why paganism was at length known in the world as a single religion." On religious grounds, what was there to fight about? It is easy to judge how far the Christian world had relapsed into paganism by January 29, 1965, when Paul VI returned to the Turks the banner wrested from them by Catholic blood and prayer at the battle of Lepanto, accompanying his gesture with the declaration, "Wars of religion are ended forever!" Were this true, the Church Militant would even now have passed out of existence.

+

What put the faithful at risk and would eventually produce untold numbers of candidates for the Roman Martyrology was another article of faith implicit in St. Paul's talk on the Areopagus: When he declared that the God of the Christians was "Lord of heaven and earth... not far from every one of us," and in whom "we live and move and have our being," he intimated that this God, who "made of one all mankind, to dwell upon the whole face of the earth, determining appointed times and the limits of their habitation," was not only supreme, but was the *only* God there is, ever had been or ever will be. To obliterate at one stroke the entire panoply of gods, goddesses and in-betweens who peopled the pagan cosmos, must have struck his hearers as intolerably arrogant, if not blasphemous.

To believe, furthermore, that this supreme God was the god of an insignificant nation like Israel, who had revealed His identity by a specific historical revelation in time and space, was too much to ask of educated minds. Celsus would ask, "Is it only now after such a long age that God has remembered to judge the life of men?" And Julian in his tract against the Galileans would want to know why Judea was "the only land that he chose to take thought for.... If he is the God of all of us alike and the creator of all, why did he neglect us?" No Supreme Being would behave in a fashion so repugnant to reason.

He proposed as self evident, "That the human race possesses its knowledge of God by nature and not from teaching is proved to us first by all the universal yearning for the divine which is in all men whether persons or communities, whether considered as individuals or as races. For all of us, without being taught, have attained to a belief in some sort of divinity, though it is not easy for all men to know the precise truth about it, nor is it possible for those who do know it to tell it to all men" (52b).

We are indebted to St. Augustine for incorporating into the *City of God* the arguments of Porphyry, who pointed out, "No doctrine has yet been established to form the teaching of a philosophical sect which offers a universal way for the liberation of the soul; no such way has been produced by any philosophy, nor by the moral teachings and disciplines of the Indians, nor by the magical spells of the Chaldeans, nor in any other way." Symmachus would say, "We cannot attain to so great a mystery by one way." If all this sounds familiar, that is because it forms the basis of modern ecumenism, now let loose even among Catholics.

That men might aspire to some degree of divine status was generally acknowledged in pagan civilizations. The Romans were not above deifying their Emperors, and St. Lactantius tells us that many of the Greek gods were known to have once lived earthly lives before rising to Olympus, but St. Paul informed the Athenians that the God who was so far unknown to them "hath appointed a day wherein he will judge the world in equity, by the man whom he hath appointed, giving faith to all by raising him up from the dead" (Acts 17:17-34). In many ways the pagan found this claim to be the most offensive to reason. How could a purely spiritual God, especially if He were the only one, capable of making something out of nothing, deign to reveal himself through His own material creature, let alone transfer His supreme power to him? How is it possible to believe that having ascended into heaven, "from thence he shall come to judge the living and the dead?" Worse still, how could such a man be the sole means of establishing contact with God?

How could Christians set themselves above human experience by presuming to say that their God alone was the supreme deity? Overriding every ethnic loyalty by offering salvation to all indiscriminately, not only had He decreed from eternity, "Thou shalt have no other gods before me," but He had declared through His Psalmist that "all the gods of the nations are devils!" (Ps. 95:5). Suetonius reflected the common consensus when he labeled Christians "a class of men given to a new and mischievous superstition," for such a revolutionary concept of religion automatically branded them as political subversives. Tacitus made a point of the fact that those executed under Nero suffered not so much for their imputed arson as for their antisocial tendencies. Rarely if ever officially prosecuted on religious grounds *per se*, by refusing public honor to the gods of officialdom they proved themselves guilty of adulterating the collective *pietas* which was the very lifeblood of good government.

Of the many martyrs made by Julian the Apostate during his ephemeral reign, the most famous are the brothers Sts. John and Paul who for centuries have been commemorated in the *Communicantes* of the Latin Rite Mass. From their beautiful mansion, an architectural gem which is happily still extant on the Coelian Hill above the Coliseum, they were engaged in charitable works made possible by funds left to them by Constantine's daughter Constantia when Julian invited them into his personal service. There was no question of renouncing their faith by accepting positions in the royal household, for as Dom Guéranger pointed out, "The most exacting casuist could not find it a crime... to dwell in a court where nothing was demanded of them contrary to the divine precepts." The same might be said today of Catholics working for the U.S. government.

Yet they refused to be employed by an apostate, despite the fact that close contact with Julian might have led to influencing him "to relax somewhat of those administrative trammels unfortunately imposed on the Church by his prejudicial government. For aught one knew, the possible conversion of his soul, the return of so many of the misled who had followed him in his fall, might be the result." Lulling his conscience with prospects of this kind, the average Christian then as now would have gladly accepted the appointment, but John and Paul were of the stuff of saints: "The frank expression of their sentiments and this boldness infuriated the tyrant and brought about their death." Now required to pay homage to Jupiter because of their insubordination, they refused, even though they would have been permitted to do so before an official in the privacy of their own home. The upshot was that the Emperor had them executed and buried in the house to avoid adverse publicity to himself.

On reading the Martyrology today it is easy to forget that for every name gloriously inscribed on its rolls were hundreds of other Christians who saw no harm in complying with what they regarded as a mere bureaucratic formality. What harm in burning a little incense in honor of a civic deity whose function was largely symbolic and very few believed in anyway? To read the accounts of the trials, the judges were as often as not sympathetic to the defendants, if not in some cases related to them, and eager to let them off if possible. That the majority of the Catholics accused opted to join the ranks of the incense-burners is therefore not to be wondered at.

The Abbot of Solesmes reminds us, however, that it was from a church dedicated by St. Hilary of Poitiers to Sts. John and Paul "that Clovis on the eve of the battle of Vouillé beheld streaming towards him a mysterious light, presage of the victory which would result in the expulsion of Arianism from Gaul, and in the foundation of monarchical unity." He deplores the day when "merely because sin does not stare them in the face, Christian souls stoop from the lofty height of their Baptism to compromises which even a pagan would avoid!" Mindful that "Julian's plan of action is once more in vogue," he entreats the two martyrs "to uphold the new militia raised by the necessity of the times" and "to bless our harvest ripe for the sickle." [31] Time will tell how modern generations measure up to their forbears in the Faith.

+

Pagans, who in every age have maintained on principle that there are many ways of reaching God, find it hard now as always to accept that Jesus of Nazareth alone is the way, the "door" to salvation, and that "if anyone enter by me he shall be saved... He that entereth not by the door into the sheepfold, but climbeth up by another way, the same is a thief and a robber" (John 10:1-9). Porphyry wanted to know, "If Christ says he is the way, the grace and the truth, and claims that only in himself can believing souls find a way to God, what did people who lived in the many centuries do before Christ?" And pagans today still ask, what do they do now who have never heard of Him?

If the arguments advanced by Celsus, Porphyry and the apostate Emperor sound familiar, that is because they are being heard more and more as the world reverts to paganism. Hear what the London Professor Cyril Joad wrote to Sir Arnold Lunn back in the 1930's, in an exchange of letters published under the title *Is Christianity True?* He derides the conclusion "that a supreme revelation of the nature of reality, of the origin of the earth, of the personality and intentions of its Creator and of the purpose and destiny of mankind took place in Palestine just under two thousand years ago; that this revelation was the central event in the history not only of this planet but of the universe; and that unless and until it is repeated, nothing of even approximately equivalent importance can occur. It is implied, further, that our remote descendants... will still be living on the income of the religious capital of this event, and that their own religious experiences will be limited to confirming and endorsing it.

"... Let us consider the claims of your creed in the light of the equally assertive claims of rival creeds. It is the parochialism of your view that shocks while it amuses me. I can only smile at the naiveté of one who assumes that while all the other gods have passed away – Isis and Astoreth, Zeus and Athene, Janus and Vesta, and Yahweh himself once mentioned with awe and venerated by millions – his own will abide forever.... I cannot stomach a religious absolutism which, believing in a single supernatural revelation, infers that human souls can be saved only if they accept its official view of the nature of its exclusive god. Anybody who has tried his hand at governing the British Empire knows perfectly well that... his only course is to treat all religions as absolutely equal." [32]

Ecumenism in religion, like pluralism in politics, is indeed the only sensible, natural way of integrating irreconcilable differences. As we have noted, there were no wars of religion in classical times. Only by healing the wound to paganism can the Beast with so many heads and crowns be put in condition "to make war with the saints and to overcome them" (Apo. 13:7) Pitting its prefabricated "unity" against the unity of the Church, not since the days of Julian the Apostate has the Beast shown us so clearly how to compose our differences in a civilized manner. Soaring above every creed or dogma which takes into account our dual existence in matter and spirit, the neo-paganism which revived with the Enlightenment would have us abandon matter altogether as inconsequential and take refuge in a Supreme Being who appears to be purely spiritual, but is in fact simply an immaterial abstraction, having no real existence, like the universal God of the American Thanksgiving Day.

+

Under the circumstances it is no surprise to find that Rousseau's *Social Contract*, the acknowledged Bible of the modern pagan revival masquerading as democracy, ends with a final chapter on "civil religion." Pretending to show how the spread of Christianity systematically destroyed social unity by giving man two sets of laws, human and divine, which put him in contradiction with himself, Rousseau admitted that "in speaking of a Christian republic, each of these two words excludes the other." He had read sufficient history to know, moreover, that separation of church and state is a political fiction of recent coinage, for "it might be proved that no State was ever founded without religion serving as its basis." Belief in an "omnipotent, intelligent, benevolent divinity that foresees and provides" he takes for granted.

He maintained the real solution lay in "the religion of man," which he calls true Christianity, "not that of today, but that of the Gospel, which is quite different. By this holy, sublime and pure religion, men, children of the same God, all recognize one another as brethren, and the social bond which unites them is not dissolved at death." Again, if this sounds familiar, it is only because we are hearing it once more from modernists, liberation theologians, ecumenists and other alleged reformers. Rousseau laid the groundwork for them by recommending "the purely civil profession of faith, the articles of which it is the duty of the sovereign to determine, not exactly as dogmas of religion, but as sentiments of sociability, without which it is impossible to be a good citizen or a faithful subject.

"Without having power to compel anyone to believe them, the sovereign may banish from the State whoever does not believe them; it may banish him not as impious, but as unsociable, as incapable of sincerely loving law and justice and of sacrificing at need his life to his duty." Essentially this was the accusation leveled against the Roman martyr, as it was against Christ and is now against His disciple today. After quoting in a footnote the Marquis d'Argenson's famous definition of morality: "In the commonwealth each is perfectly free in what does not injure others," Rousseau defines, "The dogmas of civil religion ought to be simple, few in number, stated with precision and without explanations or commentaries. The existence of the Deity, powerful, wise, beneficent, prescient and bountiful, the life to come, the happiness of the just, the punishment of the wicked, the sanctity of the social contract and of the laws; these are the positive dogmas. As for the negative dogmas, I limit them to one only, that is, intolerance; it belongs to the creeds we have excluded.

".... Now that there is, and can be, no longer any exclusive national religion, we should tolerate all those which tolerate others, so far as their dogmas have nothing contrary to the duties of a citizen. But whoever dares to say: 'Outside the Church no salvation' ought to be driven from the State.... Such a dogma is proper only in a theocratic government; in any other it is pernicious."

While the French political theorist Rousseau was putting the finishing touches on his *Social Contract*, his contemporary the German philosopher Immanuel Kant was declaring God not quite dead but nearly so, being metaphysically unknowable and beyond the reach of reason. By virtue of the school Kant left behind him, God's essential unattainability would once more become official dogma as in pagan times. Watching

Napoleon's *Grande Armée* passing by, another German philosopher, Georg Hegel, plunged the world one step deeper into error by declaring, "The Universal is to be found in the state... the state is the Divine Idea as it exists on earth.... We must therefore worship the State as the manifestation of the divine on earth." The revolutionary Karl Marx, famous for dismissing religion as "the opiate of the masses," would pinpoint socialism as "the functional equivalent of religion." All of which serves to prove G.K. Chesterton's dictum that "when men cease to believe in God, they will not believe in nothing, they will believe in anything!"

The first nation in the world to be put together according to a pre-fabricated written Constitution, the United States of America was already providing the working model for the new pagan society before it left the drawing board. Although God is nowhere mentioned in the founding document, He was not absent from the deliberations of its framers, whose Deism was simply another name for the cult of the old pagan Supreme Being, lately installed as the God of Masonry. Why else would George Washington have deleted the name of Christ from his proclamation of the first Thanksgiving Day? America may well have been Christian at one time and may still be so in places, but this could never have been said of the United States, whose Founding Fathers were aware even as the Constitution was adopted, that God must be kept within juridical bounds if their experiment were to succeed.

Always careful not to mention Him by name, the first Article of their very first Amendment, the so-called "Bill of Rights," provides that "Congress shall make no law respecting an establishment of religion or prohibiting the free exercise thereof." As Rousseau postulated, intolerance belongs only to the creeds we have excluded. Properly interpreted, however, Article I means that the new government, like any pagan state, must not only transcend all religions, but must use vigilance in preventing the pre-eminence of any one of them. There must be no legal loophole whereby a particular religion proclaiming itself *the* religion, outside of which there is no salvation, might set limits to freedom by preaching right and wrong to the state.

All creeds are indeed tolerated, but only provided they keep their place in the private sector under an undefined Entity unofficially accepted as supreme. Because the God of pagan society must remain sufficiently nebulous to absorb all professed creeds, suit all circumstances and hold sway over every contradiction, it is best to keep Him unnamed. At most He is the Life Force, a purely spiritual energy animating the world. By now the Unknown God of the Athenians has been accredited to the United

States, where he reigns as the God of their dollar bill, and where at least once a year on Thanksgiving Day, gratitude for His many benefits pours forth publicly from sea to shining sea from the hearts of Catholics, Protestants, Jews, Muslims, Buddhists and all, without shadow of discrimination Democratic or Republican. In the fall of 1986, this same indeterminate deity was implicitly acknowledged by the Pope of the one, holy, universal and Apostolic Church, when he invited Christian and non-Christian church leaders from all over the world to pray together in Assisi where "each religion will have the time and the opportunity to express itself according to its own traditional rite."

Their formula for a union of heterogeneous states having proved feasible, at the beginning of the twentieth century the States hatched a world League of Nations created in its own image which at the century's close would give way to a grander United Nations. Like its prototypes, this august international body displayed little interest in religion beyond ignoring it, but this may no longer be the case. According to Marguerite A. Peeters of Centre New Europe's Interactive Information Services, a new Earth Charter up for ratification by the General Assembly by the year 2000, bids fair to be "a new paradigm of development." In May 1997 in Zurich she reported, "The Earth Charter will not be an environmental charter, but the Charter of 'sustainable development,' therefore of social equity, the charter of 'quality of life for all'... It will be the charter of the new social consensus, the charter of" – ah, yes – "the new social contract, the charter of the new world order," equivalent in its own way to the Universal Declaration of Human Rights proclaimed in 1948.

In the words of its main inspirer Maurice Strong, it should embody "the basic principles for the conduct of nations and peoples with respect to the environment and development to ensure the future viability and integrity of the Earth as a hospitable home for human and other forms of life." As Rousseau said, "No State was ever founded without religion serving as its basis," and apparently the UN will be no exception, for as Ms. Peeters pointed out, "The Earth Charter has a spiritual/religious/ethical component. This is new in the UN consensus. The main idea is that the 'crisis' (the social, economic, environmental crisis) is such that it transcends religions and cultures. It transcends them, therefore it carries imperatives of its own. Religions of the world must come up with a consensus about the new values and behaviors to adopt. These values must be compatible with the principles of sustainable development."

+

Have we heard this before? Many times, for until the allegedly unknowable God entered history and manifested Himself as man, this was
the generally accepted norm of cooperation among all pagan peoples. So
why not again, now that the world has returned to paganism? The Incarnate Jesus Christ alone can refute paganism, whose airy, unsubstantial
God of all is God of nothing. Christ's Mother the immaculate Mary
destroyed every heresy when she vested the Son of the God of Israel with
a material body and made Him visible to the world at a specific place and
time decreed from eternity. In his vision on Patmos St. John heard Him
say, "I, Jesus am... the root and stock of David, the bright and morning
star." Although at the end, "He cometh with the clouds... every eye shall
see him, and they that pierced him," and those who have overcome "shall
see his face: and his name shall be on their foreheads," where the Beast
would have set his mark. (Apo. 22:16; 1:7; 22:4).

Nearly every false god holds out hope of deification to his devotees by
some form of ecstatic identification with himself. Only the omnipotent God
of the Christians, whose delight is to be with the children of men, has by His
own power "humanized" Himself, becoming Man in order to identify with
them. Neither Zeus nor Mithra nor Buddha nor Mohammed ever died on a
cross for them out of an excess of love as did God's only-begotten, substantial Son made Man. When the centurion Longinus thrust his lance into the
breast of the divine Man on the Cross, the bystanders saw nothing more
than the merciful consummation of a death sentence, but St. John, who
viewed the proceeding close up and from the proper perspective, reported
more correctly that "one of the soldiers opened his side" (John 19:43).

What he saw was a *coup de grâce* delivered in its fullest possible
sense, for by that bloody cleft in the Rock of salvation grace and mercy
were set flowing over the whole world. For the first time in history man's
way to the Godhead was clear, having opened suddenly and materially in
the gaping side of Christ. The physical, stricken, Sacred Heart of Jesus,
resurrected and glorified, is God's final answer to paganism and all its
theological vapors. The wound of the Beast was healed, for it was only a
superficial wound to one of its heads and was bound to close over in time.
The wound of Christ will never heal, for it was a vital one to the heart of
God and is eternal. What could heal the Wound that heals every other?

84 APOSTASY

ONE WORLD, TWO CROWDS

Rather than dignify the evil beast looming in vision on Patmos with a name, St. John designated him by a number, reckoned as "666." The Apostle knew whereof he spoke, having been present on the shores of Lake Genesareth when our Lord exorcised the local demoniac who was terrorizing the neighborhood. Compelled to identify himself, the possessing devil admitted publicly that he was characterized by quantity rather than by quality when he said, "My name is Legion, for we are many" (Mk. 5:9). He didn't say how many, but in the *Apocalypse* St. John would tell us that before the end of time, "when... Satan shall be loosed out of his prison and shall go forth and seduce the nations which are over the four quarters of the earth... and shall gather them together to battle," he will dispose of forces "whose number is as the sands of the sea" (Apo. 13:18; 20:17). They would rival in number the descendants of Abraham, to whom God promised progeny multiplied "as the sand that is by the seashore," a throng estimated by St. Paul "as the stars of heaven in multitude ... innumerable" (Gen. 22:17; Heb. 11:12).

This being the case, the Christian pitted against the devil can expect sooner or later to face the raw might of sheer numbers, for Satan is always "many" and prefers faceless anonymity. In the course of His ministry our Lord constantly encountered large numbers of people who "followed him from Galilee and from Decapolis and from Jerusalem and from Judea and from beyond the Jordan," avid to hear Him speak or to receive some miraculous benefit from His hand. Scripture says that on one occasion the swarm was so overpowering that "he went into a boat and sat, and all the multitudes stood on the shore." Out of compassion He fed thousands, not only with bread and fish in the desert, but by word of mouth throughout Judea and Galilee, and after the Sermon on the Mount, "great multitudes followed him" (Matt. 4:25; 13:2; 8:1).

When He entered Jerusalem in triumph before His Passion, "A very great multitude spread their garments in the way: and others cut boughs from the trees and strewed them in the way," crying out, "Hosanna to the Son of David!" at the top of their lungs. Throughout the city "the people said: This is Jesus the prophet, from Nazareth of Galilee" (Matt. 21:8-11). Yet, only a few days later, after the fateful deliberations of the Sanhedrin, a "whole multitude of them rising up, led him away to Pilate," where "they began to accuse him, saying: We have found this man per- verting our nation and forbidding to give tribute to Caesar and saying that he is Christ the king... He stirreth up the people, teaching through- out all Judea" (Luke 23:1-2).

"A tumult was made" clamoring for His execution, and when Pilate publicly washed his hands "of the blood of this just man," the accusers were only too ready to relieve him of further responsibility by declaring, "His blood be upon us and upon our children!" (Matt. 27:25). This avouch- ment did not issue from the ringleaders only, for Scripture is at pains to record that it came from "all the people answering" (Matt. 27:24-25). A landslide of such proportions would normally lead to the conclusion that the huge crowds who till then had acclaimed our Lord so enthusiastically throughout Judea and Galilee had never been anything but a mob, easily induced to mob rule by the use of mob psychology.

It would be hard to refute such an assumption were it not for the fact that the chief priests and scribes who "sought how they might put Jesus to death" had nonetheless so "feared the people" that they dared not act openly. When Judas Iscariot therefore "went and discoursed with the chief priests and the magistrates, how he might betray him to them," they were only too "glad, and covenanted to give him money." Clearly the decisions of the establishment were far from enjoying universal sup- port, for "he sought for an opportunity to betray him in the absence of the multitude," and on our Lord's way to Calvary this other crowd comes out in its true colors where Scripture says, "There followed him a great multitude of people and of women."

Unlike those clamoring for His Crucifixion, they "bewailed and la- mented him," and afterwards, "all the multitude of them that were come together to that sight and saw the things that were done, returned strik- ing their breasts" (Luke 22:2-6; 23:27,48). Obviously, in the numbers milling around Christ wherever He went, there must have been two radi- cally dissimilar crowds all along. One would accompany Judas to betray Him in Gethsemane, demand the release of Barabbas in Pilate's courtyard and deride their Savior in agony on the Cross, whereas in the ranks of the other would be found the condemned thief who prayed, "Lord, remember me when thou shalt come into thy kingdom," and the Roman centurion who publicly acknowledged that the criminal capable of "crying out with a loud voice" at the very moment of expiring had to be "a just man!" (Luke 23:42,47).

After the Resurrection this second crowd, till then largely indistinguishable from the other, would turn out to be that "multitude of the believers" which St. Luke characterizes as having "but one heart and one soul: neither did any one say that any of the things which he possessed was his own, but all things were common to them" (Acts 4:31-2). What they held most in common, of course, was the Holy Ghost, for this crowd had never been anything but the Church, the body of the predestinate of whom Christ said, "You shall give testimony, *because you are with me from the beginning*" (John 15:27), and to whom He would say on the last day, "Come, ye blessed of my Father, possess the kingdom prepared for you *from the foundation of the world*" (Matt. 25:34).

They are our Lord's crowd, for as He said, "I know mine and mine know me.... a stranger they follow not" (John 10:14,5). After Pentecost they would all meet "with one accord in Solomon's porch" at the Temple, but then as now, "of the rest, no one durst join himself to them," for though "the people magnified them" (Acts 5:12-13), and some may even have expressed a degree of support in private, the crowd which seeks safety in numbers will never stand up to be actually counted. It was a mob to begin with, and will never be anything else. Members of the judaic hierarchy figured prominently in its ranks, but as Daniel had prophesied, "the people that shall deny him shall not be his" (9:26), regardless of the authority God saw fit to confer on them.

Our Lord had told "the chief priests and magistrates of the temple and the ancients" who were present at His betrayal in Gethsemane that they were able to lay hands on Him only because "this is your hour, and the power of darkness." When "laying hold on him, they led him to the high priest's house," St. Peter, who had never at any time belonged to that crowd, "followed afar off," for he knew his Lord. Although he was about to deny Him through all too human weakness in Caiphas' courtyard, "the Lord turning, looked on Peter" after that wrenching defection, even then recognizing Him as one of His own. (Luke 22:52-54,61).

+

The two crowds first distinguished themselves within the family. In Eden two brothers, Cain and Abel, "fixed a great chaos" which would forever divide human generations into those headed for hell and those headed for heaven. As Abraham tells the rich reprobate in the parable, "They who would pass from hence to you cannot, nor from thence come hither" (Luke 16:26). St. Augustine would call the two contingents the City of Man and the City of God, for the family is the nucleus and source of all human society, and what happens there happens everywhere. Our Lord was not speaking idly when He said, "Think ye that I have come to give peace on earth? I tell you no, but separation: For there shall be from henceforth five in one house divided, three against two and two against three.... For I am come to set a man at variance... And a man's enemies shall be they of his own household" (Luke 12:51-52; Matt.10:35-36).

On October 14, 1943 Maria Valtorta heard Him speak of family members who, "while living in their families, 'leave' them out of love for Me more than if they were to set themselves beyond the double grill of a monastery.... Those who, going against the selfishness, derision and incredulity of relatives, are able to... come to Me, those who do not grow disturbed or cold under the daily assault of unjust remarks and the religious indifference of others. But rather, they suffer this and labor to augment the light in themselves and bear it into the midst of their obfuscated families, and they exhaust themselves in protecting the interests of their God within the first of human societies - the family - and go so far as to give Me their lives provided they can obtain life for the dead in their families – the spiritually dead." [33]

Doing only what He sees the Father doing, the Son of God continues on earth the inexorable separation which began with creation itself, when God "divided the light from darkness," and the good angels from the bad. Our Lord's own family was no exception to this bitter legacy of the angelic fall, for even among His relatives there were two crowds. This became evident at the Feast of Tabernacles before the Passion, where although "many believed in him," some of them even daring to profess, "This is the Christ!" St. John notes dryly that "neither did his brethren believe in him," who had actually urged Him to "go into Judea," where there was price on His head, in order to "manifest thyself to the world." When He refused, preferring to attend the Feast "after his brethren were gone up... not openly, but as it were in secret," even the Apostles were puzzled, and after the Last Supper St. Jude would ask Him, "How is it that thou wilt manifest thyself to us, and not to the world?" Because, our Lord replied, "He that loveth me not keepeth not my words."

As He had told His importunate relatives, it was perfectly safe for them to appear publicly at the Feast of Tabernacles, for "your time is always ready. The world cannot hate you," because the world loves its own, "but me it hateth: because I give testimony of it, that the works thereof are evil" (John 7: *passim*; 14:22). As in any other family, it was not physical relationship that constituted membership in our Lord's crowd. Of His own Mother and relatives He would say, "Who is my mother and who are my brethren? ... My mother and my brethren are they who hear the word of God and do it" (Matt. 12:47; Luke 8:21).

Unfortunately, the refusal of His relations to acknowledge His divinity carried inordinate weight, for humanly speaking they were among those most intimately acquainted with Him. They were in the best position to ask, "How came this man by this wisdom and miracles? Is not this the carpenter's son? ... Is not this the carpenter, the son of Mary, the brother of James and Joseph and Jude and Simon? Are not his sisters here with us?" Small wonder that the inhabitants of Nazareth and vicinity where He grew up "were scandalized in regard of him," a man who had lived in obscurity like themselves and was now proclaiming Himself the Son of God. Ironically enough, He "could not do any miracle" in Nazareth for those who claimed to know Him best, to the point that "he wondered because of their unbelief." He therefore only "healed a few that were sick," concluding sadly, "A prophet is not without honor but in his own country and in his own house and among his own kindred" (Matt. 13: 54-55; Mark 6:3-6).

This crowd, we might say, knew Him too well to recognize Him. And it must be admitted that a higher degree of faith was required of them than of those who had not shared His humdrum existence for years at close quarters. That is eminently true of the Blessed Virgin and His virginal father St. Joseph, who displayed incomparable faith in believing their own miraculously conceived Child was truly God, thereby exceeding even the great faith of their ancestor Abraham, who on God's word had believed that sacrificing his only son would not prevent his becoming the father of nations. St. Elizabeth proved that she was "filled with the Holy Ghost" when she greeted her young cousin Mary with the words, "Blessed art thou among women and blessed is the fruit of thy womb," and ascribed her divine Maternity primarily to the fact that "thou hast believed" that her Son "shall be called the Son of the most High, and the Lord God shall give unto him the throne of David his father" (Luke 1:42, 45, 32).

As intimately acquainted with our Lord's human origins as the others in the family, the believers knew exactly who Jesus was as soon as their relative St. John the Baptist pointed Him out on the banks of the Jordan. They would report, "We have found the Messias! ... We have found him of whom Moses in the law and the prophets did write, Jesus the son of Joseph of Nazareth!" (John 1:45) They were convinced of the true identity of "the carpenter's son," precisely on account of His parentage, the very reason alleged for unbelief by the others. This may explain why St. Luke, probably under the direction of our Lady, chose to insert our Lord's genealogy at this particular point in the narrative. He supports Jesus' messianic claim by tracing His human descent from His foster father St. Joseph back to King David, Abraham, Adam and God himself, who first promised the Redeemer in Eden. Actually he is tracing our Lady's bloodline, for not only were she and St. Joseph of the same tribe and closely related, but St. Joseph's father-in-law Heli, who was our Lady's father St. Joachim by another name, is cited there as St. Joseph's legal parent.

St. Matthew opens his Gospel with another genealogy, which starts from Abraham and ends with "Joseph, the husband of Mary, of whom was born Jesus who is called Christ." The one reinforcing the other, the two geneaologies serve to establish Christ's human filiation beyond any reasonable doubt. When at the Feast of Tabernacles one crowd insisted, "We know this man whence he is: but when the Christ cometh, no man knoweth whence he is," our Lord therefore retorted, "You both know me and whence I am!" (John 7:27-8). All Jews expected the Messiah to come from the line of King David, to whom God had solemnly declared through the prophet Nathan, "I will establish the throne of his kingdom forever ... and thy throne shall be firm forever" (2 Kgs. 7:12-16).

This promise had been many times ratified by the prophets, and when the last of them solemnly announced that God had finally fulfilled it, they were not surprised, and rejoiced. Although the scepter of the kings of Judah had long since fallen, along with their patrimony, to Roman procurators and tetrarchs like Pilate and Herod, the royal line itself had descended in full vigor to Joseph of Nazareth, who would have been its reigning head. The devout among our Lord's relatives interpreted the Scriptures correctly and were not misled by appearances, as were those who expected the Messiah to arrive with worldly pomp and circumstance. They believed our Lord's messianic claims because, unlike the others, they believed God's promise to the royal line of David, and like the monarchists of our own day, they knew perfectly well who the legitimate pretenders were. To this day St. Joseph is referred to as "Prince of Judah" in Eastern liturgies.

+

Lest misapprehensions arise regarding the preeminence of the family in which the Incarnation had taken place, the angel who appeared to St. Joseph in sleep to acquaint him with the divine origin of his blessed wife's Offspring addressed him not by name only, but by his royal title as "Joseph, son of David," rightful successor to the kings of Judah (Matt. 1:20). Edward Healy Thompson, who in the last century compiled the *Life and Glories of St. Joseph* from the most authoritative sources, concluded, "There is not a more splendid genealogy than was his; among all the monarchs of the earth there is none to compare with him .... Joseph is the glory of nobles and the consolation of workmen; he is the condemnation of those sectaries who, born of ignoble blood, desire to reduce all to one vulgar level, destroying all distinction of name, rank or property, by which process society itself would soon be entirely destroyed." [34]

All classes nonetheless meet in Joseph, for in his person he joined poverty to royalty, thus leaving neither the lowly nor the great of this world any grounds for offense. We leave aside the fact that St. Joseph was the first saint of the New Testament canonized by the Holy Ghost himself, who pronounced him "just" in Scripture. According to a strong theological opinion entertained by authorities from Chancellor Gerson, St. Bonaventure and St. Thomas on down, he was sanctified in the womb, if not actually immaculately conceived like Mary. According to St. Bernardine of Siena, Suarez, St. Francis de Sales, St. Leonard of Port Maurice and many others, it may be piously believed that he was among those "saints who slept" who rose from their graves at the Resurrection of his divine foster Son and "came into the holy city and appeared to many" before accompanying Him to heaven body and soul at the Ascension (Matt. 27:52-53).

Joseph's portrayal in modern times as an ignorant artisan departs so irrationally from the facts that it can only be attributed to the prevailing democratic perversion Edward Healy Thompson referred to, whose craze for equality demands that everyone be reduced to the lowest common denominator. It is of a piece with those scriptural meditations which depict the Apostles as roughshod illiterates and make of Mary, the wealthy, exuberant socialite of Magdala, a woman of the streets. This is part and parcel of the new religion of democracy, which has been set up as a rival to Christianity. As Jean Madiran pointed out so ably in his correspondence with Fr. Yves Congar, its basic dogma is that "no individual nor body may exercise authority which does not expressly emanate from popular sovereignty. The authority of the father over the family, of parents over children, of the teacher over students, the economic authority of the company head, professional authority, the spiritual authority of the bishop over his diocese and that of the Pope over the Church are abolished...." for since the Declaration of the Rights of Man, no authority exists beyond that of man himself. [35]

It follows that Catholics weaned on the democratic heresy that "all men are created equal" are inclined to think souls are basically alike, differing only in achievements, talents, bodily characteristics and other accidentals. To think otherwise is "elitist." Retreat masters accustomed to telling housewives that our Lady was "a woman just like you" leave the impression that the inestimable privilege of the Immaculate Conception was the only thing that really set her apart from others, and that we can all become great saints if we apply ourselves as she did, as if saints were self-made. Saints we should be, but how great is not for us to determine, for "to every one of us is given grace according to the measure of the gift of Christ" (Eph. 4:7). Like our Lady, we can become only what God created us to be.

Souls are not clones. Speaking from his own experience as a spiritual director, St. John of the Cross said he never found two who resembled each other by so much as by half. "One is the glory of the sun, another the glory of the moon and another the glory of the stars," says St. Paul, and even then, "star differeth from star in glory" (1Cor. 15:41).

In this life as in the next, not only is no man equal to any other in rank, attributes or essential being, but all are subject to one another in intricate ways. All have superiors greater than themselves to look up to and be grateful to, as well as inferiors on whom to bestow benefits. Each fills a place to which he is not so much appointed as created in, which can be occupied by no other.

As our Lord made clear to Pilate, all authority, however wielded, comes not from the governed, but from God. Christ's birth was a Blessed Event not only to shepherds and Magi, but first of all to the Royal Family into which He had been born. Almost immediately after He had been conceived, a mystery called the Visitation was enacted at the core of the Davidic monarchy at the home of Zachary and Elizabeth in "the hill country," for Mary, Elizabeth and Joseph were all first cousins. Tradition, reinforced by Benedict XIII, avers that our Lady's mother St. Anne and Elizabeth's mother were sisters of Joseph's father Jacob, making of Our Lord and St. John the Baptist second cousins.

Nor did the royal lines stop there, for St. Joseph had a younger brother called Cleophas or Alpheus, three of whose sons were the Apostles Simon the Zealot, James the Less and Jude Thaddeus, and two others were the disciples Joseph Justus and Simeon. Cleophas also had two daughters, one of whom was Mary Salome, the mother of the Apostles St. James the Greater and St. John the Evangelist, and the other is believed to have been the mother of John Mark. All belonged to the one royal family instituted by God in the loins of David, who was once commonly understood to have been the ancestor not only of St. Joseph and our Lord, but of every legitimate monarch of Christendom. How else explain democracy's satanic, statutory hatred for the very principle of hereditary kingship?

So much for the liberal fiction that Christ was a revolutionary risen from down under, or that the Church was the first democratic institution, composed almost exclusively of "common people," publicans, prostitutes and underprivileged sinners. That the first pillars of the Church were well-meaning louts bereft of education may be dismissed by the same token. God did not entrust His only-begotten Son to the care of darkened intelligences. Scripture vouches for the fact that our Lord had not received formal academic training, yet His detractors are left to wonder, as they did at the Feast of Tabernacles, "How doth this man know letters, having never learned?" (John 7:15). Even when He was teaching in the synagogues in His own country, "Many were in admiration at his doctrine: saying: How came this man by all these things? .... They wondered and said: How came this man by this wisdom? (Mk. 6:2; Matt. 13:54).

It becomes obvious that He had been educated at home in the bosom of the Royal Family, primarily by Mary and Joseph, who themselves would have received excellent educations. According to tradition, Mary until her marriage resided in the Temple and would have been instructed there by learned women like Anna, who prophesied at our Lord's Presentation. It is true that the divine Child's parents could not have taught Him what as God He already knew, but He was true Man, and His Sacred Humanity was as susceptible as any other to *experiential* instruction. Doctors of the Church in fact recognized St. Joseph not only as the tutor and guardian of Christ on earth, but also as His preceptor, called *pater educativus* by St. Bonaventure and *director Christi* by St. Cyril of Jerusalem. Prefigured by Joseph of Egypt, St. Joseph would have possessed all the knowledge and talents of his prototype in their full perfection, not only in view of his guardianship of Christ and His Mother, but as predestined Patron of the Universal Church. St. Jerome maintained that St. Joseph resembled the first Joseph even as the Doctor of Egypt, for he found evidence that when the Holy Family resided there during the divine Infancy, St. Joseph had been wont to dispute the tenets of the true faith with the inhabitants, who had long since fallen into idolatry.

+

Whereas the mob tends to be relatively large, the Church on earth continues to figure in our fallen world as that irreducible "handful of defeated men" Paul VI was pleased to refer to in his speech on February 18, 1976. Apparently only in heaven will that handful add up to the victorious "thousands of thousands... a great multitude which no man could number, of all nations and tribes and peoples and tongues" (Apo. 5:11; 7:9), which St. John beheld in exile on Patmos, to which the mob had relegated him under the Emperor Domitian. Unfortunately, after two thousand years of mutual embroilment here below, the Church and the mob continue to be as difficult to distinguish from each other as they ever were by exterior signs. That is because, as the unknown writer of the elegant "Letter to Diognetus" pointed out in apostolic times,

"Christians are not different from the rest of men in nationality, speech or customs; they do not live in states of their own, nor do they use a special language, nor adopt a peculiar way of life. Their teaching is not the kind of thing that could be discovered by the wisdom or reflection of mere active-minded men; indeed they are not outstanding in human learning as others are.... They follow local custom in the matter of dress, food and way of life; yet the character of the culture they reveal is marvelous and, it must be admitted, unusual. They live each in his native land but as though they were not really at home there. They share in all duties like citizens and suffer all hardships like strangers. Every foreign land is for them a fatherland and every fatherland a foreign land. They marry like the rest of men and beget children, but they do not abandon the babies that are born. They share a common board, but not a common bed. In the flesh as they are, they do not live in the flesh."

Because the Church and the mob are so inextricably entwined in the workaday world, countless misguided attempts have been made throughout history to set them to working together in some reasonably productive way. Why can't we all be friends? As the American Cardinal Joseph Bernardin believed, isn't reconciling differences simply a matter of finding Common Ground? When he suggested on a trip to Israel in 1995 that some judicious "corrections" to St. John's Gospel would be in order to combat anti-semitism, he was not speaking without precedent, for back in 1875 Pius IX was already warning the St. Vincent de Paul Conferences of Angers about resorting to "a sort of middle ground, thanks to which truth and error could be made to embrace and an end could be put to their constant warfare, as if it were a mark of prudence to keep one's distance from both truth and error, for fear that truth should upset error in its domain, or that error should go beyond the limits foolishly assigned to it to keep it within bounds."

This temptation – which has bedeviled the Church ever since her first Pope momentarily succumbed to accommodating the obstinate judaizers who wished to incorporate the prescriptions of the old Law into the new law of grace – was foretold in the Old Testament. The story of Susanna and the Elders, which makes up Chapter XIII of the Book of Daniel, tells how "two of the ancients of the people, appointed judges that year" each "became inflamed with lust" for Susanna, "a very beautiful woman and one that feared God," and who happened to be the wife of their honorable colleague Joakim. Mutually acknowledging their infatuation, "they agreed together upon a time when they might find her alone" and demanded that she yield to their importunities. "If thou wilt not," they threatened her, "we will bear witness against thee, that a young man was with thee."

Because the chaste Susanna steadfastly refused their advances, the old men testified against her; and although her virtue was known to all, "the multitude believed them" because her accusers happened to be "the elders and the judges of the people, and they condemned her to death." That Protestants and Jews class this story among the parts of the book of Daniel they judge "apocryphal" is not surprising, for its traditional interpretation holds the calumniated Susanna to represent the Church, and the two wicked ancients to represent Jews and gentiles intent on bending her to their own purposes. Coveting her for himself, each gladly cooperates with the other in order to gain his own particular objective, and failing that, they combine forces to accomplish her destruction in the same way that the Sanhedrin and Pilate cooperated to destroy her divine Founder.

As Scripture foretells in allegory, Judaism and paganism will indeed fail to join the Church to themselves, but by misuse of the legitimate authority of the "ancient judges that seemed to govern the people," she can be expected to be reduced to the last extremity, "straitened on every side: for if I do this thing it is death to me: and if I do not, I shall not escape your hands." Thus it was that Americanist Catholic prelates operating from the first See of Baltimore sought to prostitute the Church to the purposes of democracy in the very beginnings of the United States, bringing her to her present plight. Now harnessed 200 years to the Revolution which was hatched in America, today she finds herself manipulated by a worldwide confederation created in the same revolutionary image, which intends to force her to its will.

Like the distraught Susanna who "cried out with a loud voice" to God on the way to execution, the Church can only pray that He will come soon to her defense as He did for her prototype, when He "raised up the holy spirit of a young boy whose name was Daniel." Declaring himself "clear from the blood of this woman," the youthful prophet succeeded at the eleventh hour in entangling Susanna's two accusers in their own false testimony by the simple expedient of parting them and questioning them separately on the facts of the case. Exposed by their own divergent accounts, they were promptly put to death by "all the assembly... to fulfill the law of Moses," which decreed that a false witness must suffer "as he meant to do to his brother" (Deut. 19:19).

Please God the final denouement of this cautionary tale will soon take place in regard to the Holy Catholic Church. Meanwhile, worth a passing mention, to which no undue significance need be attached, is the fact that the church of Santa Susanna in Rome, dedicated to a Roman martyr and namesake of the Old Testament heroine, who suffered under Diocletian, has long been known in the Holy City as the "American" church. Back in 1856 it had been designated as the titular church of the liberal Cardinal Alessandro Barnabò, who as Prefect of the Congregation of the Propaganda had jurisdiction over the United States, which at that time was still a missionary country. As sacerdotal adjunct to the papal Secretary of State Cardinal Antonelli, who was not a priest, but only a deacon, this prelate not only exercised enormous influence over several important congregations, but took an exceptionally personal, godfatherly interest in the new Paulist order founded by the Americanist Fr. Isaac Thomas Hecker. In 1922 the church was in fact turned over to the Paulist Fathers, who not only preserved their benefactor's name in their Constitutions, but engaged themselves to offer an annual Mass in perpetuity for the repose of his soul. Whether or not this foreshadowed the extraordinary influence Americanism would eventually exert over the Church during and after the Second Vatican Council is open to pious speculation.

+

As Daniel saved Susanna from defilement and death, Christ will save His indefectible Church, against whom the gates of hell can never prevail; but He will not prevent perverted authorities like the two old lechers in the story, "ancient judges that seemed to govern the people," from attempting to lead her members astray in practice. To people finding themselves in such a predicament Our Lord's counsel is clear: "All therefore whatsoever they shall say to you, observe and do." Those who with God's permission "have sitten on the chair of Moses" must be obeyed when they pronounce defined teaching, "but according to their works do ye not" (Matt. 23:2-3). A proper understanding of these words has never been so critical as today, for our Lord foresaw that the Great Apostasy would roll forward not so much in word as in practice. As can now be seen after the reforms of the Mass and Sacraments of the Latin Rite, dogma is perverted most effectively through liturgy, which in essence is not what the Church believes, but what the Church *does*. If the faithful would refuse to act according to her enemies' works, they would not lose the faith.

Because the Church is divinely mandated to teach and baptize that other crowd in which she is always immersed, the temptation to ingratiate herself with it has always been an occupational hazard of her apostolate. Beginning the slide down the slippery slope by permitting Galileo's unproven heliocentrism to be taught in schools, the Church's hierarchy to all practical purposes have ended by accepting as scientific dogma what is in fact a view of the universe at variance with Scripture. Once God's unique Earth was displaced as the center of the universe and reduced to the status of a planet like any other, similar aberrations were bound to follow in the political sphere, where in the same spirit of benevolent accommodation, Popes eventually rallied every Catholic nation to liberal democracy. By the close of the twentieth century, the whole Christian economy had been effectively dismantled, and now forces are actively at work to conform the divinely instituted monarchical structure of the Church to democracy by making an elective office of the Papacy.

At the Second Vatican Council the two primordial crowds were encouraged to lay aside their differences once and for all and pool their resources to build a better world based on their common humanity. Alleging that "the destiny of the human community has become all of one piece," the Pastoral Constitution *Gaudium et Spes* continues to urge pastors "by unremitting study" to "fit themselves to do their part in establishing dialogue with the world and with men of all shades of opinion." Inasmuch as "by His Incarnation the Son of God has united Himself in some fashion with every man" (Intro., 5; IV, 43; I, 22), even a degree of common worship should not be infeasible, and to promote this objective, in 1986 the Holy Father invited representatives of some 130 different religions to pray with him to the God of all at Assisi. When a decade later he declared evolution to be "more than a hypothesis," given the fact that "the convergence of results of independent research constitutes in itself a significant argument in favor of this theory," the revelations of science were put on a level with those of God and the way opened to accommodating Christian morality to Darwin's view of man.

Such is the power of the impure forces ever soliciting the Church through the channels of authority to "Consent to us and lie with us!"

Battling in the shadow of an inarticulate Magisterium, even the staunchest Catholics find themselves drawn into a kind of ecumenism peculiarly their own which leads them to tolerate in their ranks not only outright heresies, but many counter-heresies which spring up by automatic reflex. Under cover of traditionalism schismatics, evolutionists, John Bircher Americanists, sedevacantists, papolators, practitioners of neo-manichean birth control and latter day jansenists march along with sectarians who disregard the Martyrology and the constant teaching of the Church to maintain that God has bound himself absolutely by His own ordinances to damn anyone not baptized with water. Not unlike the irreconcilable denominations marching down American streets under one "pro-life" banner because they all happen to disapprove of abortion, 57 varieties of traditionalists try to maintain a semblance of "unity" in a common effort to restore the Mass, as if the Holy Sacrifice were a fetish existing on its own apart from the Church and the Catechism.

Not a few who lack the courage to stay home to pray on their own if necessary, will have the traditional Mass at any price, regardless of what priest says it or under what circumstances, without stopping to consider the spiritual consequences of celebrating or attending contrary to God's will. Growing numbers find it expedient to settle for the new Mass, provided its heretical ambiguities are suitably rendered in Latin, embellished with good music, and the whole is performed *reverently* by a minister properly attired. For two thousand years the only serious rivals to the Church's authority have been the schismatic Eastern Orthodox, but following on the outrage justly generated by the modernist "reforms" of the Second Vatican Council, she has had to contend increasingly with what might be described as the Latin Orthodox. A new variety of schismatics possessing valid clergy and Sacraments, and operating independently of the Holy See with or without challenging its supremacy.

Whatever show of concord might be achieved by all such factions, it remains that inextricably entwined in them, as everywhere, are the mob and the Church, between which only extrinsic unity of a most superficial kind is ever possible. The two crowds might conceivably join forces to manufacture a product or repel a military invasion, but close collaboration on a moral level is the stuff of illusion, given that their underlying motivation can never be the same. To rally around whatever unites at the price of disregarding whatever divides only breeds further chaos. As St. Paul told the Corinthians, "Bear not the yoke with unbelievers. For what participation hath justice with injustice? Or what fellowship hath light with darkness?... Wherefore go out from among them and be ye separate, saith the Lord" (2 Cor. 6:14,17), before total confusion obliterates every saving demarcation.

There are only two crowds. There is no third party of "independents," because there is no middle ground between truth and falsehood. What is so false as the partly true? Somewhere in the revelations of the mystics it is said that those angels who attempted to remain neutral in heaven by refraining from active participation in Lucifer's rebellion were thrown into hellfire with him all the same, because they failed to defend God's glory. Didn't He tell us when He was on earth, "He that is not with me is against me: and he that gathereth not with me scattereth?" (Matt. 12:30).

Please God the holy angels and saints rally the troops soon, for the battle plan was laid out long ago, and everyone has a part in it somewhere. When the people asked St. John the Baptist, "What then shall we do?" he answered, "He that hath two coats, let him give to him that hath none; and he that hath meat, let him do in like manner." He told the tax collectors, "Do nothing more than that which is appointed you," and to the soldiers he said, "Do violence to no man: neither calumniate any man: and be content with your pay!" (Luke 3:10 -14). In this war the pay is eternal life, and desertion is, well, what this book is all about.

As the veteran Donoso Cortés said, "And don't tell me you don't wish to fight, for the moment you tell me that, you are already fighting. Nor that you don't know which side to join; for while you are saying that, you have already joined a side. Nor that you wish to remain neutral; for while you are thinking to be so, you are so no longer. Nor that you want to be indifferent; for I will laugh at you, because on pronouncing that word you have already chosen your party. Don't tire yourself seeking a place of security against the chances of war, for you tire yourself in vain; that war is extended as far as space and prolonged through all time. In eternity alone... can you find rest, because there alone there is no combat. But do not imagine, however, that the gates of eternity shall be opened for you, unless you first show the wounds you bear. Those gates are only opened for those who gloriously fought here the battles of the Lord Crucified!"

100 APOSTASY

POURING THE JORDAN INTO NIAGARA

When the Assyrian general Holofernes was laying siege to Bethulia - the last Israelite city to offer resistance to Nebuchadnezzar's world empire - the Book of Judith relates that "in going round about," he "found that the fountain which supplied them with water, ran through an aqueduct without the city on the south side: and he commanded their aqueduct to be cut off. Nevertheless, there were springs not far from the walls, out of which they were seen secretly to draw water, to refresh themselves a little rather than to drink their fill." Acting on the advice of his allies in the neighborhood, he decided to overcome them "without joining battle," being persuaded that he need only "set guards at the springs, that they may not draw water out of them," whereupon "they will yield up their city, which they suppose, because it is situate in the mountains, to be impregnable" (Jud.7:6-9).

Like the wily Holofernes, the devil is too good a strategist to dissipate his forces needlessly where his prey is on home ground in naturally fortified territory. Incapable of stanching grace at its supernatural source in God and His saints, over whom he has neither power nor influence, he was astute enough not to launch immediate search and destroy operations against the last remnants still in a position to withstand him. Like his prophetic prototype he therefore began his final assault of latter times by targeting the most ordinary, most essential material agent of man's natural and supernatural life. He planned to force the submission of the City of God by the simple expedient of exploiting its dependence on WATER.

This would not be feasible were it not that created nature was specially designed by God as a foundation for the supernatural, by which it acquires a perfection utterly beyond itself. According to St. Thomas, God endowed man with a *potentia obedientialis* to this end, a responsive power which can provide the locus of connection between his nature and the higher one offered to him by God, if he so desires. This innate human capacity is implicit in St. John's Last Gospel, where he says that as many as received our Lord, "He gave to them power to be made the sons of God, to them that believe in his name. Who are born, not of blood, nor of the will of the flesh, nor of the will of man, but of God."

When our Lady pronounced her *Fiat* to God's proposal she acted in her person as *potentia obedientialis* for all creation, for it was only after her free consent that the Word, "the only-begotten of the Father, full of grace and truth... was made flesh and dwelt among us." A permanent liaison between the divine and the human was established which would ultimately transfigure temporal, natural creation into an eternal, supernatural one, when "the creature also itself shall be delivered from the servitude of corruption into the liberty of the glory of the children of God. For we know that every creature groaneth and is in labor even until now. And not only it, but ourselves also, who have the first fruits of the spirit... whom he foreknew... predestinated to be made conformable to the image of his Son" (Rom. 8:22-29).

The new relationship to God has been characterized as adoption, for only Jesus Christ is God's son by nature, but it is a kind of adoption beyond the usual sense of the word. An adopted child can be given his foster father's name and become his legal heir, enjoying all the external benefits of true sonship, but there is no real affiliation of body and blood. Only God has the power to share His Sacred Body and Most Precious Blood in the Holy Communion of a mutual contract with a child he chooses to endow with His own Spirit, making of him a new creation. St. Paul tells the Roman converts, "You have received the spirit of adoption of sons, whereby we cry: Abba, father! For the Spirit himself giveth testimony to our spirit, that we are the sons of God. And if sons, heirs also: heirs indeed of God and joint-heirs with Christ" (Rom. 8:15-16).

Alas, this does not take place automatically. Universal salvation is not only outrageously wishful thinking, but major heresy, for to men was confided only the "power" to become children of God, provided they met the proper requirements. Because every individual must freely posit his own fiat to the divine invitation to higher life, as our Lady did, or elect to withhold it, as Lucifer did when he flaunted his *Non Serviam* in the face of God, the devils labor to create an environment on earth which will incline man to their own option. If, as has been said, a Christian society is the greatest external grace predisposing to eternal life, then obviously outside influences can predispose to damnation as well.

Because supernature has no other foundation to build on but nature, which it presupposes, and which God joined to himself in the Incarnation for that very purpose, any subversion of nature de-stabilizes the divine edifice resting on it. This is effected all the more easily because, incredible as it may seem, the juncture point of the two orders is the will of man. Created free to begin with when God appointed Adam Lord of the material universe, his will became increasingly unreliable as the effects of the Fall began making themselves felt more and more in his descendants. The Immaculate Conception of the Virgin Mary alone escaped mankind's genetic weakness.

The devil understands this all too well, who knew exactly how to go about subverting the will of Eve even while she still enjoyed a perfectly integrated nature. Inexorably cut off from supernatural existence by sin, which is irreversible in angels by reason of the simplicity of their being, it is true that he is restricted to natural means, but these unfortunately include abilities which, although they are ordinary endowments of the higher angelic nature, are "preternatural" as far as we are concerned and lie beyond our grasp. These render the devil an opponent so formidable that without God's grace to balance the odds, no human being could successfully oppose him, let alone outmaneuver him or bring him to terms.

This being the case, the devil uses all the prodigious natural means at his disposal to intercept the flow of grace, by which alone man is made equal to him. Blind as he is to the supernatural, he can nevertheless deduce its operations by closely observing its otherwise unexplainable outward effects. He had ample reason for suspecting that in the unfathomable judgments of the Godhead, water was a fundamental building block of the universe. There is no substance so common, nor so mysterious as water. Underlying both natural and supernatural existence, its significance remains beyond human understanding, science being unable to explain its essence. When God drew the world out of absolutely nothing, water seemed to be already there before anything else, for its creation goes unmentioned in Genesis.

The second verse of Scripture tells us that before light was created and days as we know them had even begun, when as yet "the earth was void and empty... darkness was upon the face of the deep." This revelation follows immediately on nothing less than the pre-revelation of the Most Blessed Trinity with which the Bible opens. Confiding the ineffable Mystery to future generations, its first verse reads, "In the beginning God created heaven and earth." Unfortunately the deeper meaning of this simple sentence is not conveyed by the vernacular translations, for it lies hidden not so much in the vocabulary as in the syntax. Whereas in the Hebrew the plural noun Elohim is used to designate God, best translated as "Strong Ones," the verb "created," is singular in form, denoting superhuman Persons acting as One.

The mystery is intimated again prior to the creation of Adam where God says, "Let *us* make man to *our* image and likeness." The text does not say how many persons are speaking here, but that there are in fact three may be inferred from later passages in the Old Testament, such as the story of the three mysterious visitors entertained by Abraham before the destruction of Sodom. Not only do these divine representatives foretell the miraculous birth of Abraham's son Isaac in Sarah's old age, but they accept his worship as their due without demur. This example is expounded at length among others by the Talmudic scholar Rabbi David Paul Drach, a famous nineteenth century French convert from Judaism who became Librarian of the Roman Propaganda.

In *De l'Harmonie entre l'Eglise et la Synagogue* he demonstrated conclusively that before the Hebrew scriptures were falsified by the unbelieving Jews after the destruction of the Temple, doctrine on the Blessed Trinity was well known to those who "have sitten on the chair of Moses" (Matt. 23:2) and were faithful to tradition. Part of the genuine Mosaic *kabbala*, the mystery was taught to the learned in the synagogues, but not to the generality of believers, because its full revelation was believed to be reserved to the Messiah. This explains why good Pharisees like Nicodemus and later Gamaliel were able to recognize Jesus as the Son of God by what He taught on the subject, and why those "blind guides" who denied Him despite the testimony of the ancients did so wilfully without excuse. As our Lord told them at the Feast of Tabernacles, "My doctrine is not mine, but his that sent me," so that whoever does God's will, "shall know of the doctrine, whether it be from God or whether I speak from myself" (John 7:16-17).

Immediately after the revelation of the divine plurality, Genesis speaks of one of the Persons in particular by stating in the very next verse that in the primordial dark void, "the Spirit of God moved over the waters." Taking place even before the creation of light, this action argues for extraordinary intimacy between water and God, especially the Holy

Ghost. It would seem that water is the first element of all things. It is the "blood" of creation, both animate and inanimate. St. Francis of Assisi called water "unfathomable, restless, full of riddles and force, a true likeness of the mysterious origins from which life streams forth and death calls." Not only is it the main constituent of human blood, but of the Precious Blood, sweat and tears with which the God-Man Jesus Christ redeemed the world. From His pierced side on the Cross "there came out blood and water," (John 19:34), for water gave divine life to the Second Creation as it had given natural life to the First.

Thus, beyond the reach of history and natural reasoning, Genesis pictures the world as emerging from its birth waters, as from an amniotic sac. After light was created and separated from darkness, the vivifying waters were parted by a firmament, so that those below, when "gathered into one place," would disclose the first "dry land." At the time of the Flood, when "all the fountains of the great deep were broken up and the floodgates of heaven were opened," the upper waters would break, destroying "all the substance that was upon the earth from man even unto beast." These same destructive waters nonetheless supported the Ark of Noah, just as the stormy waves of Lake Genesareth would support the feet of the Savior and His Vicar.

From these second birth waters, the sinful earth re-emerged purified, prefiguring the second, supernatural creation in grace which would take place when water, mixed this time with the saving Blood of Christ, would issue from the Redeemer's side to put the Church into the world. As our Lord told Nicodemus come to Him by night, "Amen, amen I say to thee, unless a man be born again of water and the Holy Ghost" - those close collaborators from the beginning of time! - "he cannot enter into the kingdom of God".... If I have spoken to you earthly things, and you believe not: how will you believe if I shall speak to you heavenly things?" (John 3:5,12).

If all references to water were deleted from the Bible, its essential message would be lost. To list them all would require many pages. Suffice it to say that at the end of time the "rivers of living water" (John 7:38) our Lord promised would flow from the belly of the man who believes in Him, find their final outlet as "the river of water of life, clear as crystal, proceeding from the throne of God and the Lamb" (22:1), which St. John saw flowing through the celestial Jerusalem in the *Apocalypse*. The origin of the salvific stream seems to have been a mysterious spring which "rose out of the earth, watering all the surface of the earth" before paradise was planted. Functioning as a kind of *potentia obedientialis* in the heart of natural creation, it must have supplied the water in the "slime of the earth" from which God created Adam, into whose face He breathed "the breath of life."

The same primordial spring presumably fed the river which watered Eden, where God subsequently "placed man whom he had formed," and from whence it "divided into four heads," the Phison and the Gehon, and the storied Tigris and Euphrates. Because earth's original land mass was jumbled by the Flood and broke up into continents after the trouble at Babel, it is impossible to identify the remnants of these streams with any degree of certainty, let alone chart their courses throughout the world. We are at liberty to suspect, however, that the Jordan is a close affiliate of the primal headwaters, if only because it is the most important river in the Holy Land, which was once the capstone of the world and geographical center of the "dry land" God drew from the "waters that are under the heaven" in the beginning, and where God "wrought salvation in the midst of the earth" (Ps. 73:12).

+

The Jordan is aptly named, for the word means "downcomer." Traveling headlong from north to south through a great geological rift from three pure, high sources nearly 2000 ft. above the Mediterranean, it broadens into the Sea of Galilee to become a sluggish, filthy stream dropping into the Dead Sea at some 1200 ft. below sea level. What its course symbolizes in Scripture is not hard to guess, for it is a visible representation of the Fall of man, who sprang innocent from the hand of the triune God only to run downhill all the way to death in sin. It figures prominently in both the Old and the New Testaments, where, given the river's precipitous banks, expressions like "crossing the Jordan" and being on "this side" or "the other side" of it convey considerable spiritual significance.

Because the Jordan provided the background for so much of the activity of the prophet Elias and his successor Eliseus, who prefigured the Christian sacraments by directing the Syrian general Naaman to wash seven times in its waters to cure his leprosy, it is not surprising that our Lord began His public life on its banks, where the new Elias, His cousin

St. John the Baptist, would point Him out as the Messiah. Not only were the Jordan's running waters privileged to baptize the Incarnate Word by the hand of the Baptist, but a tremendous theophany took place there to ratify the event, which was more than reminiscent of the opening lines of Genesis. When Jesus came "from Galilee to the Jordan ... to be baptized" by the last of the Old Testament prophets, the Three Persons of the Blessed Trinity, whose presence amid the first creative waters was only suggested without being actually revealed, openly manifested Themselves over the waters of the second Creation at the Jordan.

As the Sacred Humanity "went up presently out of the water," emerging from it much like the land which disengaged itself from the depths in the beginning, "behold the heavens were opened to him: and he saw the Spirit of God descending as a dove and coming upon him, and behold a voice from heaven saying, this is my beloved son in whom I am well pleased!" St. John the Baptist had objected to baptizing Jesus, "saying, I ought to be baptized by thee, and comest thou to me?" but relented when our Lord assured him "it becometh us to fulfill all justice." The Fathers of the Church explained that although our Lord was holiness itself and in no need of Baptism, His words conferred authority on St. John's ministry while at the same time providing an outstanding example of the humility which must henceforth accompany the Good News.

St. Ambrose, however, pointed out another reason. He said our Lord's Baptism sanctified the waters of the Jordan, giving them the power of washing away men's sins as they had Naaman's leprosy. In the Roman liturgy the second nocturn for the Feast quotes St. Gregory Nazianzen, saying explicitly, "John is baptizing; Jesus draws near; that he may sanctify John by whom he is baptized. He draws near that he may bury the old Adam in the water, and especially that through this, *the flood of the Jordan may be hallowed*... Jesus comes out of the water, drawing from it and raising with him, in a figurative sense, the submerged world."

St. Cyprian wrote, "As often as water alone is spoken of in Holy Scripture, Baptism is foretold, as ... pointed out in Isaias. 'Remember not,' he says, 'former things, and look not on things of old. Behold I do new things, and now they shall spring forth .... I will make a way in the wilderness and rivers in the desert, to give drink to my people, to my chosen.' Here God has foretold by His prophet that in later times rivers would flow forth from the Gentiles in places that before had been waterless," for "those who by the rebirth of Baptism have become children of God." [36] The Eastern liturgy, in which the Baptism of the Sacred Humanity has figured as a major feast since the second century, marks the occasion with an antiphon taken from Psalm 114, declaring, "The sea saw and fled: backward flowed the stream of Jordan!" By an act of God the "downcomer" as it were had been empowered to run back uphill to its trinitarian source, reversing the direction of the Fall. "O Lord, when thou hadst been baptized in the Jordan, the mystery of the Trinity was revealed, for the voice of the Father bore witness to Thee, calling Thee his beloved Son; and the Spirit, in the form of a dove, confirmed this statement... Today Thou hast revealed thyself to the universe."

Not to accept the role played by matter in man's eternal salvation is to reject the sacramental system ordained by God, which begins with water. In fact St. Cyril of Jerusalem says in his Mystagogical Catechism, "*Water is the principle of the world, and the Jordan the principle of the Gospels*," for like the river of Paradise which "divided into four heads," in order to water the whole world, the Jordan branched out into the four books of Matthew, Mark, Luke and John to refresh it with grace. "Christ, who is the river, is announced throughout the world by the quadruple Gospel," says St. Hippolytus of Rome in his Commentary on Daniel. Echoing the prophecy of Isaias, "All you that thirst, come to the waters!" (Is. 55:1), St. Gregory of Nyssa bids all to "Hasten to my Jordan, not at the call of John, but at the voice of Christ!"

Satan was well aware that the prophet Ezechiel had promised in God's name that "every living creature that creepeth withersoever the torrent shall come, shall live: and there shall be fishes in abundance after these waters shall come hither and they shall be healed, and all things shall live to which the torrent shall come." When St. John saw from Patmos that "on both sides of the river, the tree of life bearing twelve fruits, yielding its fruit every month, and the leaves of the tree for the healing of the nations" (Apo. 22:1-2), the Adversary must have known his time was short. With good reason the Book of Job said of him, "Behold, he will drink up a river and not wonder, and he trusteth that the Jordan may run into his mouth!" (40:18).

Commenting on this verse, Pope St. Gregory asked, "And who is meant by the river if not the flowing stream of the human race? The race that flows from the beginning unto the end; and like water runs from the river of humanity to its appointed end. What is the Jordan but a figure of those who are baptized? For as the author of our Redemption deigned to be baptized in the Jordan, so by the name Jordan is signified the multitude of those who are protected within the sacrament of Baptism. The ancient enemy of mankind therefore drank up the human race, because from the beginning of the world until the coming of the Redeemer, a few of the elect escaping, he dragged mankind down into the maw of his own iniquity.

"Rightly then is it said of him, 'Behold he will drink up a river and not wonder,' for he holds it as nothing when he snatches up the unbelieving. But what follows is truly grievous: 'And he trusteth that the Jordan may run into his mouth,' for after he has overcome all who have not believed from the beginning of the world, even now he is confident he can make his own those also who believe. For by the mouth of his deadly persuasions he daily devours those whose wicked life is opposed to the faith they confess." [37]

+

To frustrate the Redemption of the human race, which would take place through the same element which endowed men with life in the first place, the devil in his overweening pride resolved to replace water in their lives by a universal element of his own choosing. He is not called Lucifer, the Light-Bearer, for no reason. Created second only to God himself in the angelic hierarchies, had he not fallen from grace, we may presume he had been destined to prepare the way of the Messiah who was "the true light which enlighteneth every man that cometh into this world" (John 1:9) by casting heavenly light on earth. Unable to act contrary to his nature even when intending the rashest evil, he therefore chose as his preferred instrument a form of light, the least material, most "angelic" of created elements, which in his fallen state turned out to be connatural FIRE.

Demonic exemplar of the Titan Prometheus who gave men fire stolen from heaven, Lucifer would gradually impart its secret natural properties to perverted minds who would cooperate with him in accomplishing his design. By putting his fire into their hands, he would construct an artificial world in his own image which would enter into competition with the world God created for Christ and His elect. By God's permission it would even prevail for a time, for the *Apocalypse* predicts that "it was given to him to ... overcome them" (Apo. 12:7). Lucifer's fire must therefore not be thought of in terms of the log crackling merrily on the hearth or the candlelight glowing on the altar. It is not the fire of the burning bush seen by Moses, nor the pillar of fire which guided the Israelites through the desert by night. Most certainly it is not the fire which our Lord said He had come to kindle on the earth, nor the tongues of flame which descended on the Apostles at Pentecost.

It is more akin to the fire which rained like water from heaven to destroy Sodom and Gomorrah, or "the everlasting fire which was prepared for the devil and his angels" which is the specific material torment of the damned. It is pinpointed by Supreme Grand Master Albert Pike in *Morals and Dogma*, the "bible" of speculative Masonry, where he writes, "The elementary fire is evidently Electricity or the Electric Force, primarily developed as magnetism." In other words it is the "secret fire" of the ancient alchemists who, in pursuit of what they called the Great Work, laid the foundations of the revolutionary electronic civilization presently invading every corner of the globe and modifying every facet of human life. Pike defined the Great Work as "above all things, the creation of man by himself: that is to say, the full and entire conquest which he effects of his faculties and his future. It is, above all, the perfect emancipation of his will, which assures him the universal empire of Azoth, and the domain of magnetism, that is, complete power over the universal magical agent."

Writing in the mid-nineteenth century, when electronics and nuclear power were still in embryo, he went on to say, "Man as yet knows little of the forces of nature.... He is the slave of these forces unless he becomes their master....There is in nature one most potent force, by means whereof a single man who could possess himself of it and should know how to direct it, could revolutionize and change the face of the world.... It is a universal agent.... If science can but learn how to control it, it will be possible to change the order of the seasons, to produce in night the phenomena of day, to send a thought in an instant round the world, to heal or slay at a distance, to give our words universal success and make them reverberate everywhere."

Today these wonders are taken for granted, but many years before the magus Pike penned these lines, our Lady had already warned at La Salette that "the seasons will be changed" and "voices will be heard in the air." For now, she said, "the time has come for the most astonishing wonders to take place on the earth and in the air.... There will be extraordinary wonders every place *because the true faith has been extinguished and a false light illumines the world.* " Twice in the Secret she mentions "water and fire" in combination, and it is worth noting that she puts water first in its proper hierarchical order. In the first instance she says they "will lend convulsive motions to the earth's sphere," as if these two universal elements had been set at variance for the life or death of the world. In the second instance, however, she says that in the end "water and fire will purify the earth and consume all the works of men's pride, and everything will be renewed: God will be served and glorified."

For his part Pike was predicting, "We may be sure that so soon as religion and philosophy become distinct departments, the mental activity of the age is in advance of its faith; and that, though habit may sustain the latter for a time, its vitality is gone." Subsequent events have unfortunately proved his prognosis correct, for truth is sought more and more in science rather than God's word and even theology is being adjusted to human knowledge. As we have seen, the false theory of evolution was admitted into the Christian spectrum by the Pope of Rome, who declared to the Pontifical Academy of Sciences on October 23, 1996 that "new knowledge leads us to recognize in the theory of evolution more than a hypothesis .... It is indeed remarkable that this theory has been progressively accepted by researchers, following a series of discoveries in various fields of knowledge."

Increasing tolerance for unproven scientific speculation is only the logical aftermath of the decree *Gaudium et Spes*, whose authorship has been largely attributed to His Holiness at the Second Vatican Council before he assumed the papacy. Therein can be read, "Technology is now transforming the face of the earth," and "intellectual formation is ever increasingly based on the natural and mathematical sciences and on those dealing with man himself, while in the practical order the technology which stems from these sciences takes on mounting importance"(5). Inasmuch as "a culture resulting from the enormous scientific and technological progress must be harmonized with an education nourished by classical studies as adapted to various traditions" (56), the faithful are urged, "Let them blend modern science and its theories and the understanding of the most recent discoveries with Christian morality and doctrine. Thus their religious practice and morality can keep pace with their scientific knowledge and with an ever advancing technology" (62).

Grandmaster Pike admitted that for a very long time "science had to conceal itself" from Christians. "It enveloped itself in new hieroglyphs, concealed its efforts, disguised its hopes. Then there was created a jargon of alchemy, a continual deception for the vulgar herd greedy of gold, and a living language for the true disciples of Hermes alone." Now that so many men no longer believe in God, however, the wraps are off. The old reprobate science has not only emerged as a creative force at the service of men, but has achieved a degree of penetration into the highest echelons of the Church. Pike believed that in electricity is to be found "perhaps the secret of life or the vital force." Indeed, how construct a whole new world without also creating its inhabitants?

+

For the devil, who unlike God cannot create, and unlike man cannot even procreate with God's help, producing life is the ultimate ambition, the only objective proportioned to his pride. What he cannot generate, he will therefore seek to reproduce, using for this purpose some highly sophisticated forms of the elementary fire which may already have served him in the past. There is reason to believe that his attempt to fabricate his own world in these apostate times is not his first, for Genesis tells us that once before, "The earth was corrupted before God and was filled with iniquity," to such a point that "it repented him that he had made man on earth," and "seeing that the wickedness of men was great on the earth and that all the thought of their heart was bent upon evil at all times," God sent the waters of the Flood to destroy them and all their works.

This old world won to the devil had apparently reached such a pitch of evil that Scripture will relay no details of it, lest the very knowledge of its baneful achievements contaminate future generations. Except for the geneaology of the patriarchs from Adam to Noah and his three sons, the sum of what Genesis tells us about this long period of history is contained in three or four verses which so far have defied authoritative interpretation. We are told only that after "men began to be multiplied upon the earth and daughters were born to them, the sons of God seeing the daughters of men, that they were fair, took to themselves wives of all which they chose.... Now giants were upon the earth in those days. For after the sons of God went in to the daughters of men and they brought forth children, these are the mighty men of old, men of renown" (Gen. 6:1-2,4). The prophet Baruch said these giants, perhaps the fabled Titans, were "of great stature, expert in war," but they "did not find the way of knowledge" and "perished through their folly" (3:26).

Whether or not this indicates genetic manipulation on a massive scale, of which dinosaur fossils might be residual evidence, their technical accomplishments may well have surpassed anything seen thus far in modern times, for in the days of Adam there had already been unmistakable portents of the direction the world was taking. In the fifth generation from Cain, Lamech is singled out as the first man to take more than one wife at a time. Whereas the name of the first is Ada, meaning "ornament," that of the second, Sella, means "shadow," as if signifying an illusory status. God would permit polygamy to the patriarchs after the Flood, when the world had to be repopulated by men whose lifespans had been radically shortened by the new climatic conditions ushered in by the cataclysm; but there was no excuse for polygamy in Lamech's day, when people normally lived for hundreds of years in the company of their ancestors and descendants, like blossoms and fruit on the same branch.

Lamech was moreover a malefactor, who acknowledged his guilt in the world's earliest recorded fragment of poetry, which reads,

"*Hear my voice, ye wives of Lamech, hearken to my speech:*
for I have slain a man to the wounding of myself,
and a stripling to my own bruising.
Sevenfold vengeance shall be taken of Cain:
but for Lamech seventy times sevenfold" (Gen. 4:23-4).

Hebrew tradition says it was Cain whom Lamech killed, mistaking his forbear for a wild beast while hunting, having acted on information supplied by his grandson, the "stripling" whom he subsequently beat to death in retaliation for the fatal error.

Scripture mentions three of Lamech's sons by name, each of whom was responsible for opening up hitherto unknown fields of human endeavor. By Ada he had Jabel. Described as "father of such as dwell in tents, and of herdsmen," Jabel was the first professional non-farmer, the head of a family with no permanent ties to the land beyond good grazing for his wandering flocks. His brother Jubal, on the other hand, inaugurated the arts. As "father of them that play upon the harp and the organs," he invented the first musical instruments, seeking to supplement by devices of his own contrivance the voice God gave him to sing His praises.

Although descended from the reprobate Cain, Ada's two sons were nevertheless lawful progeny. Pioneering variations of Adam's duty to "Increase and multiply, and fill the earth and subdue it" (Gen. 1:28), their activities were not intrinsically incompatible with the service of God. Men can save their souls in professional life without being tied to the soil which sustains them, as long as their professions remain subsidiary to Adam's primordial agricultural calling, which is meant to be served by all others in the temporal order without being dictated to by any of them. History proves that wherever professions have flourished at the expense of agriculture, disaster has resulted for the family and the whole of society.

Jubal's endeavors were also legitimate, but fraught with greater danger, because the arts, and music in particular, operate on the senses at the borderline of the spiritual faculties. They can impinge on man's intimate relations with God as well as condition his emotions. Before their fall from grace, Adam and Eve had been accustomed to hearing "the voice of the Lord God walking in paradise at the afternoon air" (Gen. 3:8), to which they presumably lifted their own voices in reply, carrying on ineffable conversations possible only in the state of innocence. As mouthpiece for material creation, the human voice was constituted by God to sing the divine praises, a supreme duty constituting the essential *Opus Dei*. After the Fall, when this work was beset with difficulty like everything else and recreation became a necessity, Jubal's subventions must have filled a genuine need.

Catholics today who wince on hearing guitars in church are not likely to look upon the organ as an abuse, yet organ-playing entered the sanctuary through the back door, by way of the theater and the circus, and before the twelfth century rarely accompanied the celebration of the sacred mysteries. It was only after the Reformation, when that latter day Jubal, Johann Sebastian Bach, perfected his "ill-tempered clavichord" that this artificial aid to piety became an overnight quasi-necessity, along with stationary pews and other comforts for fallen nature. In most churches today, the organ no longer merely accompanies the choir but actually leads the singing, when not replacing it entirely.

To the great credit of the major Eastern rites, the use of instruments is still excluded from their liturgy, in which *a cappella* singing on the part of both clergy and laity is required. Even in the Latin rite, before the Second Vatican Council the organ was strictly relegated to the choir loft along with the singers, and except for *Gaudete* and *Laetare* Sundays, not played during the penitential seasons of Advent and Lent. Now, as often as not it occupies a position adjacent to the Altar so as to figure prominently and visibly at any and all ceremonies and to set off to advantage the soloists forbidden by St. Pius X's *Motu proprio* on Sacred Music. To speak of the music itself would lead too far from the present subject, from which we have strayed considerably already.

+

If the human activities pioneered by Ada's legitimate sons provided built-in occasions of aberration without actually setting themselves in opposition to God, this was apparently not true of those pursued by Sella's son Tubalcain, "who was a hammerer and artificer in every work of brass and iron." A Cainite descendant born of Lamech's "shadowy" union with the illegitimate second wife, Tubalcain, "the smith," fathered the kind of technology which would eventually delude man into proclaiming himself independent of God. As Scripture reveals, Lucifer did not abandon his original project after the Flood swallowed up his first successes, and he was always in need of trained technicians. By the time Noah's descendants had multiplied to the point of having to migrate from the east, while the earth was still in one piece and mankind "of one tongue and of the same speech," he was already hard at work reconstructing the empire he had lost.

When the early technocrats in the plain of Senaar set themselves to brick making, the devil's inspiration could hardly have been suspected, for in that locality where building stone is scarce, such an occupation would not be exceptional. Scripture reveals his influence, however, by adding a detail of apparently little significance. Instead of merely drying their products in the hot sun, "each one said to his neighbor: Come let us make brick, and bake them with *fire*." That they bound the new fired bricks together with what the Vulgate designates as *bitumen* instead of the customary mortar may also be significant, for although asphalt is a natural substance, it is peculiarly flammable, and it served their purpose.

However long it took them to realize the possibilities opened up by the new technique, they decided to "make our name famous" by constructing a whole city for themselves which would incorporate the famous tower of Babel, "the top whereof may reach to heaven." God in his infinite mercy intervened by scattering these neo-Jubals over the already fragmenting continent and confounding their language, but not before they had laid the main lines of the electronic society which reigns today, whose fiery seeds would be carried with them in secret wherever they went. Although the men of Babel "ceased to build the city," they did not relinquish their aspirations any more than did the devil who inspired them. We have God's word for it that they had only "begun to do this," and that they would not "leave off from their designs till they accomplish them in deed."

Today the devil has every hope of bringing his enterprise to completion, for the old tower-builders' ambition to conquer heaven by human instrumentality has become a world goal. Primarily to this end has fire been pitted against water, those two immiscible entities created by God each with power over the other, the one to evaporate, the other to quench. Water is substantially composed of hydrogen and oxygen, yet these two elements will combine only through the agency of electricity, which was ordained to serve water rather than command it. Whereas water, as we have seen, seems to have existed before creation, fire seems to have played no part in it apart from light, as if it had no existence of its own. Like evil, which manifests itself by distorting some good, fire normally comes into being by the rapid disintegration of other substances. Thus fire and water, at the root of unfathomable mysteries in the natural order, serve to exemplify the most unfathomable in the supernatural order: the mystery of iniquity.

The Electronic Age was centuries a-dawning. Its closely guarded secrets, preserved after the Flood by the ancient Chamite priesthood of Egypt, were in due time transmitted clandestinely to men like Pythagoras and Paracelsus until such time as the first flickers of the Age of Enlightenment broke out openly and they could be disseminated throughout the world in the wake of democracy. Electricity's geneaology is demonstrably anti-Catholic. The very word was coined by Dr. William Gilbert, the apostate Queen Elizabeth's personal physician, who derived it from *elektron*, the Greek word for amber, a substance whose magnetic properties had been studied from antiquity. He invented an electroscope to detect electromagnetic energy in the body, and in the next century, promoters like Mesmer and Benjamin Franklin would begin popularizing electricity as the hope of the future.

Once out of the closet, by the close of the nineteenth century the alchemy of the occultists had transformed itself into the science of the scientists. By 1837 Samuel F.B. Morse had invented the telegraph, and the first wireless S.O.S. from a ship at sea was sent by the ill-fated super-liner Titanic which sank over submerged Atlantis, taking with it the pseudo-serial number NO 9093 painted in block numbers just below its waterline which if read in a mirror spelled "NO POPE." To make a long story short, electricity was gradually brought under human control and submitted to measurement in terms of standardized units named after men like Volta, Ohm, Ampere and Hertz. At the same time, men like the Scot mathematician James Clerk Maxwell, who first proposed that the various forms of electricity depended on frequencies of oscillation, set seriously to work concocting theories to explain its extraordinary behavior.

Ominously enough, among the first practical uses to which electricity was put was the execution of criminals. Thomas A. Edison, the acknowledged electrical wizard of the day, opened the way by sponsoring Saturday demonstrations for news reporters of the electrocution of stray dogs and cats rounded up by schoolboys from the city streets. The hapless animals were forced onto a metal sheet wired to a thousand volt alternating current, and on one occasion an assistant trying to coerce a wildly protesting puppy was accidentally shocked. Although the man survived, it was with a lifelong "awful memory of body and soul being wrenched asunder... the sensation of an immense rough file thrust through the quivering fibers of the body."

Nonetheless, on August 6, 1890, feast of the Holy Transfiguration, the first legal execution of a human being by electricity took place at New York State Prison, where a condemned murderer named William Kemmler was strapped to an electric chair and dispatched into eternity. The initial charge being too weak, a second was required, prompting a witness to describe the event as "an awful spectacle, far worse than hanging." Despite this gruesome introduction to society the electric chair was adopted as a common means of execution, and only marked the beginning of the human carnage which would offset the much publicized benefits of electricity. A little more than a half century later, again on the feast of the Transfiguration, on August 6, 1945, the same nation which pulled the switch on William Kemmler deemed it expedient to drop the first atomic bomb on civilian populations it perceived as proper targets in Hiroshima and Nagasaki, traditional enclaves of Christianity in far off Japan.

At two minutes past eleven, 8000 Christians were killed in Nagasaki. By midnight the cathedral had caught fire and was incinerated. On the night following the nuclear explosion, nuns were heard singing Latin hymns. By the next morning all were dead, along with many Catholic girls, who had been singing, "Mary, our Mother, I offer myself to you." In the words of the Christian doctor Takashi Nagai, who died of the effects six years later, "Wherever He went the Lamb of the Apocalypse was followed by a choir of singing virgins. The holocaust of Calvary gave meaning and beauty to the holocaust of Nagasaki.... Wasn't Nagasaki the chosen victim, the spotless lamb offered on the altar of sacrifice for the sins of the nations during World War II?... The little flock of Christians of Nagasaki retained the Faith throughout three hundred years of persecution.... It was there that was found the all pure lamb for the sacrificial holocaust." This conclusion was voiced by many Japanese. [38]

+

On April 20, 1895, five years after Kemmler's execution, a material representation of the coming satanic takeover of the remains of Christendom took place at Niagara Falls in the same state of New York. It may have marked the official opening of the Electronic Age, for on that day was manifest the indenture of God's living water to the devil's fire. Harnessed to the production of the secret force by which modern alchemy would literally spark the transformation of life on earth, North America's mightiest cascades were set to turning the giant turbines of the Niagara Mohawk Power Company, conferring electric light on the nearby town. The following year the current reached Buffalo, where it ran the street cars, proceeding thence to metropolitan New York to run the elevateds.

Ere long it was running the machinery of the whole civilized world, not to mention some segments in outer space. Where the current fails today, not only does communication falter and commerce collapse, but private homes are disrupted for lack of the heat, light and assorted appliances which have become the normal adjuncts of everyday life. Where electric pumps are used, water itself can be lacking. This may be only the beginning of water's servitude, however, for experiments are already far advanced for turning water into pollution-less fuel, using high voltage electricity to create energy by fracturing its molecules. Seducing every society it penetrates with unprecedented material comforts, electricity has lately succeeded in imprisoning mankind in an inextricable global web of cybernetics, whose principles were largely developed by the same genius who performed the first miracle at Niagara Falls.

He was Nikola Tesla. At the end of the long line of prophets who heralded the Age of Electricity, he stands out unquestionably as its messiah. Born in Croatia during an electrical storm in 1856, when that country was still part of the Austro-Hungarian Empire, he was the son of a well educated Serbian Orthodox priest who expected him to follow in his footsteps. An uncle was a monk. The child's destiny, however, obviously lay elsewhere, for from the time he was five he was producing original designs for paddle-less waterwheels, constructing insect-powered motors and rigging experiments in flight from the top of the family barn. The first time he saw Niagara Falls was in a steel engraving in a book at his uncle Col. Brancovic's house in Carlstadt, and the sight so fired his imagination that he immediately announced his intention of one day going to America to harness the falls for the production of power. Years later he could say, "I saw my ideas carried out at Niagara, and I marveled at the mystery of the mind."

After working as an engineer in Budapest, Paris and Strasbourg, he began carrying out his plan in 1884, the year he went to the United States to work with Thomas Edison, who unfortunately cheated him of promised compensation for months of work improving a series of dynamos the American inventor had designed. Tesla subsequently formed a happier association with George Westinghouse, and having become an American citizen in 1891, spent the rest of his life in independent research in his adopted country, for which he had only enthusiastic praise. "I was a good American before I ever saw this country," he once told a reporter. "I had studied its government.... Its people are a thousand years ahead of the people of any other nation.... I could not have accomplished in any other country what I have here." At the end of his life he would say, "All my inventions are at the service of the United States Government."

Needless to say, he was not the first to dream of harnessing the Niagara River's 164-foot torrent. A first plant had been built there in 1852, but the technology of the day was insufficiently advanced to lend the project any great commercial significance. A seventeen-man international Niagara Falls Commission had been set up under Lord Kelvin, however, to explore possibilities, and in the fall of 1893 the Westinghouse Corporation was awarded a contract to build three generators using Tesla's revolutionary polyphase system for the production of alternating current, winning out over Edison's proposal, which was designed for direct current. The superiority of Tesla's generators had already been established earlier that same year at the great Columbian Exposition held in Chicago, which was the first World's Fair to be illuminated by incandescent lighting.

Lighted up there at the same time was the first World Parliament of Religions held in conjunction with the Fair, in which Archbishop Ireland, brandishing "the Gospel in one hand and the Constitution in the other," took an active, enthusiastic part along with Cardinal Gibbons and other Americanist prelates. While these waxed eloquent on "the common humanity" binding all denominations together and on "putting an end to religious divisions and antagonisms," Nikola Tesla was lecturing to the public, playing magician by allowing a million volt high frequency alternating current to pass through his body without ill effect. He also delighted audiences by improving on Columbus' famous method for standing an egg on end, by spinning metal ones on end electrically and thereby demonstrating the principle of the rotating magnetic field which underlay his induction motor.

Over and beyond such parlor tricks, Tesla seemed to have been gifted with powers bordering on the preternatural. He recalled that even in childhood he suffered from "a peculiar affliction due to the appearance of images, often accompanied by strong flashes of light which marred the sight of real objects and interfered with my thought and action. They were pictures of scenes and things which I had really seen, never of those I imagined. *When a word was spoken to me the image of the object it designated would present itself vividly to my vision and sometimes I was quite unable to distinguish whether what I saw was tangible or not.*" Lest he be judged unbalanced, his sister was often detailed to accompany him to social events. She would let him know how much of what he saw was visible to others, especially on occasions when he might be seeing "all the air around me filled with tongues of living flame" and tempted to mention it in conversation.

His unusual power of visualization would stand him in good stead as an inventor, for unlike Edison, his nearest rival, who had to proceed by ordinary methods of trial and error, he was able to work out his ideas perfectly in his mind beforehand without recourse to experimental models. He was also gifted with a phenomenal photographic memory, making it possible for him to store in his head logarithmic tables or any other mathematical aids required for making calculations. In an article for "The Electrical Experimenter," he explained,

"I do not rush into actual work. When I get an idea I at once start building it up in my imagination. I change the construction, make improvements and operate the device in my mind. It is absolutely immaterial to me whether I run my turbine in my thought or test it in my shop. I even note if it is out of balance.... Invariably my device works as I conceived that it should, and the experiment comes out exactly as I planned it.... Why should it be otherwise? Engineering, electrical and mechanical, is positive in results. There is scarcely a subject that cannot be mathematically treated and the effects calculated or the results determined beforehand from the available theoretical and practical data."

Believing that remembered images were simply reflex actions from the brain to the retina of the eye, he wrote, "It should be possible to project on a screen the image of any object one conceives and make it visible. Such an advance would revolutionize all human relations. I am convinced that this wonder can and will be accomplished in time to come," As a matter of fact experiments are now being conducted on transferring thoughts directly to photographic film and electronic printers. Had Tesla known of the images of Bl. Juan Diego and Bishop Zumárraga which were later discovered in the eye of the image of Our Lady of Guadalupe, would he have only been confirmed in his belief that the retina contained untold secrets?

A tall, urbane gentleman with oversized hands, always impeccably attired, Tesla lived an irreproachable moral life by any external standards. He was an accomplished linguist, a lover of good cuisine and polite society who had hosts of friends, among them Mark Twain, whose works he had admired in translation in his native country. Wedded exclusively to his work and never known to take a vacation, he found no time for contemplating marriage, and one wonders if any woman could have lived with him. Habitually sleeping only about an hour or two a day, he exhibited many other eccentricities, among them a close friendship with a gray pigeon, from which some believed he hoped to extricate the secret of birds' homing instincts. He had a morbid fear of germs and women's earrings. Super-sensitive to light and noise, once during a strange illness in Budapest he heard a watch ticking from three rooms away.

"The sight of a pearl would almost give me a fit," he admitted, "but I was fascinated with the glitter of crystal objects with plane surfaces. I would not touch the hair of other people except perhaps at the point of a revolver. I would get a fever by looking at a peach, and if a piece of camphor was anywhere in the house, it caused me the greatest discomfort." He compulsively "counted the steps in my walks and calculated the cubic contents of soup plates, coffee cups and pieces of food – otherwise my meal was unenjoyable. All repeated acts or operations I performed had to be divisible by three, and if I missed I felt impelled to do it over and over again if it took hours."

Despite his pious upbringing, Tesla was in no sense a practicing Christian, his friend Underwood Johnson once suggesting he pray to his "No-god" in a difficulty. Convinced that biblical miracles all had scientific explanations, he held that Moses had been an electrical adept and that Aaron's sons were killed by high tension discharge from lightning when they touched the Ark. To his friend and confidant George Sylvester Viereck he said, "There is no conflict between the ideal of religion and the ideal of science, but science is opposed to theological dogmas because science is founded on fact. To me, the universe is simply a great machine which never came into being and never will end.... Man, like the universe, is a machine.... In the course of ages mechanisms of infinite complexity are developed, but what we call 'soul' or 'spirit' is nothing more than the sum of the functionings of the body."

A few days before Tesla died on January 7, 1953 in his apartment at the Hotel New Yorker, he is supposed to have watched a thunderstorm from his window and remarked, "I have made better lightning than that!" Although he had made and spent several fortunes in developing his scientific ideas, he left only about $2,000 worth of assets. His remains were cremated following a Serbian Orthodox funeral service at St. John the Divine, and eventually were returned to his native land. Because so many of his ideas were pirated, he had become increasingly secretive about his work, keeping much of it in his head. What happened to the tons of research papers and the 85 or so trunks of apparatus he left behind has never been revealed to the public, but after the enactment of the Freedom of Information Act it became apparent that the U.S. government had shown more than a passing interest in them. Oddly enough, the code name of the Army Air Force's top secret project is said to have been "Project Nick."

Tesla died alone without leaving a will, and although he had been a U.S. citizen for over fifty years, the F.B.I. unaccountably turned everything over to the Office of Alien Property, which subsequently both claimed and disclaimed any knowledge of the consignment. According to Margaret Cheney in *Tesla: Man out of Time*, in 1952 everything was supposed to have been shipped off with his ashes to Yugoslavia, where some of his scientific apparatus is now on view at the Tesla Museum in Belgrade. Whoever or whatever parties have had access to his vast output, almost every major invention since his death can be traced in one way or another to principles discovered by him, and appropriately enough, the flux of magnetic induction is now measured in terms of a standard unit dubbed the *tesla*.

+

Although he enjoyed considerable notoriety at various periods of his life, he fell into quasi-oblivion outside the scientific subculture, where a veritable cult has grown up around his memory. He is credited not only with the AC power technology and the "Tesla coil" for which he is famous, but also with fluorescent lighting, robotry, diathermy, weather control, television, radar, lasers, remote control, guided missiles, cybernetics and last but not least the "Tesla shield" which was supposed to underlie the "Star Wars" defense strategy. If he did not actually invent UFOs, their capability for vertical takeoff may be attributable to him. That he had perfected all the components necessary for radio transmission back in the 1890's is well known, and in fact eight months after his death the U. S. Supreme Court ruled that he, and not Italy's Guglielmo Marconi, was the actual inventor of radio.

Dreaming of a huge industrial utopian city, Tesla had actually exclaimed like the men of Babel, "I will build a Tower!" and had proceeded to do so. Designed by his architect friend Stanford White and torn down in 1917, a gigantic 172-foot structure called the Wardenclyffe arose on Long Island under his direction which may have supplied the most palpable clue yet to the true nature of its famous predecessor at Babel. Financed by J.P. Morgan, it was built with the understanding that it would operate as a monster antenna for a worldwide radio network, but engineers suspected at the time that it was more like a giant Tesla coil whose purpose was the transmission of wireless power rather than radio waves. Tesla himself, who once lit 200 lamps from 26 miles away without wires, had long maintained that limitless electricity could be drawn directly from the earth by means of inexpensive connections to the ground.

He once wrote Morgan, "What I contemplate and what I can certainly accomplish ... is not a simple transmission of messages without wires to great distances, but it is the transformation of the entire globe into a sentient being as it were, which can feel in all its parts and through which thought may be flashed as in a brain.... From one single plant thousands of trillions of instruments could be operated, each costing no more than a few dollars, and situated in all parts of the globe." In one of his lectures he predicted that eventually,

"We shall have no need to transmit power at all. Ere many generations pass, our machinery will be driven by a power obtainable at any point in the universe.... Throughout space there is energy.... It is a mere question of time when men will succeed in attaching their machinery to the very wheelwork of nature." He also told Morgan, "If you will imagine that I have found the stone of the philosophers, you will be not far from the truth!" That his dream was not put into effect in his lifetime was due largely to opposition from businessmen like Morgan and inventors like Edison, who looked to electricity as a source of revenue to be gleaned from miles of wires attached to meters. Apparently even the devil is not always a match for human greed.

One of Tesla's more frightening predictions, that future wars would be fought by electrical waves rather than explosives, was amply supported by his experiments in resonance and vibration. On one occasion when he was testing different frequencies emitted from an alarm-clock size electromechanical oscillator he had attached to a Manhattan building, he accidentally set off a miniature earthquake. Shaking substructures and shattering glass caused widespread consternation in the neighborhood, emptying the local police station and adjacent sweatshops of their occupants before he could take a sledgehammer to his device to stop the tremors. Years later he admitted, "I told my assistants to say nothing. We told the police it must have been an earthquake. That's all they ever knew about it."

He never divulged the secret, but he had proved to his satisfaction that he could create forces capable of splitting the earth "as a boy would split an apple, and forever end the career of man." He declared that a disaster of such magnitude might take months of careful timing, but that the destruction of the Empire State building or the Brooklyn Bridge would be the work of a moment, and the same principles could be used to detect submarines or locate ore deposits. Equally sinister is the invisible "death ray" capable of stopping aircraft in flight, which the *Colorado Springs Gazette* for May 30, 1924 reported had been invented by Tesla while he was experimenting there in 1899. He refused to comment on the matter, but it is known he took out a patent on something similar in 1922. That he is suspected of having accidentally set off the mysterious nuclear-type catastrophe which occurred in Siberia in 1907 is therefore not surprising.

In an article for *Liberty* magazine in 1935 he disclosed his discovery of a charged particle beam which could "make any country, large or small, impregnable against armies, airplanes and other means of attack ... approaching within a radius of 200 miles.... Many thousands of horsepower can thus be transmitted by a stream thinner than a hair, so that nothing can resist." We now know this was the famous "shield" by which he hoped to outlaw war by making whole countries impregnable to outside attack. "This wonderful feature will make it possible, among other things, to achieve undreamed results in television," to which he said he had devoted twenty years of research, but apparently leaving others to pursue the idea to completion.

The gradual substitution of pushbuttons and levers for brawn and muscle has had many unexpected repercussions in society, but one of the most far-reaching is the rise of feminism. As women become less and less dependent on men's superior muscular strength, they are rapidly emancipating themselves from male authority and pursuing vocations hitherto restricted to the stronger sex. Automated weaponry opens up even active warfare to women, who can manipulate electrical devices as easily as men. Inasmuch as this aspect of female liberation probably began with the electric kitchen demonstrated in the Woman's Building of the same World's Fair which first established Tesla's reputation, it is not surprising to discover that the inventor was long resigned to feminism.

In an interview for *Collier's* magazine entitled "When Woman is Boss," he prophesied, "The struggle of the human female toward sex equality will end in a new sex order, with the female as superior.... It is not in the shallow physical imitation of men that women will assert first their equality and later their superiority, but in the awakening of the intellect of women.... But the female mind has demonstrated a capacity for all the mental acquirements and achievements of men, and as generations ensue that capacity will be expanded.... Women will ignore precedent and startle civilization with their progress."

He even envisaged "desexualized armies of workers whose sole aim and happiness in life is hard work," and spoke of a time when, "The acquisition of new fields of endeavor by women, their gradual usurpation of leadership, will dull and finally dissipate feminine sensibilities, will choke the maternal instinct, so that marriage and motherhood may become abhorrent and human civilization draw closer and closer to the perfect civilization of the bee."

In a letter to Viereck he predicted, "The year 2100 will see eugenics universally established.... The trend of opinion among eugenists is that we must make marriage more difficult.... Certainly no one who is not a desirable parent should be permitted to produce progeny. A century from now it will no more occur to a normal person to mate with a person eugenically unfit than to marry a habitual criminal." He said he actually constructed robots, "but the principle has not been pushed far enough. In the twenty-first century the robot will take the place which slave labor occupied in ancient civilization."

Convinced that he had received a "one-two-three" patterned message from Mars or Venus back in 1899 while working alone one night in his Colorado Springs laboratory, Tesla believed that interplanetary communications would dominate the next century. The existence of intelligent beings in outer space he accepted as probable, declaring in an article for *Century Magazine* in 1900, "We cannot with positive assurance assert that some of them might not be here, in this our world, in the very midst of us, for their constitution and life manifestation may be such that we are unable to perceive them." He told reporters for *Time* magazine in 1931, "I think nothing can be more important than inter-planetary communication. It will certainly come one day, and the certitude that there are other human beings in the universe working, struggling and suffering like ourselves will produce a magic effect on mankind, the foundation of a universal brotherhood that will last as long as humanity itself."

Having apparently dissolved the devil along with God in the course of his scientific experiments, Tesla would ascribe nothing to the machinations of demons, disavowing any traffic with the occult at every opportunity and betraying not the slightest interest in it. But as Arthur C. Clarke, author of the gnostic science saga *2001*, put it, "Any sufficiently advanced technology is indistinguishable from magic." Inasmuch as alchemical science and the black arts began as one, when exactly did they part company? Where draw the line between the two? What was the source of Tesla's inspiration? To do the devil's work, does one have to be in conscious league with him? Isn't ignorance on the part of the recipient actually an advantage to the Adversary, who St. Teresa said is accustomed to working among us "like a noiseless file?" Tesla had acknowledged that he felt he was on the brink of a great revelation during the course of his experiments in Colorado, and that "there was present in them something mysterious, not to say supernatural."

The principle of the rotating magnetic field which would electrify Niagara and the world had occurred to him in Budapest while walking in the park at twilight with a classmate, to whom he was reciting – believe it or not – a well known passage from Goethe's *Faust*. When he came to, "The glow retreats .... Ah, that no wing can lift me from the soil, upon its track to follow, follow soaring!" suddenly, without the slightest warning, "The idea came like a flash of lightning, and in an instant the truth was revealed." Picking up a stick, he began drawing on the ground a diagram of what he had conceived, the details of which he would expose six years later to the American Institute of Electrical Engineers. Recalling the incident in his maturity, Tesla wrote, "Pygmalion seeing his statue come to life could not have been more deeply moved."

Small wonder that Kenneth M. Swezey, in an article on Tesla for the old *New York Herald Tribune* back in July, 1931, had called him "an arch conspirator against the established order of things!" Long before that, at a celebratory dinner given after the initial triumph at Niagara

Falls, Tesla himself had said, "We know that light, heat, electrical and magnetic actions are closely related, not to say identical. The chemist professes that the combination and separation of bodies he observes are due to electrical forces, and the physician and psychologist will tell you that life's progress is electrical. Thus electrical science has gained a universal meaning, and with right, this age can claim the name, THE AGE OF ELECTRICITY."

+

The visitor to Niagara Falls today is privileged to see a nine-foot bronze statue of Nikola Tesla enthroned on Goat Island in the midst of the thundering waters. A replica of an original by the sculptor Frano Krsinic, it was presented as a gift from the people of Yugoslavia on the occasion of the American Bicentennial in July 1976. Characterized on the pedestal as "independent inventor" and "citizen of the world," the electrical genius is portrayed in a godlike attitude, his huge hands raised slightly from the arms of the chair, contemplating his extraordinary handiwork which, according to the statue's inscription marked "The Beginning of the Revolutionary March of Electric Energy." Illuminated at night amid the deafening roar of the cataracts, the scene is both majestic and ominous, luciferian in every sense of the word. A worthy companion piece to the statue of Liberty Enlightening the World, who wields her electric torch over sunken Atlantis in New York Harbor, is this effigy at the Great Lakes of the mastermind who supplied the technology proper to her ideology.

Created resplendent without intermediary from absolutely nothing by the hand of God, the Fallen Angel has well calculated contempt for man, a creature who was also produced from nothing, but conjoined to pre-created matter, being, in God's own words, "formed from the slime of the earth." Man's consort Eve is no better, having been "built" from a rib God took from the pre-created Adam. This means that if Lucifer is to re-fashion the world to his own immaterial image, he cannot limit his efforts to souls. He must "angelize" matter itself.

In the wake of the electronic revolution launched at Niagara Falls, the remotest third world barrio is not safe from the alluring temptation to short-circuit the forces of nature by "mind-control." Man, divinely condemned by his own fault to wrest his daily bread from recalcitrant matter "with labor and toil ... in the sweat of thy face" (Gen. 3:17-19), is now being led to believe he has found an intelligent way out of his punishment. Although as long as time endures, matter can neither be created nor destroyed, it can be transmuted, and he has been shown how to do it electronically, in its deepest center, not by the sweat of his face, but by the flick of a switch at molecular level. It is a simple case of mind over matter.

Now that Lucifer the lightbearer proclaims himself light of the world, darkness can be said to have dawned, and it dawned in America, where he began his final assault after many previous failures and half-triumphs. If Nikola Tesla was in any sense correct in saying that the earth itself could be split by vibrations generated by human ingenuity, there is no reason to believe that the principles he discovered had not been mastered back in adamic times, when man's intellect was far stronger and fresher than it is now. At the time of the Flood, when "all the fountains of the great deep were broken up and the floodgates of heaven were opened" so that "all things wherein there is the breath of life on the earth died," it is just possible that God had wreaked punishment on men by allowing them to engineer that disaster for themselves. Scientifically disrupting the equilibrium of the waters of the firmament above and those below, they succeeded in submerging the whole earth.

The builders of the Tower of Babel were obviously headed down a similar path before God mercifully thwarted their plans, no doubt in view of the Incarnation yet to be accomplished in the fullness of time. This is no longer the case. It is impossible to know the exact nature of the great chastisement which so many saints and mystics have seen looming ever closer, but man could be bringing worldwide catastrophe down on himself for the second time in history. However it happens, God promised that "there shall no more be waters of a flood to destroy all flesh" (Gen. 9:15), so it is not unlikely that this time it will arrive as some form of fire. With the canopy of the firmament no longer sheathing the earth to protect it as before the Flood, what limits could be set to a conflagration set off in the upper atmosphere?

This may serve to explain why our Lord spoke of "great tribulation" reserved for the latter days, "such as hath not been from the beginning of the world until now, neither shall be. And unless those days had been shortened, no flesh should be saved" (Matt. 24:21-22). Also He told the crowds, "Yet a little while, the light is among you. Walk whilst you have the light, that the darkness overtake you not: and he that walketh in the darkness, knoweth not whither he goeth. Whilst you have the light, believe in the light!" (John 12:35-36).

Against that day of darkness, Jesus the son of Sirach warned that God "*hath set water and fire before thee: stretch forth thy hand to which thou wilt*! Before man is life and death, good and evil; that which he shall choose shall be given him" (Ecclus.15:17-18). Written after the time of Esdras, this passage does not form part of the Hebrew canon. It is a special legacy from the Holy Ghost to the Catholic Church, who vouches for its divine origin through apostolical tradition. *Water or fire*? Heaven or hell? Three times the candidate for Baptism in the universal Jordan is asked, "Do you renounce Satan? All his pomps? All his works?" Isn't that what the choice comes down to in the end?

THE AMERICAN
RESISTANCE

By the time Nikola Tesla died, the electronic machinery calculated to insure the satanic takeover of the world was firmly in place and operative. Nearly the whole of Catholic America already had a vested interest in apostasy, nation after nation having for one reason or another forsworn the rule of Christ the King in order to experiment in various forms of democracy inspired by the U.S. Constitution. The territories of Catholic France in Canada and parts of the United States had fallen prey early on to Protestant England and her American offshoot on the Potomac. At the close of the Spanish-American War in 1898, Catholic Spain had been forced to her knees and had ceased to figure as an international power, having relinquished the last of her colonial possessions. Cuba was declared independent, with Puerto Rico and Guam handed over to the victorious United States, who claimed even the Philippines in far off southeast Asia as spoils of war. Catholic Portugal had already disappeared from the American scene in 1889, when the independent constitutional monarchy set up under Prince Pedro was overthrown in favor of a republic modeled on the U.S.

If the faith survived anywhere in America, it would have to do so without political protection of any kind from any direction, for the same conditions pertained throughout Christendom. Whatever cultural or religious subjugation remained unaccomplished by force of arms, economics or diplomacy was left to the more arcane strategies of Freemasonry, whose lodges honeycombed the entire western hemisphere by the end of the eighteenth century, and whose members occupied key posts not only in government but even in the Church. By the time the Second Vatican Council opened, world wide apostasy was in full swing and well represented, especially among the American *periti* of that august body. If any resistance was mounted in the New World, it was useless to expect it from the United States, where the Faith had rarely if ever been taught in its integrity, if only by lack of emphasis on those doctrines diametrically opposed to democracy. During the persecution which raged there briefly before the War of Secession, it was already all too evident that the Catholic prelates were congenitally unprepared to recognize, let alone excoriate the true nature and logistics of the current apostasy.

But what of those from other American countries? How is it possible that so few of the Bishops who convened in Rome for the Second Vatican Council seemed to be aware of what was afoot in the Church for her destruction? Even *Nostra aetate*, the Declaration on the Relationship of the Church to Non-Christian Religions, the most hotly contested of that body's promulgations by reason of its statements regarding the Jews, drew only 250 *non placets* out of 2,312 votes cast during the debates, which centered largely around the initial text absolving the Jews of all responsibility for our Lord's Passion and death. The Declaration on Religious Freedom *Dignitatis humanae*, the other document meeting with determined opposition, produced a similar count of 249 objections during the debate, but out of the total of 2,386 voters, only 70 *non placets* were finally entered.

Was there no warning of the direction the Council would take? Of course there was. Information was certainly not wanting, much of it available even to the laity who knew where to look for it. Seniors may recall an impressive 700-page book called *The Plot against the Church* which was published in the U.S. by St. Anthony Press of Los Angeles in 1967 under the pseudonym "Maurice Pinay." The first edition had appeared in Italy by the fall of 1962, and by the time the Council opened in 1963, it had been followed by German, Austrian and Spanish editions.

Writing from Rome, the anonymous author began the Introduction to the first edition by telling his readers, "The most infamous conspiracy is in progress against the Church. Her enemies are working to destroy the most holy traditions and thus to introduce dangerous and evil-intended reforms, such as those Calvin, Zwingli and other false teachers once attempted. They manifest a hypocritical zeal to modernize the Church and to adapt it to the present day situation; but in reality they conceal the secret intention of opening the gates to Communism, to hasten the collapse of the free world and to prepare the further destruction of Christianity. *All this it is intended to put into effect at the coming Council.* We have proofs of how everything is being planned in secret agreement with the leading forces of Communism, of world Freemasonry and of the secret power directing these."

Before outlining the strategy which would be employed to achieve these ends, the writer ruefully predicted that "the Progressive bloc forming at the beginning of the Synod will be able to count upon the support of the Vatican, in which, so it is said, those anti-Christian forces possess influence. This appears unbelievable to us and sounds more like boastful arrogance by the enemies of the Church than sober reality." Alas, 35 years later, the veracity of his words appears incontestable. Invoking St. Bernard's dictum, "Pray to God and hit out with the stick!" he deplored that "for writing this very documentary book we have taken more than fourteen months, and there remain only two until the opening of the Second Vatican Council. God will help us to overcome all resistance in order to have ready the printing of this work either by the beginning of the Synod or at least before the enemy can cause the first harm."

An unknown private benefactor was said to have provided the wherewithal to put a copy of the book into the hands of every Bishop, but if so, it is impossible to ascertain how many of them actually read it. As it stands the work gives every evidence of having been put together in considerable haste without proper editing. The Preface to the German edition admits that "the style in many chapters leaves much to be desired and repetitions also occur," but the contents were conscientiously "compiled by a group of idealists who are Catholics of strict belief and who as Catholics firmly believe that the Catholic Church is now passing through one of the most dangerous periods in its history."

Needless to say, *The Plot* was furiously attacked by the leftist press as soon as its existence became known, and every effort was made to suppress it. Overnight it became what the *Agora* of Lisbon, a Catholic periodical, called "a bibliographic rarity," as many copies as possible having been bought up by parties unknown. An article dated March 1, 1963 imparted that "any person of elemental culture can divine that the compilation has been made by clerics.... There are those that affirm that the authors were Italian prelates, in collaboration with elements of English Catholicism; others speak of a group of priests, including some bishops from an unidentified country of South America."

According to the editor of the Spanish edition in Caracas, the secular world press believed the book was put together by the Roman Curia, "to cause the destruction of those reforms which the left wing of the Catholic clergy is attempting to bring about, reforms which if realized would completely subvert the bases on which the Holy Church rests. There are newspapers which ... affirm that it was the so-called 'Syndicate of Cardinals' who prepared the book," referring to "the heroic group of Cardinals of the Roman Curia who are struggling in the Second Vatican Council to prevent a group of the clergy – which in a strange manner is found at the service of Masonry and Communism – from imposing on the Holy Synod a whole series of theses, subversive, and some heretical, designed to cause the ruin of the Church." The book "deals with a magnificent and imposing compilation of documents and sources of undeniable importance and authenticity, which demonstrates with no room for doubt the existence of a great conspiracy, which the traditional enemies of the Church have prepared against Holy Catholic Church and against the Free World.... The most useful instruments in this conspiracy are those Catholic clergymen who, betraying Holy Church, attempt to destroy her most loyal defenders..."

Exactly who put together *The Plot against the Church* was never made public, but there is every reason to believe that several, possibly the majority, of its authors were in fact Americans. Not from the United States, to be sure, but from America's Catholic countries. The Mexican Jesuit Dr. Saenz y Arriaga was an outspoken and courageous critic of the Council and the new religion hatched in its back rooms,[39] but no members of the hierarchy dared support him openly in that masonically controlled nation so close to the United States. This was the case in many other countries – even the U. S. – where isolated priests and a few indignant laymen consistently spoke up against the heresies being promulgated, but where ranking prelates maintained an eloquent silence.

A rare exception was Brazil,undoubtedly "the unidentified country of South America" cited by the Lisbon paper as a stronghold of embattled traditionalists. At Fatima our Lady told Sr. Lucy that "the dogma of the faith would always be preserved in Portugal," and at this point in history it would seem that she may have included that nation's erstwhile colonies in that happy prediction. Almost immediately Portuguese speaking Brazil was alerted to the danger. Not only outstanding laymen of the caliber of Arnaldo Xavier da Silveira and Dr. Plinio Corrêa de Oliveira, founder of the international TFP, but bishops like Msr. Castro-Mayer of Campos rose in defense of the faith.

Whether another Brazilian prelate, Archbishop Geraldo de Proença Sigaud, SVD, Bishop of Diamantina, was one of those unknown "clerics" who put together the text of *The Plot*, is not known with certainty, but it is more than likely. A main organizer of the embattled traditionalist minority at the Council who officiated as Secretary of the *Coetus Internationalis Patrum*, he remained virtually unknown to the English-speaking Catholic world, but he was singled out easily enough by Gary McEoin in *What Happened at Rome* as an affiliate of "reactionary groups ... in various parts of Latin America," who "openly identified himself both in Rome and in Brazil as opposed to the Johannine *aggiornamento* and the major reforms voted by the Council." His opposition to the Pastoral Constitution on the Modern World as too "phenomenological" was also deemed worthy of mention by the well known "Xavier Rynne" in his account of the Council's fourth session, but the prelate's adversaries seem to have been most impressed by his stand against collegiality in the third session.

A footnote to the Rynne book quotes a circular in which the Archbishop declared categorically, "Collegiality has no basis either in the Bible, in tradition or in the history of the Church ..... It would give rise to lack of discipline in the Church, whether with respect to the bishops and the Pope, or priests and bishops .... Bishops would be subjected to episcopal conferences, that is, a collective authority, *the worst kind there is...*" In *The Open Church* Michael Novak reported Archbishop Sigaud as saying that "a bishop has jurisdiction outside his own particular diocese only when he attends one of the rare ecumenical councils of history, and only then because the Pope approves the acts of the Council. National episcopal conferences have juridical effect only when approved by the Pope or by the bishop in his own diocese. A permanent 'world parliament' in the Church was unknown to Christ and never heard of for twenty centuries!"

+

Once Pope John XXIII had convoked the Council, he was at pains to solicit input from all quarters in the Church in regard to its agenda. According to Réné Laurentin in *Bilan du Concile*, in 1959 "he set up machinery for free consultation with all the bishops, as well as Roman congregations, religious superiors and universities. That was known as the ante-preparatory phase: preparation for the preparation. It was the conciliar undertaking's first outlay. The answers were often dull and timid. Very few had dared accept at face value the unprecedented invitation to speak out 'with total freedom'." An informant says that most of the thousands of replies which poured into the Vatican between mid-1959 and mid-1960 were brief and dealt with matters of limited or local consequence. Few if any voiced any serious misgivings about the state of the Church.

Not so Bishop Sigaud's reply, which numbered fifteen pages and was promptly dispatched from Jacarézinho, Brazil on August 22, 1959. It began by assuring the Holy Father that it was not his intention to accuse superiors or to deal with dogmatic or juridical questions, but to point out certain practical fundamentals bearing on the future of the Church. Needless to say, this correspondence was highly confidential, delivered to the Holy See *sub secreto* in the common Latin, but now that all the responses are in the public domain, anyone who can manage the language is free to read them. Although Cardinal Ruffini complained at one Council session that Church Latin was "Not expected to be Ciceronian, but [was] in spots hardly Latin," the Archbishop's letter is marked by singular spontaneity and common sense quite transcending the medium.

The letter is too long to quote in full, but a few excerpts are sufficient to demonstrate its continuing relevance. Pope John would certainly have classed its writer among those "prophets of doom" he referred to in his opening speech at the Council as "always forecasting disaster," to whom "we sometimes have to listen;" but after 35 years of devastation, the reader can judge the Archbishop's grasp of the situation for himself where he says, "When I consider current Catholic life in my country and other parts of the world, I see many signs of life, certainly calculated to warm the heart of one who loves the Church of Christ. Nevertheless I also see things which cause me intense pain. They are so serious that I find them worthy of attention on the part of the Ecumenical Council's Pontifical Preparatory Commission and eventually of the Council proper.

"I see the spirit and principles of the revolution working their way into the Christian clergy and people, just as the principles, doctrines, spirit and love of paganism once entered medieval society and produced the pseudo-Reformation. Many among the clergy have yet to see the errors of the Revolution and are still not resisting it. Others among the clergy love the Revolution as an idealistic cause, as it were, propagating it and collaborating with it. They persecute the Revolution's adversaries, calumniating and impeding their apostolate. Most pastors say nothing. Others espouse the errors and spirit of the Revolution and support it either in public or in secret, like the pastors in the days of Jansenism.... Seminarians leave the seminaries and the Holy City itself imbued with revolutionary ideas...."

He believed "the Church should organize a systematic fight against revolution throughout the world," just as the revolutionaries themselves have done, whom he holds responsible for "the rise of worldwide, simultaneous, uniform *Christian democracy* in many nations immediately after a terrible war," resulting in "Revolution by Catholic consent ... We must take note of the deadly battle being waged against the Church in every field, identify the *enemy*, decipher his strategy and battle tactics and observe his logic, psychology and dynamism, in order to be able to interpret every stage of this war correctly and organize a properly directed counter-offensive. For six centuries our implacable enemy ... has been waging war to the death, slowly and systematically overturning and destroying nearly the whole Catholic order, *actually the City of God*, ... in order to construct *the city of man* in its place, with a whole new order of human life, a society and humanity without God, without the Church, without Revelation, based on sensuality, greed and pride..... Yet many Catholic leaders dismiss what I am saying as a bad dream...."

Pinpointing Freemasonry as "the main force in the implacable war against Catholic society," the Archbishop directs the Pope's attention to the American dollar bill as evidence of the conspiracy afoot. There "we see a pyramid built on a vast uncultivated plain. The stones which compose it are squared and polished. The meaning of the allegory is given on an inscription reading: *Novus ordo seclorum*. The pyramid stands for the new humanity composed of men enlightened by Freemasonry, whose symbol is a polished stone, into which men created by God the Creator are transformed ... by the Great Architect of the Universe. The base of the pyramid proclaims the founding of this New Order of the Ages: 1776, which is the date of birth of the American States.

"The U.S.A. are therefore the base of this New Masonic Humanity. There is no top to the pyramid, which means the New Order of the Ages is not yet completed, but little is lacking. The work will certainly be finished, for above the whole pyramid is set 'God,' not the Father of Jesus Christ, who is the 'evil' Creator, but the Gnostic God, the Architect, represented by an eye in a triangle surrounded by rays. We are in full gnostic-manichaean dualism, which is the theological basis of the Masonic sect. This 'God' *annuit coeptis*, as can be read above the pyramid, as if to say, he blesses the undertaking, approves it and concurs with it.

"...This is a vital matter for the Church. The Masonic Order is in opposition to the Catholic Order. Soon the Masonic Order will encompass all humanity, yet many Catholic leaders do not see it, and even more remain silent. After Leo XIII, no more encyclicals about this Sect have been forthcoming. What is taught about it in universities and seminaries?... In studies and orientations for the priesthood not a word is said about the program, methods or system of this whole Masonic sociology, about its objectives, spirit, means, tactics or strategy. In fact a French Jesuit, Fr. Berthelot, wrote a book on the possibility of harmonious collaboration between the Church and the Sect!"

The Archbishop puts Communism in focus by remarking, "The Masonic sect gathers up the 'bourgeois,' Communism organizes the 'proletariat.' The objective of both is the same: a society which is socialist, rationalist, without God and without Christ. Both have a common head," which he identifies as International Judaism. "We condemn all persecution of the Jews on account of their religion or for ethnic considerations. The Church is against 'anti-semitism,' but the Church cannot ignore International Judaism's past deeds and avowed assertions. For centuries Jewish leaders have conspired against the Catholic Name and with methodical, undying hatred they are planning the destruction of the Catholic Order and the construction of a Jewish World Empire.

"Masonry and Communism serve this end. Money, the media and world politics are largely in the hands of the Jews. Although they are the biggest capitalists, and should therefore be Russian Communism's biggest opponents, they not only do not fear it, but actually underwrite its success... This is a reality. Then hate them? No! But vigilance, clear-sightedness and systematic, methodical warfare should be directed against the systematic, methodical warfare of this 'Enemy of Man' whose secret weapon is 'the leaven of the Pharisees which is hypocrisy.'"

Actually, "The overwhelming power of the Revolution comes from *the cunning use of human passions*. Communism created *the science of revolution*, and its principal weapons are *unrestrained human passions*, systematically aroused. To destroy Catholic society and construct atheist society, Revolution makes use of two vices: sensuality and pride. These inordinate, turbulent passions are scientifically directed toward a precise end.... A kind of central government, dynamic and highly intelligent, directs the whole process: A human Center which is the instrument of Satan himself. Thus even so-called 'right wing political parties' like Fascism and National Socialism spearheaded that same fight against the Church of Christ."

+

What positive measures can the Church take against the satanic offensive? The Archbishop believed "the condemnation of perverse doctrines is very necessary but not sufficient. Condemnations were not lacking in the battle against Protestantism, Jansenism, Modernism and Communism. They had their proper effect. Some came too late. What is needed is an organized campaign against errors and the promoters and propagators of those errors.... Such organized warfare should take on the errors and spirit of the Revolution even in their disguised forms." These, he said, are sometimes the logical consequence of errors which have been applied in practice, or again, erroneous doctrine is presented in such a way that the less informed faithful cannot detect it, and "are gradually imbued with the principle and spirit of revolution without realizing it."

In the Archbishop's estimation Pope Pius IX's *Syllabus* was nothing less than "a providential collection of the most pernicious errors of our age which retains all its pertinence. However, it should be completed by including current new errors." He is aware that their propagators are often "promoted to positions of power in the Church. In seminaries can be found teachers who expound error and are enamored of the Revolution. Priests who remain neutral in the fight get ahead. Those openly fighting the Revolution are disbarred. They often suffer persecution and are forbidden to speak out. Pastors don't protect the sheep from the wolves, yet they keep the dogs from barking!" These words, written in the 60's, prove that the so-called "spirit of Vatican II" had long been abroad. It was never loosed by the Council, but on the contrary, actually produced it.

The letter goes on to deal with the widespread misunderstanding of the familiar doctrine of the "lesser evil," which the Archbishop characterizes as the Trojan horse by which the Revolution made its way into the Catholic camp. He explains, "Catholic doctrine teaches that if we are unable to avoid evil, we may allow a lesser evil in order to avoid a greater one, as long as we do nothing positively wrong. In practice Catholic resistance often gives way under this pretext. Actually they think that a lesser evil is necessarily a *small* evil, against which a fight would not be justified. "Most Catholics, even priests, think that fighting is harmful to the Church, as if she were not the Church *Militant*. Therefore under the pretense of prudence, charity, or the demands of the apostolate, they permit evil without a contest. They do not reflect that even a lesser evil is still an *evil*, and therefore they do not try to restrain or abolish it. In their daily contact with "lesser evil" they forget the greater good to which the evil is opposed, and in the course of applying the 'hypothesis' they forget the 'thesis' and end by considering the evil as normal and hating the good. For instance, separation of Church and state; permitting divorce among non-Catholics lest it be imposed even on Catholics."

The Archbishop did not neglect to excoriate the evils of conforming to the world by compromise, which he calls "the second secret door through which the enemy enters the Catholic ark.... There can be no compromise as to principles. It is important to insist on this point, so that the faithful can understand the necessary contradiction between the world and the Church.... Even where principles are observed, compromise with the world can injure the Catholic cause when it draws human weakness into evil, because of the scandal.... If the failure to compromise irritates our adversaries, that is not necessarily a bad thing. Indeed it can be very good. Even the Savior did that. War cannot be waged, nor victory won without painful conflict.

"Our adversaries perceive as if by instinct what favors the Church and what is detrimental to the Revolution, and that distresses them." Assuming a good faith on their part which must not be troubled, "Catholics believe non-Catholics are caught up only in intellectual errors, ready to convert to Catholic truth on the spot, provided it is presented to them in a friendly way. They even believe that all polemic is bad, and that the zeal and severity with which the Church defends the Faith is prejudicial to the conversion of individuals. The consequences of widespread cooperation with non-Catholics in community affairs are very serious for the Catholic cause.

"Certainly in particular circumstances ... the Church may draw some good from such cooperation. In general, however, true collaboration is not possible, for the principles, objective and spirit are too different. Non-Catholics gain little from the association, and Catholics lose a great deal. Many evils make their way into the Catholic camp because of the myth of 'good faith,' especially when positions of high importance are entrusted to persons whose loyalty has not been tested. In peaceful times it is true that 'no one is guilty until tried,' but when the city is besieged, no one qualifies for dangerous guard duty before his loyalty has been proved. For that, 'no one is innocent until tried.'"

Not confining himself to generalities, Archbishop Sigaud lashed out at what he termed "vehicles of corruption." Television was in its infancy when he wrote, but he deplored the pernicious effects of "romantic" movies which excite the passions to no purpose and lead to abnormal fantasizing. "Educational" films whereby "the faithful are led to watch dangerous scenes under the pretense of art and technique, as if fantasy and concupiscence could be bound and loosed at will by means of electric current," he called "a diabolical joke." "Perhaps the creation of a crisis center in Rome with worldwide authority under the direction of the Holy See would be a practical solution. Not only must the immediate moral problem be considered, but also the propaganda value for the dynamics of the Revolution. Films classed as 'good for persons of mature judgment' [roughly a "P.G." rating in the U.S.] should be severely examined under this aspect. Intimate dancing and rock-and-roll "should be strictly forbidden to Catholics the world over." Some women's fashions, especially for the beach, should also evoke serious concern. Beauty contests "must be absolutely condemned. It seems to me that contestants as well as promoters, judges or those providing financial support to such traffic in human flesh should all be punished by excommunication.... This should be done throughout the world."

The *Index of Forbidden Books*, abolished by Paul VI in 1966, was still in operation when this letter was penned, and thus we read, "The condemnation of books made by the Holy Office is very beneficial to Catholics. The faithful for the most part avoid those books. Of course others read them, but knowing that the Church has condemned a book, they take into consideration that its teaching may be false and thus are less harmed by its poison. Sometimes, however, the condemnations come too late, leaving time to cause great havoc. Thus the condemnation of Gide arrived too late. Another condemnation which is very necessary is the condemnation of Jacques Maritain. His errors have done serious damage to the Church, especially in Latin America. The young clergy is beset by them. The harm caused by the errors of the 'Christian Democratic' party is a direct result of Maritain's ideas. Political agitation in America is said to be the work of his disciples. The Catholics say the Vatican approves Maritain, because he was the French representative to the Holy See. Bishops call themselves 'Maritainists.' His teachings predominate in the Catholic universities of Brazil. But Rome is silent.

"Politicians act on the principle that *the Revolution has been wrong in its methods, but is good in itself....*" There follows a plea for wholesale pedagogical reform, with emphasis on philosophy and theology rather than on historical and positivist studies. The Archbishop recommended outright condemnation of "Christian socialism," nominalism, naturalism, kantian idealism, Hegel and all his school, Sartre, Maritain and his false distinction between the human individual and the human person in sociological matters. Also on his list are evolution, positivist philosophy and juridical positivism on down to manicheanism and gnosticism as expressed in abstract art. Theosophy, Rotary, Lions and Moral Rearmament are likewise targeted for proscription.

+

The last part of the letter is devoted to defining general counter-revolutionary principles: "The revolutionary conspiracy is one and organic. This kind of conspiracy must be fought in a manner and by action which are one and organic. Catholics are waiting for the Magisterium to give a concrete and practical, fundamental and organic definition of Catholic Society – of Counter-revolutionary Society, one in which the good elements of modern life are included among the traditional ones to be retained ... To me the Catholic fight against the Church's enemies often looks like blind men fighting against people who can see. They are unacquainted with their objective, their methods, dynamics, strategy and weaponry. What does *Catholic sociology* teach about all this?

"A reconstruction of this kind is not a matter of partial corrections, but rather a new creation. Even now many things in life are not Christian, but heathen. Catholics should know when "such and such a thing does not accord with Catholic society," and exactly how "in this and that regard society should be thus and so to be Catholic." There is much latitude, but there are limits. A model of ideal Catholic society must be drawn up for us so we can see what to do. The power of the Holy See is immense. If the faithful were called out in force and set to work in an effective, clearcut, methodical manner as part of a truly worldwide offensive under the leadership of the Roman Pontiff, the triumphant march of the Revolution would be cut short and the Reign of the Most Sacred Heart of Jesus inaugurated...

"... The reconstruction of Christianity is a matter of great importance. Of highest importance is the establishment of the Reign of the Most Sacred Heart of Jesus. God can save individual souls even in revolutionary society, but when the prevailing conditions for saving them are so bad, anyone's salvation is a near miracle. Christian Order, on the other hand, is *the greatest external grace*, which gently and efficaciously moves not only single individuals but whole crowds to sanctity of life and eternal salvation. In revolutionary society God fishes with a hook; in Christian society souls are caught in nets."

The Archbishop noted the fatal mistake made by Catholics generally, who try "to deal with Communism in the same way the Church dealt with Liberalism in the last century and is still dealing with it today." Whereas coexistence with Liberalism is possible because it does not prevent the Church from preaching her doctrine or oblige her to preach liberal doctrine, even allowing her to condemn its errors, this is not true under Communism, whose "opposition to the Church is essential, radical, perpetual and total. When Communism makes peace of any kind with the Church, it is only a matter of suspending hostilities for a time.... Even the executioner pauses before delivering the death blow to his victim, in order to do it more effectively.

"Communism is the son of the Synagogue. Until the Jewish people are converted, the Jewish synagogue will be the 'Synagogue of Satan.' And Communism will be the Communism of Satan, the work and prefiguration of the Antichrist. Communism's secret power lies in *hatred of Christ*, but its power of seduction lies in the *socialist utopia*. Communism promotes a Society of Brothers – without authority, without classes, without poverty, without pain, without life's problems, without God and without hell. It promises Paradise in this life. Without God: *liberty*. Without king or father: *equality*. Without property and social classes: *fraternity*. Catholics embrace this utopia only too easily, thinking it can be baptized. They even say the early Church was socialist.

"A solemn and severe condemnation of this utopia seems to me clearly called for on the part of the Ecumenical Council. At issue is a truly global temptation on a par with the temptation in Paradise. 'You will be as gods.' Or again, 'I will give you all these things.' Earthly life isn't supposed to be paradisiacal. The cross, patience and self-denial are indispensable in attaining the end of earthly life. Charity is necessary, and not only justice. A true socialist paradise on earth will never happen. Every man seeking the Kingdom of God and His justice will obtain that measure of earthly happiness which loving Providence concedes to its sons on this earth.

"By looking for his happiness exclusively in this world and violating the laws of human nature under Satan's leadership, man is preparing the greatest slavery for himself.... At first revolutionary society will be paradise on earth; afterwards it will be hell on earth. It must be clearly taught that social and economic differences are essential for the normal life of society. This difference is not contrary to justice.... Classes must exist for the economic good of society. Socialism leads people to hatred of heaven and Christian virtues: humility, charity, poverty, chastity. Why don't the mendicant Orders preach the ideal of poverty more?

"In many parts of the world government interference in the life of individuals and families grows daily. Such interference is often necessary, due to the disintegration of collective life destroyed by Liberalism. Many things which society once undertook on its own must now be done by the state. Catholic teaching must tolerate these inroads, but obviously it must consider them as it were extraordinary, abnormal and transitory. They should be abolished as soon as possible. It is easy to look to the state for solutions to problems by changing natural traditional institutions. Problems generally arise, however, from corrupted morals. *The Catholic religion* is indispensable to moral correction. The solution to current difficulties is not to be found primarily in international conferences, but in *the rechristianization of morals*. If God and His Christ were placed at the base of individual, family and national life, the forces of nature alone would seek their connatural solutions, which must be humbly aided by intelligence and good will."

The letter closes confidently with the assurance that, "If the Ecumenical Council were to present a positive plan for counter-revolutionary action and the reconstruction of Christianity, with the details clearly worked out, and would mobilize Catholics for this work, I think the dawn of the Reign of the Sacred Heart of Jesus and the Immaculate Heart of Mary would materialize."

+

As we know, nothing of the kind ever happened at the Council, nor was it meant to happen by those who set it in motion. Returning to their dioceses after the Council's close, the traditionalist bishops submitted to its decisions to a man, the vast majority prepared to implement its decrees to the best of their ability as obedient sons of the Church. Even after

Cardinal Suenens triumphantly declared that the Church had finally undergone her "Revolution of 1789," they seemed unaware that a veritable *coup d'état* had taken place. Remaining steadfast in their opposition to the torrent of error which ensued, they strained to interpret the ambiguous verbiage in an orthodox sense in the mistaken belief that the Council's dicta were being "misinterpreted." Suffice it to say that no concerted opposition to the Council itself ever arose on the part of the traditionalist contingent.

Judging from an article by Archbishop de Proença Sigaud which was published in *La Pensée Catholique* in 1966 under the title "The Council and the Traditional Priest," it would appear that he for one deployed his considerable influence to prevent such a thing from happening. Having fought for orthodoxy tooth and nail during every session, he was well aware that the revolutionary forces had not been routed, predicting that they would labor to maintain the confusion they had roused in order to pursue their ends. In fact he quoted the Modernist theologian who had exclaimed at the Council's close, "Inasmuch as we lost the battle of the letter, let's save the Spirit of the Council!" Convinced that the doctrinal battle had indeed been won by the good guys, the Brazilian Archbishop believed that to win the war all that was necessary was to hew doggedly to the texts of the conciliar decrees without falling into the aberrations of the errant "Spirit" which had conceived them.

Today the carnage wrought by this carefree "Spirit of Vatican II," operating at large these thirty-five years without doctrinal support, is too evident to require comment. At the time, however, the Archbishop assured his readers, "The traditional priest will never rebel, will never betray his commitments to the Pope and the Bishops, masters and guides of Christ's flock. ... [He] will study the conciliar documents closely and lovingly. There he will find food for his soul ... the means for his apostolate, ammunition for the defense of his flock, food for the renewal of souls.... He will read all the documents in the light in which they were conceived, a pastoral light, not primarily dogmatic or juridical," happily greeting "regulations coming from Rome, studying to apply whatever the Church ordains to his own life and those around him, according to the immortal formula: '*Visum est Spiritui Sancto et nobis*' (Acts 15:28)."

Accepting changes to the fore-Mass as a pastoral necessity, the Archbishop was apparently unable to contemplate, let alone foresee any tampering with the Canon of the Mass, inasmuch as "stability and uniformity, as well as immutability are its characteristic marks." The priest "must understand the texts of the Constitution on the Liturgy and imbue himself with the spirit of the new principles it establishes, in order to put into practice those measures the Church expects of him," all the while he studied "to discern what is of obligation from what is merely desirable or optional" and "to exercise patience in the face of certain exaggerations occasioned by the Liturgical Reform, without allowing himself to be drawn to imitating them." He concluded the article with the statement, "The Council was not a Revolution. The Council was, and was intended to be, a Renewal, a new springtime reborn from the branches of the old and ever young tree of Tradition."

This reassuring pronouncement, enunciated in the immediate aftermath of the Council by a traditionalist leader, unfortunately helped pave the way to the working arrangement between truth and error prevailing today in the name of unity. Only too eagerly accepted by the generality of the disoriented faithful both clerical and lay, it placed them in an untenable position where the theological virtue of faith, which is directed to God alone and has no limits, is subjected to the moral virtue of obedience, which is directed to men and conditioned by circumstance. At a similar impasse, St. Peter and the Apostles had established as immutable precedent that where the Faith is at stake, "We ought to obey God rather than men!" (Acts 5:29). Had they not so decided, the Church would not have survived the first century. Nor would she have survived the twentieth had not numbers of her children elected to follow their first Pope's prescription.

One of these was Bishop Antonio de Castro-Mayer. On January 25, 1974, by which time the direction being taken by the leadership of the Church had become unmistakably clear, he and the Brazilian lawyer da Silveira sent Paul VI a book which they had authored jointly in 1969 on the recently promulgated "new Mass." Published in France as *La Nouvelle Messe de Paul VI: Qu'en Penser?* it opened by judicious inquiry into the possibility of a heretical Pope, a question long debated by St. Robert Bellarmine, St. Alfonsus de Ligouri, Suarez and other eminent theologians. The book was accompanied by two other studies, one on the Council's equivocal document *Dignitatis humanae* on religious liberty and the other on Paul VI's nearly unknown Apostolic Letter *Octogesima adveniens* on social equality.

None of these works received the slightest acknowledgement from the Vatican, and the last two were not released to the general public in view of the Bishop's reluctance to divulge their contents as long as there remained a possibility of a response from the Pope, which for obvious reasons was not forthcoming. The Bishop's analysis of the papal Letter may now be read in the first volume of A. Daniele's *L'Esprit Désolant de Vatican II* which appeared in France in 1997,[40] but the paper dealing with religious liberty still awaits publication.

In 1983, however, on the Feast of our Lady's Presentation, an open letter bearing his signature and that of the French Archbishop Lefebvre was sent to John Paul II from Rio de Janeiro begging redress of "the errors contained in the documents of the Second Vatican Council, the postconcilar reforms and especially the liturgical reforms, the false notions diffused by offical documents and the abuse of power perpetrated by the hierarchy." Inasmuch as "many are losing the faith, charity is becoming cold and the concept of the true unity of the Church in time and in space is disappearing," the Letter stated, "that is why we find ourselves obliged to intervene in public before Your Holiness, considering all the measures we have undertaken in private during the last fifteen years have remained ineffectual, in order to denounce the principal causes of this dramatic situation."

An appendix dealing with these errors under six heads was attached:

1. An ecumenical notion of the Church condemned in the *Syllabus*.

2. Collegiality as condemned by Vatican I.

3. A false notion of the natural rights of man as condemned in Pius IX's *Quanta cura* and Leo XIII's *Libertas Praestantissimum*.

4. An erroneous notion of the power of the Pope.

5. A Protestant notion of the Holy Sacrifice of the Mass and the sacraments, condemned by the Council of Trent.

6. The free dissemination of heresies following the suppression of the Holy Office.

In a long interview conducted a year later by the Saõ Paulo newspaper *Jornal da Tarde* under the title "The Church of John Paul II Is Not the Church of Christ," Bishop Castro-Mayer was quoted as saying, "Vatican II has proclaimed an objective heresy. As for those who practice and follow it, they have demonstrated a pertinacity which normally characterizes formal heresy. So far we have not accused them categorically, in order to exclude all possibility of ignorance regarding questions of such gravity." The following year, on August 31, 1985, Bishop Mayer sent the

Pope another joint letter with Archbishop Lefebvre in anticipation of the extraordinary synod called with the purpose of making the Second Vatican Council "an even more living reality." The two prelates protested particularly against the Council's Declaration on Religious Liberty, "which granted man the natural right to be exempt from any restraint imposed on him by divine law to adhere to the Catholic Faith in order to be saved," reminding the Holy Father that "your responsibility is heavily engaged in this new and false conception which is drawing clergy and faithful into heresy and schism."

On December 2, following John Paul II's visit to the Jewish synagogue and his participation in the Congress of religions at Assisi, Bishop Mayer issued a formal Declaration in conjunction with Archbishop Lefebvre wherein was stated, "Everything undertaken in defense of the faith of the Church in times past, and everything done to spread it by missionaries, even including martyrdom, is now regarded as a fault for which the Church must accuse herself and beg forgiveness... The Roman authorities are turning their backs on their predecessors, breaking with the Catholic Church and putting themselves at the service of the destroyers of Christendom and the Kingdom of our Lord Jesus Christ.... From year to year the current acts of John Paul II and the national episcopates demonstrate that radical change in the concept of the faith, the Church, the priesthood, the world, and of salvation through grace. The culmination of the break with the former magisterium of the church occurred at Assisi after the visit to the Synagogue.

"The public sin against the unicity of God, against the Word Incarnate and His Church makes one shudder with horror: John Paul II encouraging false religions to pray to their false gods – a scandal beyond measure and precedent! ... We are forced to admit that this liberal modernist religion of modern conciliar Rome is distancing itself more and more from us who profess the Catholic faith of the popes who condemned this false religion. We therefore regard as null whatever has been inspired by this spirit of denial – all the post-conciliar reforms and acts of Rome carried out in such impiety." According to Sig. Daniele, Bishop Castro-Mayer subsequently participated in the controversial Consecrations of bishops performed two years later by Archbishop Lefebvre at Ecône in hopes of using the occasion to level a formal accusation of obstinacy in error against the conciliar authorities, as the Declaration had done by implication, but he was met by a refusal to take such a stand.

As is well known, Bishop Mayer never retracted his position on the Mass, entirely aware that Pope St. Pius V in the Bull *Quo primum tempore* of 1570 had by virtue of his Apostolic authority declared that the Missal of the traditional Mass in the Latin Rite "may be followed absolutely, without any scruple of conscience or fear of incurring any penalty, judgment or censure, and may be freely and lawfully used. Nor shall bishops, administrators, canons, chaplains and other secular priests or religious of whatsoever Order or by whatsoever title designated, be obliged to celebrate Mass otherwise than enjoined by Us ... and that this present Constitution can never be revoked or modified, but shall for ever remain valid and have the force of law."

The traditional Mass had not and could not have been abrogated by a future Pope, especially one who, like Paul VI, only declared what amounted to a personal wish that a "new" one of his own choosing be celebrated. To the end of his days the Bishop of Campos Antonio de Castro-Mayer permitted any priest in his diocese to say it without let or hindrance. That every bishop of the Holy Roman Catholic Church did not follow his example is a part of the same mystery of iniquity which has prevented the consecration of Russia by the Pope and his bishops which our Lady requested at Fatima. As our Lord said to the chief priests of His day, "This is your hour, and the power of darkness" (Luke 22:53). From that point onward there was little or nothing to check the progress of the enemy forces.

Faced with the accommodations to socialistic democracy recommended to the faithful in *Octogesima adveniens*, which by now have become dominant ecclesiastical policy, Dom Castro-Mayer was constrained to remind the Pope of the existence of the unvarying "Catholic social doctrine practiced by the Church for twenty centuries, elucidated in breadth by Leo XIII and developed in accordance with tradition by St. Pius X, Pius XI, Pius XII and many Catholic moralists and sociologists." And again, "The Church has always taught that Christianity, insofar as it is a society animated by Christian culture and civilization, is founded on absolutely true and eternal principles, and that she provides a model, perfectible to be sure, but authentic, for all non-Christian peoples."

He noted how "In several passages [the Letter] presents social equality as a good and praiseworthy thing," as in Article 22, where the document speaks of a twin "aspiration to equality and participation" as "two forms of man's dignity and liberty" now making themselves felt ever more insistently "as his information and education develops." The Bishop faults the lack of "distinction between the essential equality common among men and accidental inequality. Whence the reader derives the impression that the ideal society is one without such accidental inequalities, despite the teaching of the popes, who deemed them necessary for a proper ordering of social life. In other words, *Octogesima adveniens* would desire a society without differences of birth, social condition, etc., which give life in society its hierarchical character."

In other words, what is now being preached as Church doctrine is nothing less than the star-spangled heresy first practiced as a nation and disseminated worldwide by the United States of America. It is good to know, therefore, that an American bishop from another quarter of the hemisphere could still be found to admonish His Holiness for promoting it. "When the Church no longer teaches the general lines of an ideal society and state," wrote Dom Mayer, "Catholics are allowed to think they have a free option to choose from the various models proffered by other currents without fear of wounding their conscience. Such a situation quite naturally invites them to an economic, political and social program which is not merely secular, but also open to interconfessionalism .... This was inadmissible for the Popes who were always suspicious of such communion."

And he calls to witness St. Pope Pius X in "Our Apostolic Mandate" on "the audacity and frivolity of men who call themselves Catholics and dream of re-shaping society under such conditions, and of establishing on earth, over and beyond the pale of the Catholic Church, 'the reign of justice and love' with workers coming from everywhere, of all religions and of no religion, with or without beliefs, so long as they forego what might divide them – their religious and philosophical convictions, and so long as they share what unites them – a 'generous idealism and moral forces drawn from wherever they can.'"

St. Pius also said, "We must repeat with the utmost energy in these times of social and intellectual anarchy when everyone takes it upon himself to teach as a teacher and lawmaker – the City cannot be built otherwise than as God has built it. Society cannot be set up unless the Church lays the foundations and supervises the work. No, civilization is not something yet to be found, nor is the New City to be built on hazy notions. It has been in existence and still is. It is Christian civilization. It is the Catholic city. It only has to be set up and continually restored against the unremitting attacks of insane dreamers, rebels and miscreants." Yea, and especially in America!

150 APOSTASY

LIFE AMONG THE RUINS

The world is showing all the signs normally associated with old age. If it appears to be going mad, there is every reason to believe its madness is the senile dementia of the superannuated rather than the crazed exuberance of youth. Compared with the children of adamic times and the patriarchal progeny we read about in the Bible, the youth of today appears to have been born senile. Widespread attention deficiency, loss of moral balance, carelessness in discerning the real from the imagined and a general inability to cope with any situation beyond the immediate are not symptoms of youth, but of old age, when the working connection between past and present gradually disappears with the memory, and salutary interaction with the next generation becomes as difficult as it was with the previous one.

Contemporary art babbles like old people, and science spins fairy tales for grown-ups which are taken for true. Meanwhile, frantic insistence on ever greater independence and freedom of conscience is forging an anxiety-ridden society seeking relief in drugs and compulsive rhythms, with suicide the final viable solution. Begun in earnest are the "dangerous times" St. Paul told his protégé the Bishop of Ephesus would come in the last days, when "men shall be lovers of themselves, covetous, haughty, proud, blasphemers, disobedient to parents, ungrateful, wicked, without affection, without peace, slanderers, incontinent, unmerciful, without kindness, traitors, stubborn, puffed up and lovers of pleasure more than of God:" (2 Tim. 3:1-4). These are not characteristics of juvenile vitality, but of decrepitude.

St. John Chrysostom's faithful friend St. Nilus predicted that men and women would become "unrecognizable." Having exhausted its ability to absorb proper nutrients and eliminate the toxins building up physically and spiritually, the body politic by dint of camouflaging itself with palliatives, is taking on all the allure of an embalmed corpse. Not that its condition resists diagnosis, for the world is known to have suffered all along from a congenital terminal illness. Scripture reveals in its very first verse that it cannot last forever in its natural state. Inasmuch as, "In the beginning God created heaven and earth," the world had no existence at all before time was created along with it. It is finite because it is created, but because it was created of matter, its every dimension has limits, not only in space but in duration. Without God's cooperation, nothing goes on indefinitely.

After the Fall God had to tell Adam that like the rest of material creation, "Dust thou art and into dust thou shalt return" (Gen. 3:19), and the Psalmist would sing, "In the beginning, O Lord, thou foundedst the earth: and the heavens are the works of thy hands. They shall perish, but thou remainest: and all of them shall grow old like a garment" (Ps. 101:26-27). This truth, whose disclosure conditions all human knowledge, had to be revealed to Adam, for he would have had no other way of knowing such a thing. Had God not told him otherwise, he would have expected the world to go on ceaselessly renewing itself, especially that vigorous world integrated by grace and undisturbed by temptation or any other problems which was the only one he had any experience of before sin entered it.

Scientists speaking of a universe "expanding" limitlessly are only reasoning logically from what they can see, as Adam would have. Without taking God's revelation into consideration, how can they possibly know the true state of affairs? Like Heraclitus and his ilk in every generation, they see the world's eternity in terms of constant flux and never-ending natural cycles. *Panta rei*! Constant change spells stability. So susceptible are men to this endemic delusion, that God became man in order to tell them once more, face to face, that "Heaven and earth shall pass away!" This cannot be disbelieved with impunity, for unlike material creation, "my words shall not pass away!" (Matt. 24:35).

So far there has been no way of ascertaining how long Adam had lived before the creation of Eve, but it must have been no inconsiderable while, for he had time to name "all the beasts of the earth and all the fowls of the air," which in Hebrew is a way of saying that he studied the nature and quality of every other animate being on earth and catalogued them all. He must have been quite happy by himself among all the pleasures of paradise, for it was God and not he who determined that "it is not good for man to be alone." When God brought him the animals "to see what he would call them," so that he might call "all the beasts by their names," He was in fact preparing Adam for the creation of Eve, for he had to be shown that he really was alone, and why, unlike the beasts, "there was not found a helper like himself" anywhere among them to be his mate. (Gen. 2:19).

Having seen for himself that human nature was unique and essentially different from all other forms of life on earth, Adam would have laughed heartily at the theory of evolution, which holds that men share a common ancestry with animals. But here again, errors of this kind are only to be expected where human reasoning operates independently of revelation. St. Paul is at pains to point out that Adam "was not seduced" (1Tim. 3:14) as Eve was, who had to rely on her husband's word for much of her information. Not having learned firsthand the radical distinction between carnal and spiritual natures as had Adam (who was furthermore much older than she was), Eve was less prepared to withstand on her own the sophistry of the serpent, described in Scripture as "more subtle than any of the beasts of the earth which the Lord God had made" (Gen. 3:1).

Ven. Anna Catherine Emmerich said the Tempter accosted her in the guise of "a singularly gentle and winning, though artful creature," displaying in no wise the repulsive aspect visited on it by the Fall. "I know of none other to which I might compare it. It was slender and glossy and it looked as if it had no bones. It walked upright on its short hind feet.... and its wily tongue was ever in motion. It was about as tall as a child of ten years." Although, "before the Fall, the distance between man and the lower animals was great, and I never saw the first human beings touch any of them," this particular creature "was constantly around Eve, and so coaxing and intelligent, so nimble and supple that she took great delight in it." [41] And there the trouble began.

+

Long before Eve's creation, as soon as God had put Adam "into the paradise of pleasure, to dress it and to keep it," He had warned him, "Of every tree of paradise thou shalt eat, but of the tree of knowledge of good and evil thou shalt not eat. For in what day soever thou shalt eat of it, thou shalt die the death" (Gen. 2:15-17). Catechisms usually present this injunction in terms of a "test" to which God was putting Adam and Eve. Had they been able to realize what "death" really was and taken God at His word, they would have ensured for themselves and their progeny a life on earth free of pain and crowned by eternal bliss. As Maria Valtorta's angel told her, "Man's obedience would have maintained the earth in the state of an earthly Paradise in which death, hunger, wars, misfortunes, illnesses and weariness would have been unknown. A joyous sojourn of peace and love in the friendship of God would have been man's life until his passing on to the heavenly Dwelling, the way it was for Mary most holy, who did not die, but fell asleep in the Lord and awakened in His bosom, beautiful and glorified, with her perfect spirit and faultless flesh." [42]

That God's command was a test of Adam and Eve's fidelity is beyond dispute, but considerably more was involved in the words, "Of the tree of knowledge of good and evil thou shalt not eat." Although, like the knowledge of man's spiritual nature, the interdiction was received by Adam before Eve's advent, she was nonetheless fully acquainted with it, having learned it from her husband as her head under God. The proof is that she was able to identify the tree in question readily enough as "the tree which is in the midst of paradise" (Gen. 3:3) when the serpent inquired about it. Its dominant location alone, at the very center of the garden which "the Lord God had planted ... from the beginning (Gen. 2:8), would indicate that what had been conveyed to Adam was no mere dietary prescription on a par with those figuring later in Mosaic law or the commandments of the Church. Forbidding mankind to eat of this particular tree was a promulgation of the primordial law of fast which stands at the core of creation and underlies every precept of moral theology.

The knowledge of good and evil, which God not only "hath commanded us that we should not eat," but even "that we should not *touch* it" (Gen. 3:3), is nothing more nor less than the self-determination of right and wrong, from which man must fast perpetually. It is the prerogative of self-government reserved to God alone in the Most Blessed Trinity, which man arrogates to himself when he lays down his own moral law, doing his own will without reference to God's. In the latter days, universal democratic government with religious freedom for all has institutionalized and adapted to society as a whole the divine privilege of self-sufficiency heretofore usurped only by errant individuals. For God to share His unique privilege with another, much less transfer it wholesale to a whole people, even temporarily, always remains an absolute impossibility, for it entails denying His own nature. If that were possible, the one, eternal and omnipotent God of Abraham, Isaac and Jacob who revealed himself in Jesus Christ, would at best prove to be some lesser deity with negotiable attributes.

The divine privilege was not refused to Adam by a despotic God of wrath and jealousy, avaricious of His power, for such a God is a figment of the imagination, projected by the mind of Adam and his descendants after the Fall, when they began ascribing to God the base motivation they recognized in themselves. Scripture records that it was only after eating from the forbidden tree that Adam said, "I was afraid," and that he "and his wife hid themselves from the face of the Lord God," who till then had been accustomed to speaking with them familiarly, "walking in paradise at the afternoon air" (Gen. 3:10,8). The cause of their sudden paranoia was accurately determined by St. John when he wrote, "Fear is not in charity: but perfect charity casteth out fear; because fear hath pain, and *he that feareth is not in perfect charity*" (1 John 4:18). Conversely, when love of God is cast out, as happened in Eden, fear rushes in, bringing with it every irrational phobia ever aired in the confessional or on the psychiatrist's couch. Where "the charity of many shall grow cold" (Matt. 24:12) epidemic anxiety and panic attacks will become the norm.

Eve's desire to know good and evil by eating the forbidden fruit was essentially a desire to experience evil, which she assumed had to be something good, inasmuch as till then everything she and Adam had ever known was good. Had they rested content with eating freely of all the other trees in Paradise, their every craving would have been satisfied and they would have been perfectly happy. By forbidding the fruit of one tree alone to Adam, however, God entrusted mankind with much more than the secret of happiness. He endowed them with the key to reality. The divine will being so to speak the frame on which creation hangs, willfully to "eat of the tree" is to sever moral connection not only with God, but with the world as it really is, by preferring a world of one's own, existing essentially in one's own mind.

Adam and Eve had been created by a God who is substantial love, who out of love had created them only to be happy. If this were not so, suffering would not be universally, intrinsically, repugnant to human nature, which was never ordered to pain of any kind to begin with. This being the case, the human will was designed to choose only the good. When it chooses evil, the evil must have at least a momentary appearance of good, or it would never be chosen. The serpent was well aware that Eve would never have thought of touching the forbidden fruit had she not seen "that the tree was good to eat and fair to the eyes and delightful to behold" (Gen. 3:6). Neglecting to take God's word for the consequences was her undoing.

Knowing the constitution of His creatures, the God who is Love arrived on earth as a supremely lovable, helpless human infant who would grow up and teach men to "learn of me, because I am meek and humble of heart" (Matt. 11:29). Before returning to heaven He left an official photograph of himself imprinted on His burial shroud which would be developed nearly two thousand years later, in the days when "the charity of many shall grow cold" (Matt. 24:12) and the expiring world needed to be reminded of God's essential nature in human terms it could grasp. The Holy Shroud, therefore, does not portray the Christ who castigated the money changers in the Temple or who delivered the long diatribe against the Pharisees, calling them "hypocrites ... blind guides ... serpents ... generation of vipers" (Matt. Ch. 23), but the Christ who died in torment on the Cross for love of these odious creatures.

The tortured image, true icon of the true God, documents every detail of Christ's Passion from the sole of His foot to the top of His head. It offers not only incontrovertible, visible evidence of what man does to God and his neighbor when given the opportunity, but it shows what man does to himself in the process, who cannot love himself any better than he does others. This is why by God's grace there can be victim souls. United to the immolated Christ, men can expiate for one another by the same token that they can cause one another suffering. For good or ill, our Lord's "Amen, I say to you: as long as you did it to one of these, my least brethren, you did it to me"(Matt. 25:40) works both ways. Instructing St. Timothy to offer supplications for all men, St. Paul cites no other reason than that God "will have all men to be saved and to come to the knowledge of the truth" (1Tim. 2:4). In the fullness of time, "God so loved the world as to give his only begotten Son .. not ... to judge the world, but that the world may be saved by him" (John 3:16-17).

Far from desiring to wreak vengeance on His creatures, God from the start wished to preserve them from suffering by warning their first parents of the consequences of not acting in conformity to His will, rather than let them learn by fatal experience, as proved to be the case. Centuries later He would give Moses the Ten Commandments for the same reason, not to make men miserable and lay burdens on them, but to renew in their minds the irreformable precepts of the natural law written in men's hearts, whose observance enables them to live as happily as possible in their fallen world. Strictly speaking, beyond establishing the laws upon which reality is built, God inflicts no punishments, for there is no suffering in this world or in the hereafter which man has not brought in some manner on himself or his fellows as a simple consequence of quarreling with things as they are. Didn't our Lady say at Fatima that wars are the result of sin?

+

As soon as Adam, in his capacity as divinely constituted head of creation, engaged his God-given authority to ratify Eve's disobedience by sharing the forbidden fruit with her, the whole world began dying prematurely. Left a prey to his own mortality, he was told, "In the sweat of thy face shalt thou eat bread till thou return to the earth out of which thou wast taken: for dust thou art and to dust thou shalt return" (Gen.17-19). Without the vivifying support of grace, nature began taking its course, following its hierarchs Adam and Eve into disorder. Sorrow and pain, labor and toil, thorns and thistles made their appearance in what till then had been a perfectly harmonious environment. Everything in the universe was affected, from the lowest to the highest. The serpent lost its graceful upright posture, locomoting "on thy breast"(Gen. 3:14) over the earth, and the light of heaven itself began to fail.

On the fourth day of creation God had "made two great lights: a greater light to rule the day, and a lesser light to rule the night: and the stars. And he set them in the firmament of heaven, and to give light upon the earth." Not only would these luminaries "**divide the day and the night**," but they would **"be for signs, and for seasons and for days** and years: To shine in the firmament of heaven and to give light upon the earth. And to rule the day and the night, and to divide the light and the darkness" (Gen. 1: 14-18). The plain literal sense of this passage is that the moon when created was incandescent, burning with its own light "to rule the night" instead of merely reflecting the sun's as it does now. According to Fernand Crombette,once the original sin was committed, the moon's light immediately began waning, the exact date of its final extinction apparently recorded by ancient astronomers in hieroglyphic writings. From that time forth nights are darker than they should be.

There were similar catastrophic effects in man himself, as if the primordial "slime" from which God created him had turned to mire. Not only did he have to wear clothing to cover his nakedness, but Sr. Emmerich said, "I saw Adam and Eve losing their brilliancy and diminishing in stature. *It was as if the sun went down.*" Man seemed to "draw creation into himself....It was as if man once possessed all things in God ... but now he made himself their center, and they became his master. I saw the interior, the organs of man as if in the flesh, in corporeal, corruptible images of creatures, as well as their relations with one another, from the stars down to the tiniest living thing. All exert an influence on man. He is connected with all of them; he must act and struggle against them, and from them suffer." [43]

Since the Fall every newborn child, normally conceived in pleasure, begins life wailing like the author of the book of Wisdom, who wrote that "being born, I drew in the common air and fell upon the earth, that is made alike, and the first voice which I uttered was crying, as all others do" (Wis. 7:3). Furthermore, from the moment man is conceived in the womb, everything he produces of himself is fetid. When our Lord told the crowds, "Not that which goeth into the mouth defileth a man, but what cometh out of the mouth, this defileth a man," His disciples thought to warn Him "that the Pharisees," ever sticklers for the statutory unclean, "when they heard this word, were scandalized."

The simile, chosen by Truth himself, is not one usually heard in polite society. When St. Peter requested an explanation later in private, our Lord asked the disciples wearily, "Are you also yet without understanding?" for the meaning should have been obvious to anyone from the simple evidence of his own bodily functions. "Do you not understand that whatsoever entereth into the mouth goeth into the belly and is cast out into the privy? But the things which proceed out of the mouth come forth from the heart and those things defile a man. For from the heart proceed evil thoughts, murders, adulteries, fornications, thefts, false testimonies, blasphemies. These are the things which defile a man" (Matt. 15:11-12; 16-19), for man's fallen soul produces spiritual filth fouler by far than the material filth excreted by his fallen body.

St. Paul summed up the effects of the Fall by saying, "The wages of sin is death," because sin, like death, produces separation. It parts the material body from its immaterial soul as it parted man from God, the one being a direct consequence of the other. Because "the grace of God" is "everlasting life" (Rom. 6:23), the original rupture in Eden eventually caused not only the separation of souls and bodies, which is physical death by definition, but it initiated the interminable series of separations and dislocations which characterizes a world always on the verge of decomposition. As Sr. Emmerich said, "Sin was not completed by eating the forbidden fruit." Nor did it start there, for an ever recurring fall from truth and right order runs parallel with the history of salvation. Begun in heaven among angels whose wills were created free, it has persisted in time among men enjoying the same privilege, constituting a veritable "apostatic" tradition every bit as old as that of the Church.

In its youth the sinful earth was renewed by the Flood, only to relapse into universal disorder. Eventually God became Man in order to renew it by His Blood, generating a new society of grace on earth, and in due time the political miracle called Christendom literally materialized from the petition, "Thy kingdom come, they will be done on earth as it is in heaven" which He commanded be addressed daily to our Father "who art in heaven." Like Israel of old, however, it too began disintegrating. First Byzantium fell away from the Church, and then other parts of the Church began decomposing into Protestantism. Philosophy parted company with her mistress theology, and great heresiarchs in the temporal order arose. Men like Giotto, Galileo, Bacon and Bach excised the arts, natural science and music from the executive positions they occupied in Christian society and set them to plying their trades as ends in themselves. *Ars gratia artis* was coined as watchword, and soon the people began ruling in the name of kings and princes. Economics declared its independence from the politics it was meant to serve and began dictating world policy, to the point that now, as St. John prophesied in the *Apocalypse*, "merchants are the great men of the earth" (Apo. 18:23). Labor and management having parted company, finance reigns supreme.

Just as democracy was drawing up the final divorce papers ratifying the rift between the Holy Catholic Church and human society, the Mother of God appeared in France at la Salette. On September 19, 1846, at a crucial period when the bond uniting the spiritual and the temporal in the social life of every individual and institution in Christendom was being juridically severed by the separation of Church and state, she came to prepare her children for another cleavage more calamitous yet. "Rome will lose the faith," said she, predicting at the same time that "the Church will be eclipsed, the world will be in consternation." She pled, "Do battle, children of the light, you the few who see thereby, for the time of times, the end of ends is at hand!"

+

Looming ahead is the Great Apostasy predicted by St. Paul to the Thessalonians when the Antichrist, "the man of sin" (2 Thess. 2:3), will engage mankind in wholesale flight from God and reality. From him can be expected perfect acquiescence to the three temptations by which the devil failed to seduce Christ in the desert. Turning stones into bread by substituting false teaching for true doctrine, he will confirm the satanic religion by false miracles, as it were casting himself down from the pinnacle of the temple to be borne up by spiritual hands. Given "all the kingdoms of the world and all their glory" (Matt. 4:8-9) in return for falling down and adoring Satan, Antichrist the King will establish a universal empire in the fallen angel's name. Aping as closely as possible Christ's consummation of the law and the prophets, he will capitulate in his person the whole of the world's apostatic tradition.

In the English text the word used by St. Paul to denote this catastrophic reversal of Christ's kingdom on earth is "revolt," but the Latin calls it *discessio*, and the Greek has *apostasia*, both of which mean "falling away." In other words, it will not differ substantially from the first apostasy in Eden, but will exceed it immeasurably in magnitude. The first time, man separated himself from the God who created him from nothing to natural life, but the second time he will separate himself from the God who re-created him from sin to supernatural life at the cost of His own Blood. A parent who has had the bitter experience of seeing children to whom he has given physical life, food, clothing and education turn upon him with ingratitude, misunderstanding and outright hatred has privileged insight into the true nature of apostasy.

Like the prodigal son in the parable, apostasy says in fact to God, "Father, give me the portion of substance that falleth to me!" (Luke 15:12), and taking what belongs to it by nature, declares itself independent of the sole source of its being. Its blind malice is such that it will provoke the "great tribulation" predicted by our Lord, "such as hath not been from the beginning of the world until now, neither shall be," when "the powers of heaven shall be moved" (Matt. 24: 21,29). Theophylactus said these powers are the angelic principalities on high for, "Not alone shall men tremble when the world is being dissolved, but even the angels will be fearful in the presence of such terrifying destruction of the universe." At the height of the desolation "there shall be signs in the sun and in the moon," (Luke 21:25), when "the moon shall not give her light" (Mark 13:24).

Inasmuch as from the very moment of their creation the sun and the moon were given to us "for signs" (Gen. 1:14) beyond their ordinary functions, their physical aspect cannot be irrelevant. The moon lost her incandescence as a result of the first apostasy, but it is evident that even the brightness she still reflects from the sun will fail as a result of the second, the Great Apostasy, when Scripture says even *the sun shall be darkened*," and "the stars shall fall from heaven" (Matt. 24:29). This has been interpreted to mean that the Church, symbolized in Scripture by the moon, will not be able to enlighten men as usual because Christ and His saints, symbolized by the darkening of the sun and the falling of the stars, will be obscured. The Church, said St. Augustine, "then shall not be seen, as her persecutors rage against her without measure."

Commenting on St. Luke's account, St. Ambrose explained why this would happen: "Many apostasizing from Christianity, the brightness of the faith will be dimmed by this cloud of apostasy, since the heavenly Sun grows dim or shines in splendor according to my faith. And as in its monthly eclipse the moon, by reason of the earth coming between it and the sun, disappears from view, so likewise the holy Church, when the vices of the flesh stand in the way of the celestial light, can no longer borrow the splendor of the divine light from the Sun of Christ. And in the persecutions it was invariably the love of this life that stood in the path of the divine Sun. Also the stars, that is men surrounded by the praise of their fellow Christians, shall fall as the bitterness of persecution mounts up."

When these lines were penned the events referred to were far in the future, but this is no longer the case, for it has now been over a hundred and fifty years since our Lady announced at la Salette, *"The sun is darkening!"* The four little words which follow that ominous disclosure are generally overlooked, yet they are among the most frightening in the whole Secret, increasingly verified as they are by developments in the Church since the Second Vatican Council. Whereas earlier in the text our Lady had made the shocking prediction that "Rome will lose the faith and become the seat of the Antichrist," she went on to say here that *"faith alone will survive!"*

Apparently the universal terror of those days can be expected to culminate in one final separation from the body of the Church as we know it, when the darkening of the sun precipitates that night in which our Lord said, "No man can work" (John 9:4). The whole world, and the elect in particular, will enter into a dark night of the soul similar to the one experienced by saints at the summit of the spiritual life on the threshold of union with God. It partakes of our Lord's anguished "My God, my God, why hast thou abandoned me?" uttered from the Cross at the moment of death, when by a special dispensation of Providence the Sacred Humanity was parted from any awareness of the divinity to which It was hypostatically united.

As a spotless bride perfectly conformed to her Lord, the Church is apparently destined to undergo similar torment when, for the sins of men, the exterior manifestations of divine life in her will to all appearances disappear for a time, leaving her members to subsist on naked faith, hoping against hope and loving in the void, as bereft of churches, priesthood, sacraments or other visible supports as apostate Judaism is today. What other interpretation is there of the utterly bare altar beheld in the great Trinitarian theophany granted to Sr. Lucy of Fatima at Tuy on June 13, 1929? In her account she says, "Suspended in mid-air was to be seen a Chalice and a large Host onto which fell some drops of Blood from the face of the Crucified and from a wound in His breast. These drops ran down over the Host and fell into the Chalice," [44] both of which would normally be on the altar, but were now being filled directly from the wounds of Christ, eternally on the Cross in the Most Blessed Trinity on high.

The Fathers of the Church unanimously foresaw this dereliction, for not only our Lord, but the ancient prophets made numerous references to it. Among the minor prophets the most explicit are those of Amos, who spoke of "a famine ... of hearing the word of the Lord"(8:11), and Osee, who predicted that before the conversion of "the children of Israel," figure of the Church, there would come a time when they "shall sit many days without king and without prince and without sacrifice and without altar and without ephod and without theraphim" (Os. 3:4). Daniel, one of the four major prophets, also foretold the assault on the "prince of the covenant" which would result in the failure of the Holy Sacrifice itself and the installation of the "abomination of desolation" (Dan. 8:11; 9:27; 11:21,31).

Disasters of such proportions are wont to gather momentum gradually at first. At the close of the first Christian millennium the grace of the Papacy was lost to the schismatic Orthodox, and in the course of the second millennium, at the time of the Reformation, the Holy Sacrifice of the Mass was lost to Catholics become Protestants. When, on the brink of the third millennium an unprecedented service concocted by men was celebrated under the dome of St. Peter's in lieu of the Holy Sacrifice, the fulfillment of Daniel's prophecy appeared imminent to many who were mindful of our Lord's words, "When therefore you shall see the abomination of desolation which was spoken of by Daniel the prophet standing in the holy place: he that readeth, let him understand! (Matt. 24:15). If that day has arrived, all arguments about liturgical validity, authority or jurisdiction are swallowed up in one terrible question Christ left us to ponder in His absence: "When the Son of man cometh, shall he find, think you, faith on earth?" (Luke 18:8).

+

God has only one answer to apostasy, and that is mercy. Throughout human history the abyss of man's iniquity has called forth the abyss of divine love as "Deep calleth on deep, at the noise of thy floodgates" (Ps. 41:8). Just as the apostasy of the beginning times brought on the merciful Flood which renewed the earth, the Great Apostasy of the latter times can only call forth the Greater Mercy, a deluge of grace which will ultimately transfigure all creation. Already two thousand years ago it began pouring from the riven side of the Incarnate God dying on the Cross, so that, "Where sin abounded, grace hath abounded more. That as sin hath reigned unto death, so also grace might reign by justice unto everlasting life through Jesus Christ our Lord" (Rom. 5:20-21).

Appointing Sr. Faustina Kowalska as His Apostle of Mercy for the latter times, our Lord told her in the 1930's to "proclaim that *mercy is the greatest attribute of God!* All the works of My hands are crowned with mercy.... I am Love and Mercy itself. There is no misery that could be a match for My mercy, neither will misery exhaust it, because as it is being granted, it increases..... Speak to the world about My mercy. *It is a sign for the end times.* After it will come the day of justice." Desiring that a Feast of the Divine Mercy be instituted on Low Sunday after Easter, our Lord told Sister on that day in 1935, "This Feast emerged from the very depths of My mercy.... Every soul believing in My mercy will obtain it!"

Heinous as was Judas' betrayal of his Lord, it was not the ultimate cause of the chosen apostle's damnation. In his case as in every other, the final apostasy is the refusal of God's mercy. "Before the day of justice arrives, there will be given to people a sign in the heavens of this sort: All light in the heavens will be extinguished, and there will be great darkness over the whole earth. Then the sign of the Cross will be seen in the sky, and from the openings where the hands and the feet of the Savior were nailed will come forth great lights which will light up the earth for a period of time. This will take place shortly before the last day" (301,1273, 848, 83)3 [45]

By now a good number of the woes predicted for the world in the Mother of God's little apocalypse at la Salette are of normal occurrence. The "divisions among rulers, in all societies and in all families" make the headlines of every daily paper, and alas, now beyond refutation or obfuscation is the Secret's own terrible lead line: "Priests, my Son's ministers, priests by their evil life, by their irreverences and their impiety in celebrating the holy mysteries, by love of money, love of honor and pleasures, have become sewers of impurity." Our Lady may have said as much again in the message delivered at Garabandal in 1965 when she told the young visionary Conchita, "Many priests, many bishops and many cardinals are on the road to perdition, and with them they are taking many more souls."

Her prediction at la Salette that "Many will abandon the faith, and the number of priests and religious who will separate themselves from the true religion will be great," is now abundantly supported by statistics, and that "bad books will abound over the earth" is plainly evident, leaving little doubt that "the spirits of darkness will everywhere spread universal relaxation in everything concerning God's service," and "even in homes there will be killings and mutual massacres." Thanks to worldwide acceptance of democratic principles, the twentieth century has seen how the sin of Eden has come to full flower throughout society, where "with God's holy faith forgotten, each individual will want to direct himself and rise above his peers. Civil and ecclesiastical authority will be abolished. All order and justice will be trampled underfoot. Only murders, hatred and jealousy, lying and discord will be seen, with no love of country or family.... Civil governments will all have the same objective, which will be to abolish and make every religious principle disappear."

Echoing her divine Son (Matt. 24:22), our Lady exclaimed, "Who could overcome, if God doesn't shorten the time of trial?" She had already supplied the answer, however, when she said, "Happy the humble souls led by the Holy Ghost! I shall battle along with them until they reach the fullness of maturity." Our Lord promised He would not leave

His disciples orphaned in the ruins, but would send them the spirit of truth, who "will teach you all things and bring all things to your mind, whatsoever I shall have said to you." He "will teach you all truth: for he shall not speak of himself, but what things soever he shall hear, he shall speak: and the things to come he will show you" (John 14:18,26; 16:13).

Even where priesthood and sacraments fail, every soul in the state of grace has for spiritual director the same Third Person of the Blessed Trinity who directed the Sacred Humanity on earth and even now directs the Church. As mutual Love of the Father and the Son, the Holy Ghost is that *Spiritum Sanctum, Dominum et vivificantem*, that "life-giving Lord" who, as the Nicean Creed states, *ex Patre et Filioque procedit*, proceeds from the Son and not the Father only, for the Spirit of love must proceed from the Truth. He is present in the souls of the baptized only to the degree of their union with Christ, "the way and the truth and the life" (John 14:6), for the Son ever remains the sole Mediator between mankind and God. It was He who sent the Holy Ghost to the first Christians at Pentecost, and He has continued to do so ever since. To believe that the Holy Ghost can be found in other religions apart from the Truth, as do some misguided charismatics and ecumenists, is implicit denial of the Creed. As our Lord said, "If you believe not that I am he, you shall die in your sin"(John 8:24).

The Holy Ghost comes as the fire which "sat upon each of them" individually at Pentecost (Acts 2:3). He is the quintessential *sensus catholicus* which directs the actions of every member of the Church. Like a good ear for music which tells singers and musicians when they are off key, the divine *sensus* does not function by human reason, for when attentive, the obedient soul of prayer "hears" supernaturally without intermediaries. The insensitivity of non-believers to these subtle tones may explain the sterility of that dialogue with the deaf which goes by the name of "ecumenical." Mincing no words, our Lord told the heretical Pharisees, "Why do you not know my speech? Because you cannot hear my word.... He that is of God heareth the words of God," and to the pagan Pilate He said, "Every one that is of the truth hears my voice!" (John 8:43,47;18:37).

Especially during the eclipse of the Church, in the absence of proper directives from the Magisterium and personal spiritual direction from the clergy, direct help from the Holy Ghost must be presumed. Given the *sensus catholicus* the Mother of God was able to say that in the midst of moral chaos, "the children of the true faith, my imitators," will not only not succumb to the encroaching evils, but will actually "grow in the love of God and in the virtues dearest to me.... God will take care of His faithful servants and men of good will," who "will make great progress by virtue of the Holy Ghost." She promised, "I shall battle along with them until they reach the fullness of maturity," and despite all, "men of good will will believe in God, and many souls will be comforted. They will make great progress by virtue of the Holy Ghost and will condemn the diabolic errors of the Antichrist."

+

The darker the night, the less reason for despair. As St. Paul said, "We know that to them that love God all things work together unto good!" (Rom. 8:28), and if we are to believe our Lord, the worse things get the better. Precisely when there is "upon the earth distress of nations by reason of the confusion of the roaring of the sea and of the waves: men withering away for fear and expectation of what shall come upon the whole world," He said to "look up and lift up your heads!" Not to wait till the night is over, but "when these things *begin* to come to pass, because your redemption is at hand!" (Luke 21:26,29)

The dimming of the sun and moon is a time of supreme grace, when "he that persevereth to the end shall be saved" (Matt. 10:22), for the cause of the unprecedented darkness and turmoil is not Christ's outraged exit from His world, but His imminent return to it. In the same way that "a cloud received him out of their sight" (Acts 1:9) at the time of His Ascension, our Lord's true disciples will by faith begin to discern in the current confusion "the Son of man coming in a cloud with great power and majesty" (Luke 21:25-28). The Fathers of the Church attached much importance to the words "coming" and "cloud" when interpreting this passage, pointing out that it does not refer to Christ's actual re-appearance so much as to His progressive approach, recognized by the infallible signs He predicted.

Titus, Bishop of Bostra, says, "The end of things has not yet come, but they now move toward their end, for the actual coming of the Lord, putting an end to the power of all other rulers, prepares the way for the kingdom of God." Heralding Christ's return, the clouds indicate especially His coming into the hearts of those who will receive Him. "He now comes," said St. Augustine, "in His own members, as in clouds, or in the church, as in a great cloud." The frightful apocalyptic calamities are therefore merely the turbulence accompanying the "coming" of Christ to a sinful generation "in great power and majesty" (Matt. 24:30), much like "a woman when she is in labor hath sorrow, because her hour is come : but when she hath brought forth the child she remembereth no more the anguish for joy that a man is born into the world" (John 16:21).

What looks like disintegration is transfiguration painfully begun. If Holy Mother Church is perfectly conformed to her divine Lord in His Passion, she will also be conformed to Him in His death and Resurrection, being "eclipsed" only to rise again, and like Him eventually ascend into heaven. Once having "come out of the great tribulation" she now suffers, with her "robes washed and made white in the blood of the Lamb" (Apo. 7:14), the Church will certainly also experience a peaceful interim corresponding to the blissful period of Forty Days our resurrected Lord spent with His disciples on earth before His Ascension. As our Lady said at La Salette, in the end, "Water and fire will purify the earth and consume all the works of men's pride, and everything will be renewed," but before this final denouement a respite similar to the one granted to the first Christians can be expected to occur.

Our Lady may have been describing such a period when she spoke to little Mélanie of a time to come after the devastation which "will not last long," during which "there will be peace, the reconciliation of God with men; Jesus Christ will be served, adored and glorified; charity will flourish everywhere. The new kings will be the right arm of Holy Church, which will be strong, humble, pious, poor, zealous and imitative of the virtues of Jesus Christ. The Gospel will be preached everywhere, and men will make great strides in the faith, because there will be unity among Jesus Christ's workers, and men will live in the fear of God." Isn't this essentially what our Lady promised once more at Fatima? On July 13, 1917 after the great vision of hell she in fact introduced the still undisclosed Secret by telling the children, "In the end my Immaculate Heart will triumph ... and a certain period of peace will be granted to the world."

Although this temporal peace may mark the end times, it cannot spell the end of the world, for "of that day and hour no one knoweth, no not the angels in heaven, but the Father alone" (Matt. 24:36). Those living on earth amid the ruins of Christianity can look forward, however, to a fortifying foretaste of the world's end in glory, when "God shall wipe all tears from their eyes and death shall be no more, nor mourning, nor crying nor sorrow shall be any more, for the former things are passed away" (Apo. 21:2,4). Although born into apostasy like all preceding generations and destined to endure times in which, if prolonged, "No flesh should be saved" (Matt. 24:22), they need not fear the darkening of the sun and moon, which spells disaster only for "the fearful and the unbelieving, and the abominable and murderers and fornicators and sorcerers and idolators and all liars," whose lot is "the second death" of hellfire (Apo. 21: 8).

For God's predestined, "chosen ... before the foundation of the world" to be "holy and unspotted in his sight," who "according to God's purpose are called to be saints," (Eph. 1:4-5;Rom. 8:28) the enveloping darkness augurs the eternal day in heaven predicted by the prophet Isaias, when "you shall no more have the sun for thy light by day, neither shall the brightness of the moon enlighten thee" (Is. 60:19). Shown the heavenly city in vision, St. John would likewise mark how it "needeth not sun nor moon to shine in it, and the Lamb is the lamp thereof.... And night shall be no more: and they shall not need the light of a lamp, nor the light of the sun, for the Lord God shall enlighten them, and they shall reign forever and ever" (Apo. 21:23; 22:5)."

It is true that Christ assured us that "Heaven and earth shall pass away," but as the Venerable Bede explained, "The heaven that will pass away is not the ethereal, or sidereal heaven, but the aerial, after which the birds of heaven are named. If, however, the earth shall pass away," he asks, "How does Ecclesiastes say 'The earth standeth forever?' (Eccles.. 1:4). But it is plain that He means that the heavens and the earth shall pass away in their present form, but that in their essence they will endure forever." Those days will witness the transfiguration of creation and the ascension of the Church into heaven, "prepared as a bride adorned for her husband."

Meanwhile, all that need be known is that the world in which we grew up is dying. Envisioning its final agony centuries ago, St. Eusebius wrote, "For now is the end of all perishable life, and ... the outward appearances of this world will pass away and a new world will follow in which, in place of the visible luminaries, Christ himself will shine as Sun and King of a new creation; and so great will be the power and splendor of this new Sun, that the sun which now shines, and the moon and the other stars will grow dim before the face of this greater Light."

Appendix: *ABOUT LA SALETTE*

In the foregoing pages there have been numerous references to the Secret of La Salette, confided by the Mother of God to Mélanie Calvat, the oldest of two young seers to whom she appeared in the French Alps in 1846. Attempts to discredit both the visionary and the heavenly message have never been wanting, for although the apparition was approved by the Holy See, the Secret itself was never promoted by the ecclesiastical establishment, despite papal recommendations and many *Imprimaturs*. In fact the faithful were led to believe that it had actually been placed on the *Index of Forbidden Books* then in canonical vigor. Mélanie was accused of being psychologically unbalanced by her Bishop, who eventually was the one to go mad and never recover his sanity. She was persecuted to such a degree in her own country that for long periods she was forced to live incognito in Italy, where she died at the age of seventy-two.

Today the same old accusations which were leveled against her in her lifetime, which she continued to refute to her dying day, are resurging, not only from liberal sectors as before, but even from conservative champions of the traditional Mass. Her critics maintain that the text of the Secret with which we are familiar and which Mélanie first published in its entirety in 1879 under the *Imprimatur* of Bishop Salvatore-Luigi Zola of Lecce, Italy was her own expanded and embroidered version of our Lady's real message, which Pius IX had requested her to submit to him in 1851. Emphasizing the difference in length between the two versions of the Secret, the short one set down in 1851 for the Pope and the longer one delivered to the public in 1879, some hold that Mélanie added to the original text information culled from contemporary apocalyptic literature then in circulation. Mélanie's autobiographical writings, particularly those dealing with her abused childhood and her miraculous companionship with the child Jesus, are rejected as spurious by many.

At this juncture, when so much of what our Lady prophesied in the Secret is beginning to materialize, the enemy of mankind can be expected to utilize every means of discrediting a prophecy intended to lay open his machinations before the eyes of the faithful. Whereas the arguments which proved so effective in casting doubt on the Secret's authenticity when it was first divulged are being refurbished with a vengeance, the hard facts which demolished them then have only been reinforced by subsequent events. Most of them can be found as good as new in a 40-page brochure in defense of the Secret which was published in French in 1922, bearing the *Imprimatur*, dated June 6 of that year, of no less an authority than the Dominican Fr. Albert Lepidi, then Master of the Sacred Palace and Permanent Consultor to the Congregation of the Index.

Disseminated by the St. Augustine Society under the title "The Apparition of the Most Blessed Virgin on the Mountain of La Salette," it bears a facsimile of the *Imprimatur* with Fr. Lepidi's signature, plus the following words in his own hand: *Ces pages ont été écrites pour la pure vérité*, "These pages have been written solely in the interests of truth." The first half of the brochure contains Mélanie's own account of the apparition, together with the full text of the Secret, which she set in writing in Castellamare, Italy on the feast of our Lady's Presentation, November 21, 1878 and which received an *Imprimatur* the following year from the local Ordinary, Bishop Zola. The second half is devoted to contemporary testimonials in defense of the Secret, the whole closing with an ecclesiastically approved Prayer to the Most Blessed Trinity for the canonization of Mélanie Calvat.

Seven letters from Bishop Zola to various dignitaries figure among the contents. Privileged to authorize the first publication of the Secret in its entirety with his *Imprimatur*, he never wavered in his convictions concerning La Salette, nor in his veneration for its messenger. Not only have his letters lost nothing of their force with passing time, but hindsight considerably sharpens their focus. A sampling of the longest and most informative one are offered here in translation. The Bishop wrote it May 24, 1880 in reply to questions addressed to him by Fr. Isidore Roubaud, one of the few French priests who dared undertake Mélanie's defense in the face of the dogged opposition mounted by Masonically influenced bishops like Mgr. Ginoulhiac of Grenoble, successor to the saintly Mgr. Bruillard, in whose diocese the apparition had taken place and had been originally approved.

Bishop Zola writes, "I deeply deplore France's current opposition to the heavenly Message of La Salette. We are already on the eve of the terrible chastisements with which the Mother of God threatened us because of our prevarications, and yet we prefer to reject the warnings of so tender and merciful a Mother rather than profit from her lessons, the only act on our part which could diminish the intensity of the afflictions divine wrath has in store for us. In this I recognize the work of our ancient enemy, who has the greatest interest in exploiting every means, especially among God's ministers, *ut videntes non videant et intelligentes non intelligant....*

"Only on July 3, 1851 did Mélanie herself put her Secret in writing for the first time, at the Providence convent in Corenc, by order of Mgr. de Bruillard, Bishop of Grenoble, in the presence of Mr. Dausse, head of the Department of Civil Engineering, and Mr. Taxis, Canon of Grenoble Cathedral. Mélanie filled three large pages at one sitting, without saying anything or asking any questions." [In the account of the incident given by Bishop William Ullathorne of Birmingham, England in *The Holy Mountain of La Salette* in 1854, Mélanie asked the meaning of the words *infallibly* and *Antichrist*, and how to spell the latter, but there are no other discrepancies.] "She signed without re-reading, folded her Secret and put it in an envelope. She addressed it thus: 'To His Holiness Pius IX, in Rome.'

"The next day, the fourth of July, the Secret is personally rewritten by Mélanie at the Bishop's palace in Grenoble, with the purpose of drawing a clear distinction between the dates of two events which are not supposed to happen at the same time. Having put in only one date the first time, Mélanie was afraid that the Pope might not understand correctly on that account, and some equivocation might result. On July 18 Mr. Gérin, Curate of the Cathedral of Grenoble, and Mr. Rousselot, Honorary Vicar General, both saintly priests advanced in years and highly respected in every regard, delivered to His Holiness Pius IX the letters of the Bishop of Grenoble and those of Maximin [the other little seer] and Mélanie, containing their Secrets.

"Mélanie did not send His Holiness Pius IX all of the Secret which she recently published, but only what the Blessed Virgin had inspired her to write at the time from that important document, along with many things relevant to Pius IX personally. Nevertheless, on the basis of information which I guarantee you is *very accurate*, I know that the reproaches addressed to the clergy and religious communities were *identical* to those contained in that part of the Secret given to His Holiness Pius IX. Later the blessed shepherdess of La Salette imparted other parts of the Secret to different people when she felt the proper time had arrived to disclose them. But the Secret in its entirety was made public only in the little work written by Mélanie herself and printed at Lecce in 1879 at the request and expense of a pious person.

"In 1860 one of Mélanie's directors obtained a manuscript of the Secret at Marseille. It was transmitted to me in 1869, when by order of Mgr. Petagna, Bishop of Castellamare di Stabia, I was Mélanie's spiritual director. On January 30 Mélanie put this same document into the hands of the Abbé Felician Bliard, *with a declaration of its authenticity and her signature*, but with certain small blank spaces, indicated by dots and *etc*...., to replace those parts of the Secret which she felt she should not reveal yet. The part about priests and religious, almost in its entirety, was there in its proper place. The Abbé Bliard sent a certified copy from Nice on February 24, 1870 to Fr. Semennenko, Consultor of the Index at Rome and Superior of the Polish seminary. He did the same for several Church dignitaries. Nevertheless the Secret of the shepherdess of La Salette had already been spread everywhere in manuscript form, especially among religious communities and the clergy.

"In 1873 Fr. Bliard published the document just as he had received it from Mélanie in 1870, with his own scholarly comments, in a brochure called 'Letters to a Friend about the Secret of the Shepherdess of La Salette'. This brochure appeared in Naples with the approbation given on April 30, 1873 by the curia of His Eminence Cardinal Sixtus Riario Sforza, Archbishop of Naples. I myself can certify the authenticity of this approbation, as well as the authenticity of the letter which I sent to Abbé Bliard dated May 1, 1873, a letter which was printed on the first page of the said brochure after my promotion to the See of Ugento.

"On receiving Mélanie's Secret from Mr. Bliard, Mr. C.R. Girard, the learned director of *La Terre Sainte* in Grenoble, published it early in 1872 in his book called *The Secrets of La Salette and Their Import*. This brochure was only the first of five very important little works which appeared later by the same author and were intended to vindicate and confirm the revelations of La Salette, as well as to defend them against the attacks of their enemies. These works by Mr. Girard were honored by the endorsement and blessing of His Holiness Pius IX and the support of many Catholic theologians and bishops....

"I will also say that during my many years as Abbot of the Canons Regular of the Lateran at Santa Maria di Piedigrotta in Naples, I had occasion in my capacity as Superior of that Order to maintain relations with very respected prelates and princes of the Roman Church. They were rather well informed in regard to Mélanie and her Secret. Almost all had received that document. Well then! Every one of them without exception judged very favorably of that divine revelation and the authenticity of the Secret. I shall confine myself to mentioning among others: Mgr. Petagna, Bishop of Castellamare di Stabia, who had the good shepherdess of La Salette under his guardianship for several years; Mgr. Mariano Ricciardi, Archbishop of Sorrento; His Eminence Cardinal Guidi; His Eminence Cardinal Sixtus Riario Sforza, Archbishop of Naples.... These revered and saintly Pastors always spoke to me in such wise as to confirm me strongly in my belief, now become unshakeable, in the divinity of the revelations contained in the Secret of the shepherdess of La Salette. Furthermore I have it *from an incontrovertible source*, that our Holy Father Leo XIII also received that document *in its entirety*.

"I am mindful, Reverend Sir, that the Secret contains some very harsh truths where the clergy and religious communities are concerned. Such revelations are approached with sinking hearts and fearful souls. If I dared I would ask our Lady why she didn't order them buried in eternal silence. But who are we to question her who is called the Seat of Wisdom? Our task is to draw profit from her lessons."

The good Bishop goes on to point out that there is considerable precedent both in Scripture and hagiography for rebuking the clergy in public, citing the Psalms, the Prophets, the Fathers of the Church and other sacred authors, not to mention revelations made to saints from St. Catherine of Siena on down to Bl. Anna-Maria Taigi. Nonetheless he warns that prophecy makes use of a language all its own, not meant to inspire contempt of those we are bound to respect. Reproofs aimed at the clergy in general must not be taken as addressed to all without exception, for "in the bosom of the Church there are always pastors and ministers outstanding for their learning and holiness," besides the fact that "the divine Mother's range of vision takes in the entire universe, and her chaste eye is offended by many things we can neither know nor even suspect...

"As for the Secret printed in Lecce, I assure you that it is identical to the one given to me by Mélanie in 1869. In the latter she simply filled in those small omissions and reservations which, when all is said and done, hardly added or subtracted anything from the substance of the document. I had my episcopal commission examine it according to the rules of the Church; and having found no reason to oppose the publication of the Secret, my Vicar General accorded his permission to print in the terms 'NIHIL OBSTAT, IMPRIMATUR,' to the person who desired to publish it at his own expense in accordance with his pious intentions. This approval as it appears at the end of the brochure was in fact given on November 15, 1879. The brochure was truly and entirely written by Mélanie Calvat, shepherdess of La Salette, whose surname was Matthieu. It is impossible to cast any doubts on the authenticity of this brochure.

"Here now is what concerns Mélanie personally: This pious girl, this virtuous and privileged soul whom wicked people have tried to vilify by making her the butt of their detestably gross calumnies and proud disdain, I can attest before God is in no way deceitful, crazy, deluded, prideful or motivated by self interest. On the contrary, I had occasion to admire the virtues of her soul, as well as the qualities of her mind throughout the period of time I had her under my spiritual direction, that is to say from 1868 to 1873. After that, being no longer able to undertake her direction as a consequence of my promotion to the see of Ugento as Superior of the Canons Regular, I still continued to keep in contact with her by correspondence. To this day I can affirm that her edifying life, her virtues, her writings have deeply impressed on my heart the sentiments of respect and admiration which in all justice I must entertain in her regard.

"In 1879 our Holy Father Leo XIII deigned to honor Mélanie with a private audience and also charged her with compiling the rules for the new Order recommended and requested by Our Lady of La Salette under the title of the Apostles of the Latter Days. In order to complete a draft of this kind, the ex-shepherdess stayed in Rome for five months at the convent of the Salesian Sisters. During this time she became better known and more highly esteemed, especially by these good nuns, who furnished favorable reports very much to the credit of the blessed shepherdess of La Salette.

"In fine, I know from my own sources of information that when Mr. Nicolas, a lawyer from Marseille was in Rome on Holy Saturday 1880, he was commissioned by His Holiness Leo XIII to put out a brochure explaining the Secret in its entirety, so that the public might understand it properly. I feel sure these particulars will suffice to strengthen you in your conviction. I could tell you very much more, but," concludes the Bishop of Lecce, that would require a book, not a letter.

+

The same year that Bishop Zola wrote to Fr. Roubaud, Mgr. Cortet, Bishop of Troyes, was making every effort to have the Secret put on the *Index* on the pretext that it "was causing trouble in France." When his request continued to meet with refusal on the part of the Holy Office, he threatened its Secretary, Cardinal Caterini, with the withdrawal of Peter's Pence "if something was not done in his favor." Under duress the Cardinal ended by writing him a letter dated August 8, 1880, in which he stated that the work in question had been remitted to the Inquisitors, who found it proper to reply that "it was not pleasing to the Holy See that the said work be delivered to the public," and expressed the desire that "wherever copies have been distributed, they be removed, insofar as possible, from the hands of the faithful. . . . ."

When the authentic Latin text of the letter was published seventeen years later in *Ami du Clergé*, the last sentence terminated in an extended series of dots as above, testifying to a number of missing words. Eventually Fr. Roubaud learned that the dots stood for a phrase laying down the condition, "*if as the Bishop affirms, the Secret was causing trouble in France*." This qualification had been expurgated wholesale, along with the rest of the sentence, which instructed the authorities to "*leave it in the hands of the clergy, so they may profit by it.*"

Bishop Cortet had been so disappointed on receiving this communication that rather than publish it in his diocese, he sent it to his friend Bishop Besson of Nîmes, who put out an adulterated version. Not only were the extenuating words left out of the prohibition but gratuitous additions were made to the effect that the Inquisitors "deem worthy of the highest praise the zeal you have shown in denouncing this work to them," and "that the Holy See has regarded its publication with the greatest displeasure." Removing the copies from circulation was furthermore reported to be the "*express* wish" of the Holy See.

Needless to say, this letter brought the dissemination of the Secret to a standstill in France as far as the establishment was concerned. From

Italy Mélanie would write Fr. Roubaud, "Don't worry about what the devil does by means of men; the good Lord permits it to strengthen the faith of the true believers. One of the persons I addressed in Rome belongs to the Congregation of the Index and the other to that of the Holy Office, or the Inquisition, which is the same thing. Neither one nor the other knew anything about Cardinal Caterini's letter. That's why they said it was a party acting independently of the Pope and even of the Congregations of the Index and the Inquisition."

According to the brochure, "The two people Mélanie refers to are Cardinals, one of whom was Cardinal Ferrieri. Mgr. Pennachi, Consultor to the Index, on being questioned by Mélanie, told her the same thing as the two Cardinals. It is clear from Mélanie's letter that Cardinal Caterini, by an ordinary private letter, had falsely implicated his colleagues in the Holy Office, and even the Holy See; for which the Cardinal's secretary, who had drafted it, apologized to Mgr. Zola, adding that his hand had been forced." Because poor Mélanie was unable to prove beyond a shadow of doubt that the letter had indeed been sent without the Pope's knowledge, she believed herself bound to comply with its strictures to the end of her life. Privately she admitted that the letter had "poisoned her existence" by making it impossible for her to fulfill the mission confided to her by our Lady, at least in France.

+

After Melanie's death in 1904 the enemies of La Salette hoped to deal the final blow to the Secret. Putting the capstone on the falsehoods and misrepresentations already in circulation, a decree was promulgated on December 21, 1915 which ordered "the faithful of all countries to abstain from treating or discussing this said question under whatsoever pretext or form, either in books, pamphlets or articles signed or anonymous, or in any other way." Although the action is duly recorded in the *Acta Apostolicae Sedis* for December 31 of that year, certain irregularities were soon noted in its regard.

To begin with, it carries signatures of no Cardinals or members of the Sacred Congregation, but only that of its notary, Luigi Castellano. There is moreover no mention of the date on which the Holy Office presumably met to vote this piece of legislation, nor any reference to its ever having been submitted to Pope Benedict XV for final approval. Although the decree forbids all discussion of the Secret and specifies penalties to be imposed on transgressors, no censure whatever is attached to the work itself, as would be expected in the circumstances. There is not even a prohibition against possessing, reading or distributing it!

In other words the alleged "decree" which has been brandished like a club over the heads of the faithful for over eighty years to prevent their hearing a message addressed "to all our Lady's people," has apparently never enjoyed the force of law. The faithful both lay and clerical are now, and have always been perfectly free, without exception, to avail themselves of the high ecclesiastical authorizations which were originally granted to the Secret by the Archbishop of Naples Cardinal Sforza and Bishop Zola of Lecce, not to mention those of Cardinal Ferrieri and Cardinal Guidi. So what were they waiting for?

Not only had Pope Leo XIII accepted the account of the apparition and the Secret, delivered to him personally by Mélanie on two separate occasions, but as Bishop Zola pointed out, in 1880 this same Pontiff had charged the attorney Nicolas of Marseille "to draft a brochure explaining the whole Secret so that the general public could understand it properly." When his brochure, which has provided so much of the substance of these lines, was reprinted under Fr. Lepidi's *Imprimatur* in 1922 after years of oblivion, the adversaries of La Salette were bound to react, inasmuch as any clear exposition of the facts relating to the unjust suppression of the Secret could not fail to renew public interest in it.

An unfortunate incident played into their hands when an ill-advised partisan of the Secret, a certain Dr. Grémillon of Montpellier, took it upon himself to distribute a thousand copies of the brochure to all ranks of the clergy. Under cover of the brochure's *Imprimatur* and using a pseudonym, he appended to its legitimate contents an injurious twelve-page letter dated February 2, 1923 in which, among other things, he labeled the priesthood as a whole as "sewers," taxed St. Thomas Aquinas with "obscurantism" and wound up by declaring that the Pope should impose the Secret of La Salette on the faithful as an article of faith. The copies were expedited in wrappers proclaiming, "Big News! A voice from heaven! A message from the Blessed Virgin is declared authentic by the Vatican. A bludgeon blow to the clergy. See a letter at the end from Dr. Henry Mariavé to the Abbé Z., dean of a parish in Montpellier."

Reaction on the part of the Holy Office was swift. On May 10, 1923 a decree was issued "proscribing and condemning" the entire brochure, designated by the title "The Apparition of the Most Holy Virgin on the Mountain of La Salette on Saturday, September 19, 1845." That the apparition took place in 1846 and not in 1845 would alone serve to invalidate the decree, besides the fact that for over 43 years Mélanie's account of the happening had incurred no condemnation whatsoever from any authorized quarter. To make matters worse, the Holy Office took its fateful action in a session held on the previous day, when Fr. Lepidi was ill and unable to make an appearance, either to defend the *Imprimatur* he had accorded the original publication or to repudiate the unauthorized letter which had been attached to it.

Could the brochure have suffered condemnation without Dr. Grémillon's outrageous letter? Ultimately the responsibility lay with the reigning Pope, who was then Pius XI. As it was, he was placed in the uncomfortable position of apparently proscribing what three predecessors, Pius IX, Leo XIII and St. Pius X, had actively promoted, and what, in the case of the brochure itself, one of them had actually mandated. As the years rolled on, the wistful conclusion reached at the time by many of the bewildered faithful is being heard with increasing frequency as time goes on: "The Holy Father is a prisoner in the Vatican, at the mercy of his entourage for his information!" Be that as it may, the Secret of La Salette finally broke free of all restrictions when Paul VI abolished the *Index of Forbidden Books* in 1966. By then, of course, the Church had already entered the "frightful crisis" foretold by the Secret, and there was no turning back the events which began unrolling.

+

The apparition of the Mother of God at La Salette was succeeded by two more great mariophanies. At Lourdes in 1858 she identified herself to little St. Bernadette Soubirous as the Immaculate Conception and requested the recitation of the Holy Rosary. At Fatima in 1917, while World War I was still raging on the European continent, she announced that she wished to establish devotion to her Immaculate Heart, insisting once more on the recitation of the Rosary, to which she promised to attach "a new efficacy" for the salvation of souls. She also told little Lucy dos Santos that at some future date, "I shall come to ask for the consecration of Russia." That day turned out to be Thursday June 13, 1929.

At the close of a vision of the Most Blessed Trinity granted in Tuy, Spain, our Lady told Lucy, a Dorothean sister at the time, "The moment has come in which God asks of the Holy Father to make, and to order that in union with him and at the same time, all the bishops of the world make the consecration of Russia to my Immaculate Heart," promising to convert it because of this day of prayer and worldwide reparation.[46] As we know, this request has yet to be fulfilled as specified. In a letter to Fr. Gonçalves Lucy wrote on May 13, 1936, "Intimately I have spoken to our Lord about the subject, and not too long ago I asked Him why He would not convert Russia without the Holy Father making that consecration?" She says our Lord replied, "Because I want My whole Church to acknowledge that consecration as a triumph of the Immaculate Heart of Mary, so that it may extend its cult later on, and put this devotion beside the devotion to My Sacred Heart."

At Fatima our Lady never mentioned the word Communism in relation to Russia, but only its "errors." In point of fact Communism cannot even be included among the errors proper to that nation, for as Br. Michel de la Sainte Trinité points out in *The Whole Truth about Fatima*, "One of the first important truths which must be established, under pain of dangerously deceiving ourselves concerning Russia and Communism, and consequently the words of our Lady of Fatima as well, is that *the Bolshevik revolution is not Russian*. It is fundamentally, essentially anti-Russian, as Solzhenitzyn has never tired of demonstrating to the West, which has voluntarily blinded itself on this point." Br. Michel's superior the Abbé de Nantes also pointed out, "Neither the Orthodox religion nor Slavic tradition have the least affinity with its inhuman dialectic. And if Communism took possession of this country, it is not in virtue of an illusory 'historical dialectic,' but quite simply because this great body with a sick head was easier to take and undoubtedly had no other agitating minority beside the Jewish Bolshevik clan." [47]

In other words, whatever Russia's errors maybe, they cannot be ascribed to Communism. If that great body suffers from a "sick head," the cause is *schism*, the separation from the Vicar of Christ which proved to be the fountainhead of all the subsequent separations which Christendom suffered as a consequence. The fall of Byzantium loosed the Renaissance, and the Renaissance spawned the Reformation, which in turn forged the Revolution now engulfing the world. That first debilitating rift in unity, which so many saints – and some enlightened Tsars

– have longed in vain to heal, affected not only the Orthodox millions, but the entire Church, which can be said to have kept its head, but lost its heart. Like a man whose wife has left him, the Church retained its God-given authority, but at the price of fruitfulness.

Until the erring East returns, what real hope is there to Christianize the rest of the world? When Our Lady asked the Pope to consecrate Russia in union with "all bishops of the world" is there not reason to suspect that she may have been including the schismatic bishops of Orthodoxy, who despite their illegitimacy, are nonetheless valid bishops? Would not their willing participation in such a Consecration in conjunction with the Pope of Rome constitute of itself a healing of the schism? Despite its "sick head" and longstanding disobedience, Russia still has a heart which can be appealed to, and essentially that heart is the Immaculate Heart of Mary, the Lady who appeared so spectacularly on that nation's behalf at Fatima.

Perhaps because she figures so prominently in their liturgy, devotion to her has survived every horror of Russian history from the Turks to the Communists, and let us hope, socialist democracy. The ordinary of the Mass in the Byzantine Rite is lavish in its references to Mary, whose role is as central to the sacrificial action as it is to mankind's salvation. The celebrant begins by incensing and kissing her icon along with that of Christ, beseeching her to "Open the portal of your deep mercy to us who put our trust in you, so that we may not be brought to confusion, but through you may be delivered from adversity, for you are the salvation of the Christian fold!" The First Antiphon meets with the repeated response, "Through the prayers of the Mother of God, O Savior, save us!" concluding with, "Let us remember our all-holy, spotless, most highly blessed and glorious Lady the Mother of God and ever-virgin Mary with all the saints."

During the Commemorations after the Consecration, the faithful raise their voices in the venerable hymn, "It is fitting and right to call you blessed, O Theotokos: you are ever-blessed and all-blameless and the Mother of our God, higher in honor than the Cherubim and beyond compare more glorious than the Seraphim, you gave birth to God the Word in virginity. You are truly the Mother of God: you do we exalt!" At the conclusion of the Sacrifice the Last Blessing is asked of God not only "through the prayers of His spotless and all-pure Mother," and all the saints, but specifically through those of her parents, "the holy and just ancestors of Christ Joachim and Anne." The Melkite liturgy for Corpus Christi especially dwells on the integral role of Mary as source of the Eucharist, reminding us that "the Holy Spirit formed the divine Bread for us out of her own blood.... Hail, O Virgin, who brought forth for us the Wheat of Life! Hail, O Mystical Banquet from whom we receive holy Food! O Blessed Mother, by the fruit of whose womb all the faithful are nourished," so that to receive the Eucharist is to receive Mary together with Christ.

The more sober Latin liturgy of the West is also mindful of the dignity of the Virgin Mary, according her the place of honor in the *Communicantes*, begging her intercession in the *Libera nos*, and even confessing to her in the *Confiteor*, but it cannot match the exuberance and theological sensitivity of the Byzantines. A recent convert to the Faith from Protestantism was heard to remark, "Catholics of the Latin Rite give lip service to Mary, but they aren't really devoted to her like the Easterners!" Is this why so many Marian apparitions occur in the West? True Marian devotion is certainly to be found throughout the Roman Church by anyone seriously seeking it out, but its manifestations on the whole have become peripheral to what might be described as its "official" life. What surer sign of creeping apostasy than neglect of her who "destroys all heresies!"

That our Lord wishes "*My whole Church* to acknowledge" the act of consecration may be extraordinarily significant, leading us to suspect that the consecration of Russia may be intended as much, if not more, for our benefit as for Russia's. Is something seriously wanting to the piety of the West, and to its Marian devotion in particular? It is recorded fact that all the great apparitions of the Mother of God in modern times have taken place in the West, first in America, and then in Europe, presumably always where Marian devotion was most in need of encouragement. After all, it was to the West, and not to the East, that God sent great Marian apostles like St. John Eudes and St. Grignion de Montfort.

The same radical disbelief which met the Secret confided to Mélanie Calvat of La Salette prevented the very disclosure of the Secret confided to Sr. Lucy seventy years later at Fatima, which remains secret to this day. If disbelief were not the underlying cause, why has the consecration of Russia not been made? By the same token, why are the five First Saturdays of reparation to the Immaculate Heart of Mary which were requested of Sr. Lucy at Pontevedra not a compelling priority on the agenda of the hierarchy? Isn't it possible, nay, probable, that the Consecration of Russia, on which hangs the deliverance of the long-suffering Slavic peoples, is at the same time heaven's way of demanding a concrete, long overdue re-affirmation of faith in Mary's intercession on the part of the whole Church, under its Pope and bishops?

Remonstrating with our Lord about the prevailing indifference to His wishes in the matter, Sr. Lucy said, "But my God, the Holy Father probably won't believe me, unless You yourself move him with a special inspiration." To which she said our Lord replied, "The Holy Father. Pray very much for the Holy Father. He will do it, but it will be late. Nevertheless, the Immaculate Heart of Mary will save Russia. It has been entrusted to her." When that time comes, Holy Mother Russia, please pray for the rest of us!

REFERENCES

[1] Quien fué Juan Diego? *El Eco Guadalupana,* No. 13, 2/12/74, p. 18.

[2] See *Les Cahiers du CESHE* et al. , 3 Place du Palais de Justice, B-7500 Tournai, Belgium.

[3] Hamish Fraser, "Who Was Garcia Moreno?" *Approaches* No. 19.21 Supplement 24.5.

[4] Gustavus Meyer, *History of Bigotry in the United States,* Random House, 1943, p. 200.

[5] John Cogley, *Catholic America,* Dial Press, N.Y., 1973, p. 47.

[6] Alfonso Zaratti, O.C.D., *The Work of the Catholic Church in the United States of America,* Nardini Publishing Co., Rome, 1955, p. 328.

[7] See Lydia Logan (Hertz), "Lord Baltimore's Bungle," *Big Rock Papers,* 1975.

[8] Andrew M. Greeley, *An Ugly Little Secret,* Sheed Andrews, Kansas City, 1977, p.17, 107.

[9] Maria Valtorta, *The Notebooks,* Centro Editoriale Valtortiano, Isola del Lirio, Italy, 1996. 1/26/47.

[10] William Hand Browne, *George Calvert and Cecilius Calvert, Lords Baltimore,* Dodd Meade and Co., N.Y.1890, pp. 4-5.

[11] Bernard Campbell, "Review of Hon. John P. Kennedy's Discourse on

the Life and Character of George Calvert," John Murphy, 178 Market St., Baltimore, 1846.

[12] William T. Russell, *Maryland, the Land of Sanctuary*, J.H. Furst Co., Baltimore, 1907.

[13] Michel Berger, "Le Propre du Choix Politique," *Action Familiale et Scolaire*, Paris, No. 135, Feb. 1998, p. 55.

[14] Sometimes rendered "de L'Arade."

[15] Dorothy Senior, *The Gay King, Charles II His Court and Times*, Brentano's, N.Y. 1911, p. 53.

[16] *Longinqua oceani*, 1895

[17] U.S. Treaty with Tripoli, Article XI, 1796.

[18] Manly Palmer Hall, *The Secret Destiny of America*, Philosophical Research Society, Los Angeles, 1944.

[19] Henry C. Clausen, *Freedom and Freemasonry*, published by the Supreme Council, Scottish Rite, 1977.

[20] See the Masonic Service Association's *Short Talk Bulletins*, Vol. II No. 7; XI, 7 ; XV, 2 ; XX, 11 ; XXI, 7; XXIX, 6 ; XXXIX, 5 ; CLV, 6.

[21] See J.J. Santa-Pinter, "The Great Seal of the United States of America: A Curiosity in Heraldry," *Horizontes*, Oct. 1968, Universidad de Puerto Rico, Ponce, P.R.

[22] PG 76.508c.

[23] Quoted by Dom Giuseppe Ricciotti, *Julian the Apostate*, Bruce Publishing, 1960, p. 179.

[24] *Codex Theodosianus* 13.3.5.

[25] Ricciotti, *Julian the Apostate,* p. 259.

[26] Quoted in Arnold Lunn and C.E. M. Joad, *Is Christianity True?* Lippincott, 1933, p. 79.

[27] *Commentary on Matthew,* II.

[28] *GS,* 44.

[29] De usu partium, 11.14.

[30] Robert L. Wilken, *The Christians as the Romans Saw Them,* Yale University Press, 1984, p. 199.

[31] Dom Prosper Guéranger, *The Liturgical Year,* Marian House, Powers Lake, N.D., 1983, Vol.XII, Bk. III.

[32] *Is Christianity True?* pp. 320-2.

[33] Maria Valtorta, *The Notebooks 1943,* Centro Editoriale Valtortiano, Isola del Lirio, Italy, 1996, p. 381.

[34] Tan Books, Rockford, Ill., 1980, pp. 29, 40.

[35] Jean Madiran, "Troisième Lettre,"*Le Concile en Question,* DMM, 1985.

[36] PL 4, *Epist. 63 to Cecilius*

[37] PL 76, *Sermo. 26*

[38] Quoted in a review of *Requiem for Nagasaki* by Fr. Paul Glynn in Action Familiale et Scolaire, No. 135, February 1998.

[39] See *La Iglesia Montiniana,* etc.

[40] A. Daniele, *L'Esprit Désolant de Vatican II*, Editions Delacroix, BP 109, F-35802 Dinard CEDEX.

[41] A.C. Emmerich, *The Life of Jesus Christ and Biblical Revelations*, Tan Books, Rockford, IL61105, Vol. I, p. 12.

[42] *The Book of Azariah*, Entry for 1/5/47.

[43] *Op. cit.* pp. 14,17.

[44] Frère Michel de la Sainte Trinité, *The Whole Truth about Fatima*, Immaculate Heart Publications, Vol. II, p. 474.

[45] M. Faustina Kowalska, *Diary*, Marian Press, Stockbridge MA 01263, 1987

[46] Account to Fr. Gonçalves dated Nov. 6, 1929.

[47] "L'Erreur de l'Occident," *Livre de Poche*, 1980.